IMAGES
of America

CORYDON

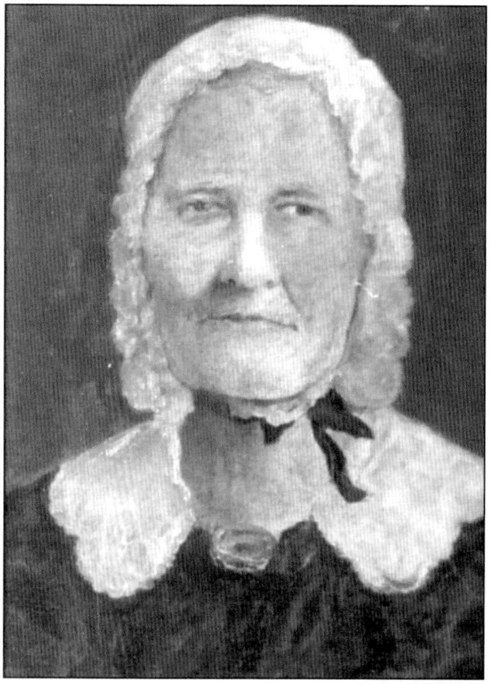

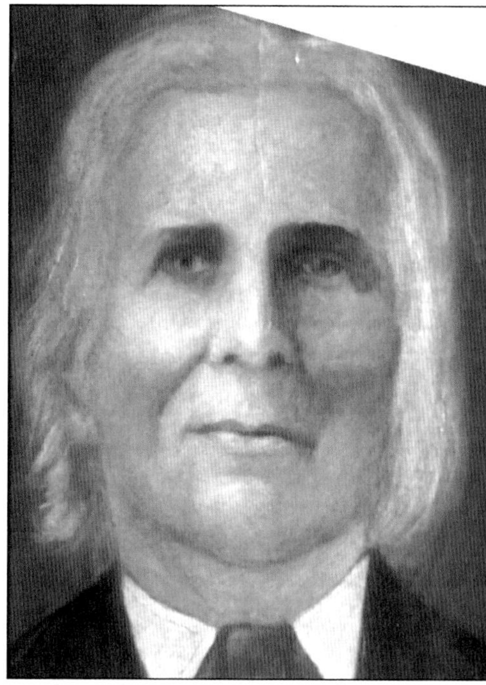

Elizabeth English and Dennis Pennington married on August 4, 1800, and came to the not-yet-named Harrison County in 1804. He built the Corydon Capitol and made certain that Indiana would be a free state. Betsy had been captured and raised by the Cherokee Indians, yet she ensured free education for all children in Indiana, and the states that came later. They are the author's great-great-great-grandparents. These portraits hang in the Governor Hendricks Headquarters at the Corydon Capitol State Historic Site. (Author's collection.)

On the cover: Mrs. Ried's Entertainment, "The Dande Drill," was staged in the 1890s. Featured from left to right are Olive Griffin, Bertha Shuck, Daisy Martin, Mary Rowland, Lizzie Chambers, Mittie Chappell, Jessie Allen, and Pfrim Zollman. (Courtesy of the Frederick Porter Griffin Center for Local History and Genealogy.)

IMAGES
of America

CORYDON

Otis Amanda Dick

ARCADIA
PUBLISHING

ISBN 978-0-7385-6050-2

Published by Arcadia Publishing
Charleston SC, Chicago IL, Portsmouth NH, San Francisco CA

Printed in the United States of America

Library of Congress Catalog Card Number: 2008940509

For all general information contact Arcadia Publishing at:
Telephone 843-853-2070
Fax 843-853-0044
E-mail sales@arcadiapublishing.com
For customer service and orders:
Toll-Free 1-888-313-2665

Visit us on the Internet at www.arcadiapublishing.com

*This book is lovingly dedicated to my mother,
Thelma Davis Dick (July 11, 1915–June 9, 2007),
my first fan, staunchest supporter, and unfailing ally in life, and
to my father, Otis Albion Dick (December 1, 1908–December 5, 1984),
our protector always.*

Contents

ACKNOWLEDGMENTS

Unless individually noted, all photographs appear courtesy of the Frederick Porter Griffin Center for Local History and Genealogy, Corydon. As with any worthwhile endeavor, many people contributed knowledge, expertise, and most of all, patience. I can name only the most outstanding. William C. Dennison is my computer guru, chauffeur, and wonderful life partner. At the Harrison County Public Library, Vi Eckert, library director, was gracious and enthusiastic from my first inquiry. At the Griffin Center, Kathy Fisher, department head; Kenney Neukam, genealogy assistant, and Virginia Fisher, genealogy assistant, steered me through voluminous files. Rick McCaffry, Bec Riley, Nancy Snyder, and Daneeta Albers, at the Corydon State Historic Site, shared information and made the site available to me whenever I needed to do research. Maxine Brown, who organized the restoration of the Leora Brown School, helps all historians interested in Harrison County. My cousins Cheryl Miller Proctor and William G. Orwick were always close by to clarify research and to set me on the right path. Of course, most of the material used for this project was collected and preserved by Frederick Porter Griffin (April 7, 1915–October 29, 2008). I had hoped to present the first copy of the book to him, but he passed away as we entered the production phase. Thank you, Fred, for your incomparable legacy.

INTRODUCTION

Long before the Euro-Americans settled in what would become Harrison County, Indiana, the American Indians came there to hunt and gather. They exploited the resources regularly, leaving traces of many temporary camps, reused for many years. The hardwood forests were filled with deer and smaller game animals, as well as sweet, oily beechnuts, hazel nuts, walnuts, and acorns. Streams were filled with fish and shellfish. They explored some of the innumerable caves found in the limestone underlying the area.

However, the particular resource of the area, which is found in archaeological sites all over the present United States, was what the settlers came to call Harrison County flint. The nodules of this particular chert were large and were relatively easy to find and gather. They fractured cleanly and predictably, and held a keen edge, which was easily resharpened. It was apparently annealed (heated to temperatures high enough to drive out impurities and harden the rock) by nature sometime in the shifting plate tectonics of the North American continent. American Indians mined this chert, packing out whole nodules, and prepared cores, from which to strike off individual blades, used to produce projectile points, knife blades, and scrapers. Harrison County flint is still sought by flint knappers of today.

French fur trappers and traders began to settle in present-day Indiana around the dawn of the 18th century, but these were small outposts, with *couers de bois* exploiting the land much the way the American Indians did—hunting, but changing the landscape very little. At the 1763 Treaty of Paris, which ended the French and Indian War, England's King George III promised that no English settlers would cross the spine of the Allegheny Mountains, thus leaving the area from the mountains to the Mississippi River safely in American Indian control.

Settlers, however, began to push down the Ohio River, exploring Kentucky and Indiana. Kentucky was settled first and became a state first. But the Northwest Territory beckoned irresistibly. Muddled land claims, profligate farming practices, which quickly exhausted the soil, and the famous "itchy foot" of American pioneers brought whites across the Ohio River into American Indian territory well before 1800.

George Rogers Clark founded Clarksville in 1783. It is considered the first permanent European settlement in the Northwest Territory (north of the Ohio River; west of the Allegheny Mountains). Settlement continued from south (Kentucky) to north (Indiana). The Clark family—George Rogers Clark, hero of the American Revolution, and his brother William Clark, who was Clark of the Lewis and Clark Expedition—and a host of early explorers and speculators measured and sold the land on the north of the Falls of the Ohio River.

Other settlers moved further into the Northwest. The American Indians were forced further north, where they began to consolidate their influence under a charismatic leader named Tecumseh. William Henry Harrison kept a wary eye on the American Indian politics as he journeyed from the territorial capital of Vincennes, to his business interests at the Falls of the Ohio River.

Harrison found it convenient to spend a night at the home of his friend, Edward Smith, who had built Corydon's first permanent home by a spring near the confluence of Big and Little Indian Creeks, in what would become Harrison County. After supper, the old *Missouri Harmony* book would be brought out and Harrison and the Smiths would enjoy singing for much of the evening. It is said that Harrison would invariably request Jennie Smith to sing the lugubrious ballad "Pastoral Elegy." In this song, the shepherdess Caroline laments the death of the shepherd Corydon. Tradition has long given credit to Harrison for giving his own name to the county, and bestowing the name Corydon on the town. A parallel tradition, however, credits Spier Spencer, first town marshal and captain of the Yellow Jackets militia, with naming his home. He kept a tavern in the yet-unnamed hamlet and chose the name from John Spencer's "Faery Queene," as the embodiment of a pastoral idyll.

However the name was acquired, the town took hold and grew in the center of rich farmland, abundant hardwood forests, and rivers and streams to connect it to the world beyond. Davis Floyd, found guilty of treason but sentenced to three hours in jail for his part in Aaron Burr's Spanish conspiracy; John Shields, veteran of the Lewis and Clark Expedition; and Squire Boone, brother of Daniel and a doughty pioneer in his own right, all settled in the environs of Corydon.

Dennis Pennington was elected to represent Harrison County in the territorial legislature and rode regularly to Vincennes to attend the government sessions. When Illinois was split off from Indiana, Pennington and others saw the opportunity of moving the capital to their districts. Early establishing his political savvy, Pennington lobbied and cajoled successfully to see the capital settled in Corydon. He also began a movement to build a county courthouse, which could serve as a territory and state capitol. He was awarded the contract in 1811 and oversaw the quarrying of limestone from the bed of Big Indian Creek to construct the 40-by-40-foot building now known as the "old capitol."

The territorial capital moved from Vincennes to Corydon in 1813. Statehood came in 1816, and the state constitution was written in the shade of a giant elm tree, the trunk of which is preserved in a shrine on High Street. Indiana came into the union as a free state. Slavery was forbidden in the Old Northwest Territory, yet Polly Strong had to bring suit against the Vincennes man who claimed her as property. The case was heard by the Indiana Supreme Court in Corydon. Strong won her freedom, but she was not allowed into the Indiana Capitol Building, where the case was heard.

In 1816, five white men were convicted of murder in the deaths of seven American Indians, at a place not far from Corydon. The case was again appealed to the Indiana Supreme Court at Corydon, and the convictions were upheld. This was the first time in the United States that white people were held accountable for murder in the deaths of American Indians.

After the capital moved to the wilderness crossroads christened Indianapolis, Corydon remained a hub of southern Indiana. The Keller family established a wagon factory, which shipped Corydon wagons all over the world. They remained in business until 1948. Dairying became an important industry in Harrison County, and Corydon was home to several creameries, which processed milk from local farmers. A bottling works carbonated the water from Big Blue Spring, in the heart of downtown, added various flavorings, and shipped out Whistle soft drinks.

In 1917, three years before the 19th Amendment to the U.S. Constitution granted women the right to vote, the board of trustees of Corydon appointed Georgia Wheat to the position of town clerk.

Corydon sent its men to fight in the Yellow Jacket militia during the War of 1812. Like the rest of southern Indiana, Corydon men fought on both sides of the War Between the States, and they "gave the last full measure of devotion" in World War I, World War II, the Korean conflict, Vietnam, Desert Storm, and Operation Iraqi Freedom.

Corydon today proudly tells the story of its history and remains a leader in the modern state of Indiana. Falling within the region dubbed "Kentuckiana," it is easy to find the footsteps that have led from perilous exploration to the firm amalgamation of north, south, east, and west, which today makes up the United States.

One

Early Days, Capitol Days

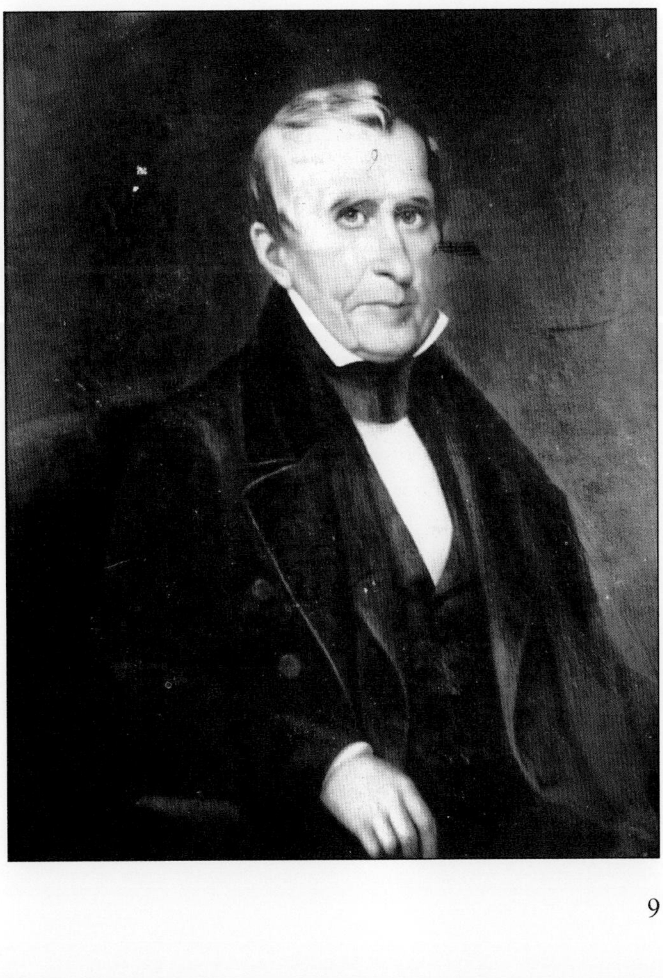

William Henry Harrison (February 9, 1773–April 4, 1841) seemed almost to emphasize the length and gauntness of his face as he aged. He emphasized his frontier life while filling his speeches with references to the Roman and Greek classics. Such a person might naturally relish the lugubrious lament of Caroline for her deceased love Corydon; but those who knew Bill Harrison are of the opinion that what he relished was beautiful Jennie Smith's lovely soprano voice.

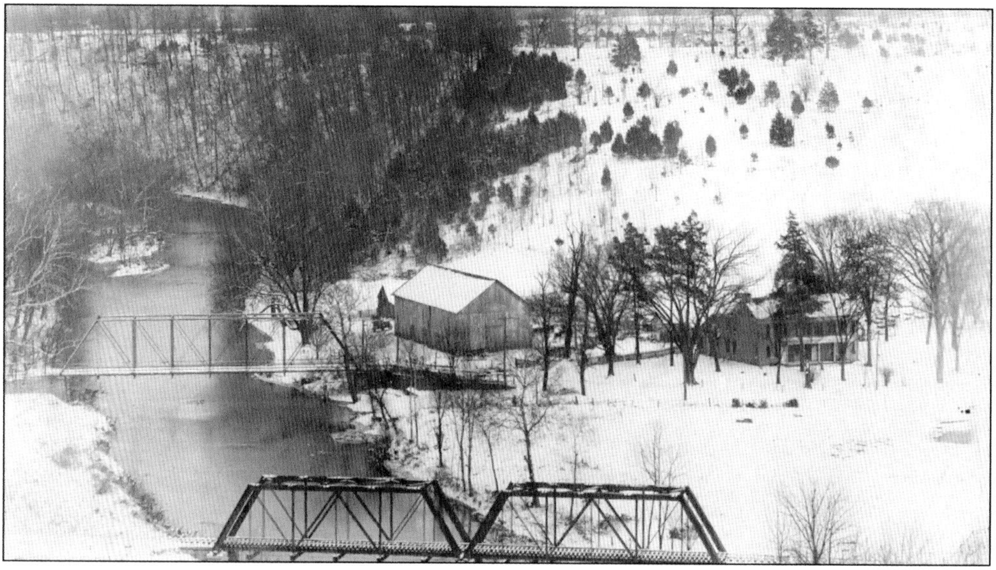

Jacob Kintner was one of Corydon's wealthiest settlers, amassing 700 acres in one parcel. Cedar Glade farm included land on both sides of present-day Highway 135, stretching from the top of the hill, past Big Indian Creek, and including part of today's Cedar Hill Cemetery. This early-20th-century photograph shows Cedar Glade house on the right and the large dairy barn, which still stands. The bridge near the buildings carries Highway 135 into town; the structure in the foreground is a railroad bridge.

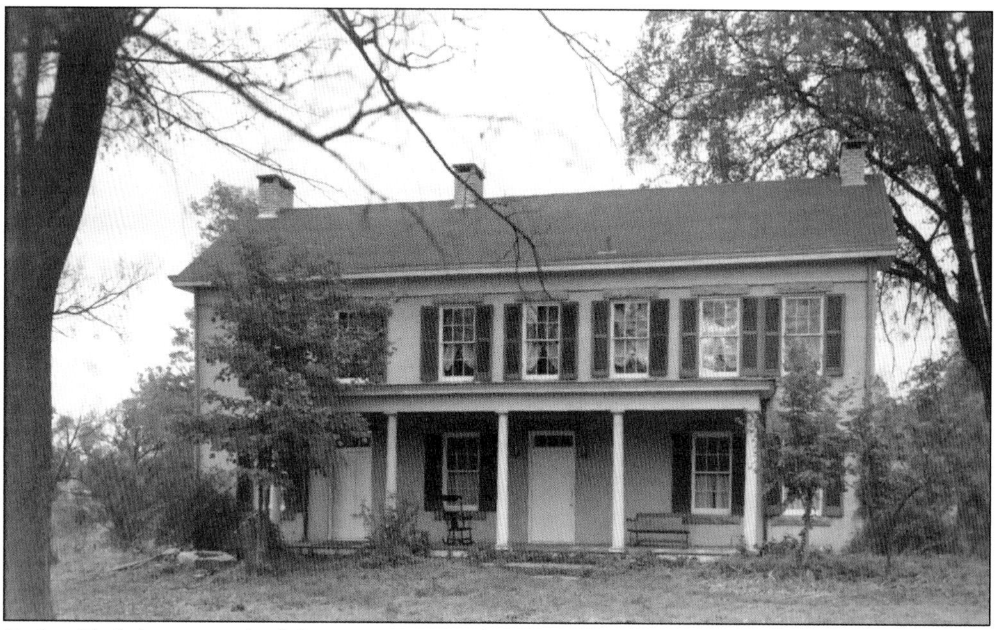

Cedar Glade house was built between 1808 and 1810. Jacob Kintner kept the property until 1819, when he traded it with Thomas McGrain Sr. for a store in Louisville, Kentucky. It remains a landmark of the community. The door on the left led to a portion of the house not connected by any interior portals. It was reputed to be the quarters for the enslaved people Jacob Kintner would bring to Indiana from Kentucky. These people would be returned to Kentucky in less than six months so as not to qualify for freedom.

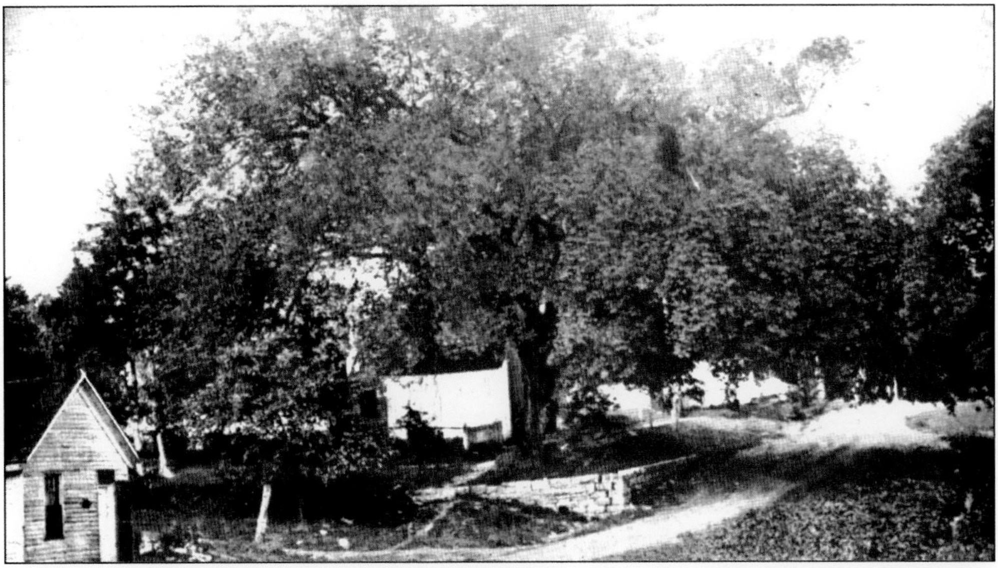

The summer of 1816 turned the "Courthouse on the Hill" into a stifling chamber, guaranteed to fray nerves and ignite tempers. The members of the constitutional convention moved down the hill to the shade of a large elm tree beside Big Indian Creek. Dennis Pennington chaired the committee; his wife Elizabeth ensured that Indiana would be the first state to provide free education for all children. The document was signed June 21, 1816. The Constitution Elm lived on until the 1920s.

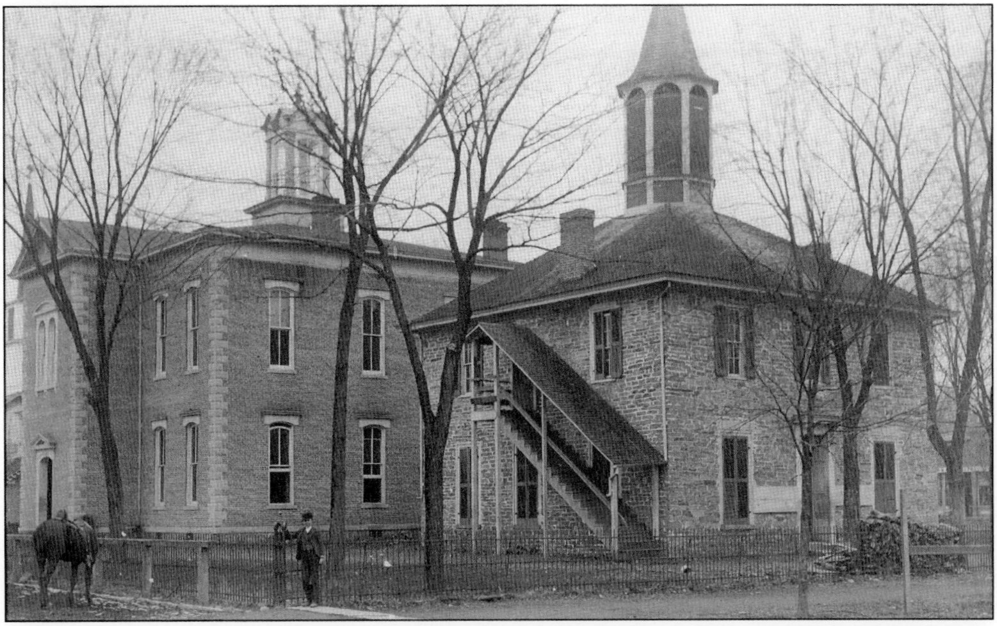

Before moving to Indianapolis in 1825, the Indiana Supreme Court ruled in two landmark cases. Five white men were convicted of murdering nine American Indians. The court upheld the death sentences. Polly Strong sued her "owner," claiming that, as slavery was illegal in the state, she was free. The court agreed with her, but she was forbidden to enter the building, even while the case was being heard. In 1882, Mast, Foos and Company replaced the split rail fence with heavy cast iron, which would in turn disappear in July 1911.

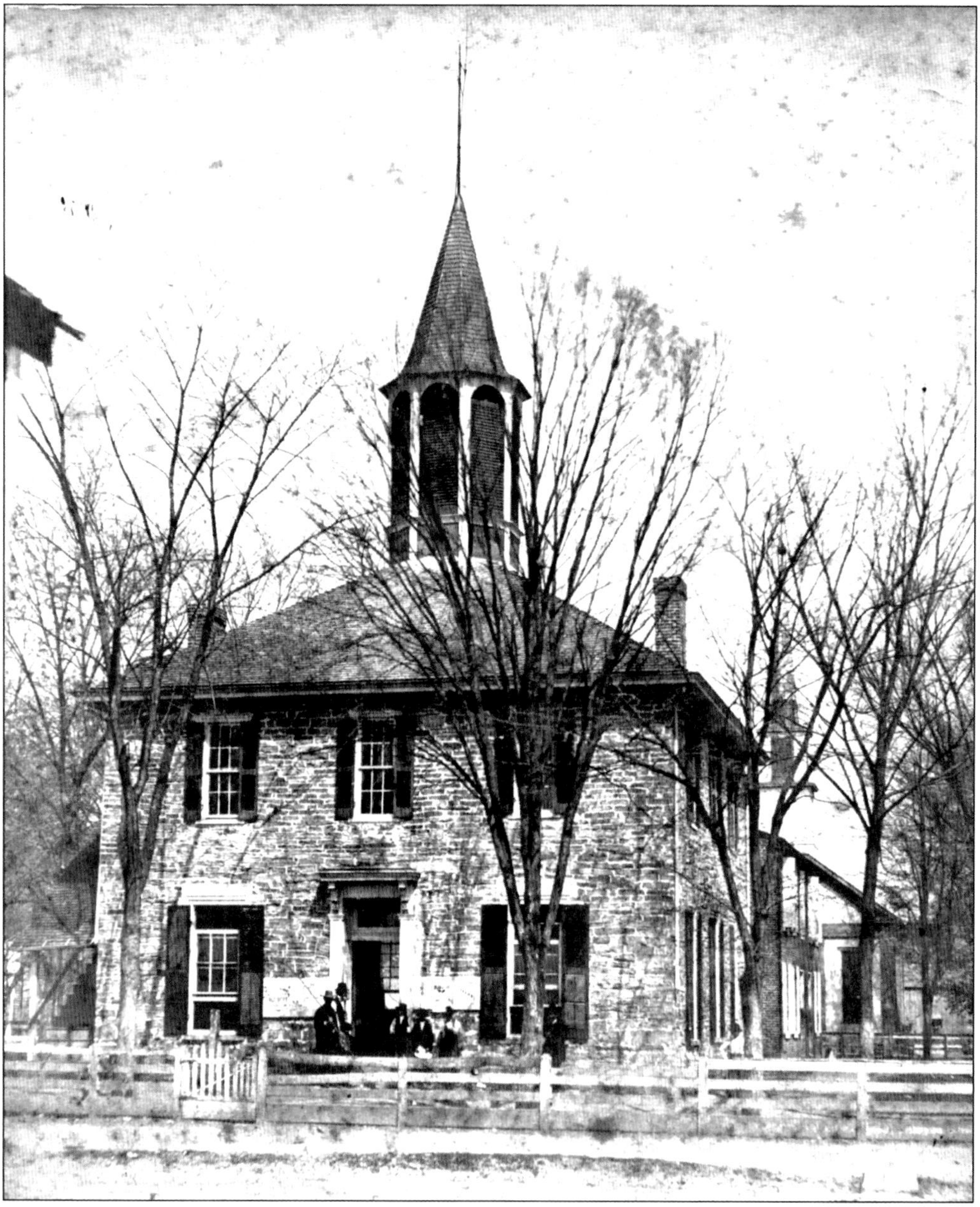

Dennis Pennington, territorial and state legislator for 29 years, advised Corydon residents that in order to secure the territorial capital for their town, they needed to build a county courthouse that would be impressive enough to serve as a state capitol, should the need arise. He was signed as the contractor and quarried the stone from the bed of Big Indian Creek. The Indiana House of Representatives met on the first floor; the Indiana State Senate and the Indiana Supreme Court occupied the second story. After the capital moved to Indianapolis in 1825, the building became the Harrison County Courthouse. This 1878 image is believed to be the oldest photograph of the building. The cupola has been heightened and an outside staircase built on the north side. The county office building and the Methodist church are visible behind the Corydon Capitol.

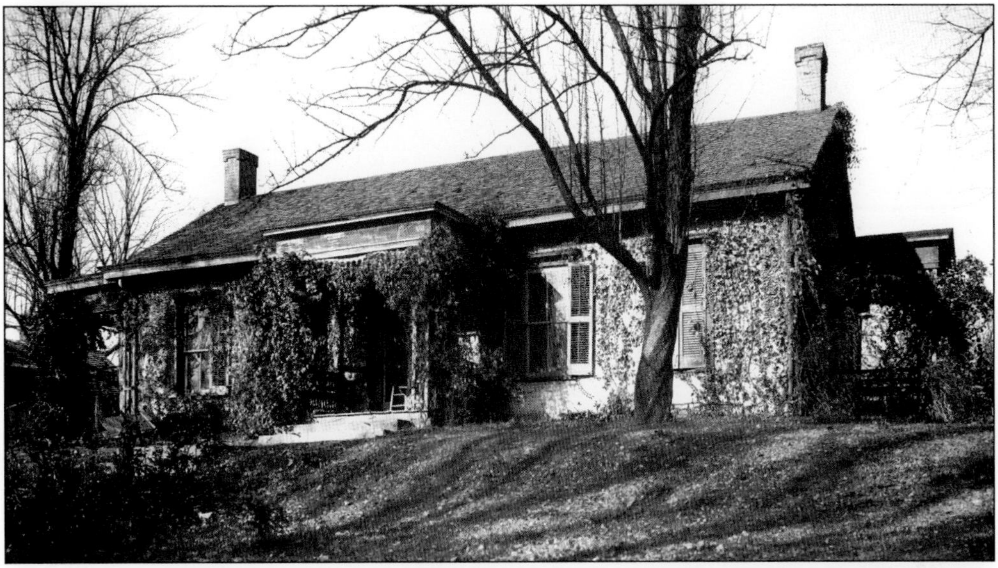

On the hill overlooking the capitol building was the first state office building. Clerks worked in the two rooms, which also held the records. The state treasury was kept safe in the cellar. Dennis Pennington drove his farm wagon to Vincennes to bring to Corydon all territorial records, papers, and funds. Four four-horse wagons and an entourage of some 30 people were required to move the capital to Indianapolis in October 1825. The building then became the home of Amzi Brewster and his family, who remained in residence until the late 20th century.

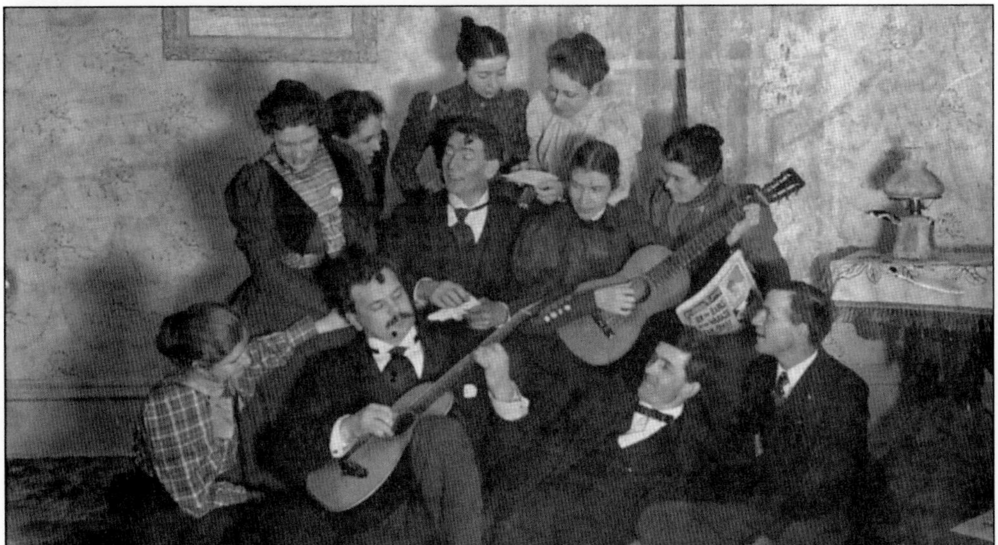

This photograph is captioned "Up at Brewsters." The individuals included are, from left to right, (first row) Nell, Ed Mitchell, Maurice, and Jim; (second row) Lizzie, Cad Shuck, Tom Wilson, Lizzie, and Olive; (third row) Jen and Harriet. After the capital moved to Indianapolis, the office building became the private residence of Amzi Brewster and his family. A large addition was put on at the back and Victorian porches and flourishes were added through the years. Numerous Brewsters contributed their talents and enthusiasm to Corydon through the years, including Aurelia Porter Brewster (daughter of Helen Porter Griffin and wife of Amzi Brewster), who edited the *1906 Atlas of Harrison County*.

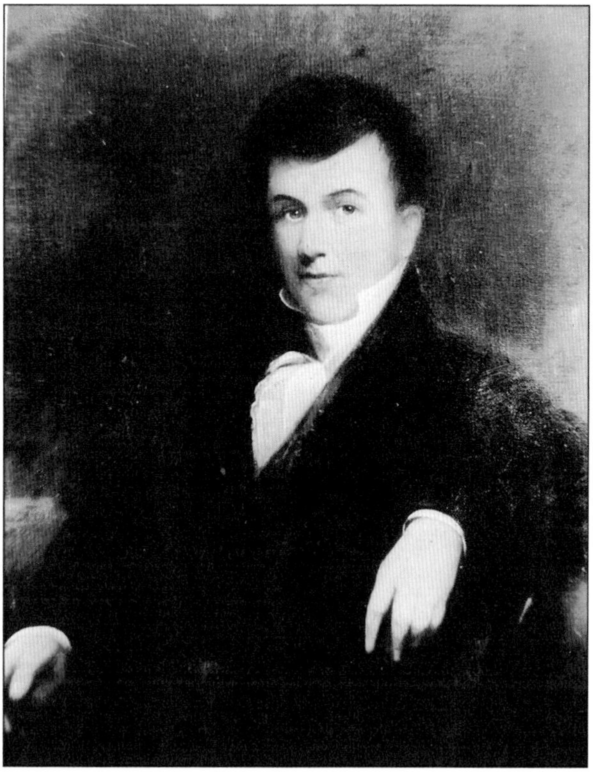

Jonathan Jennings was the first state governor of Indiana, serving from November 7, 1816, to December 4, 1822. He and his wife lived in an elegant Federal-style home on East Walnut Street. Both the Jenningses and their successors William and Sarah Hendricks were equally at home in the society of Washington City, where each man also served in the congress. They entertained both frontiersmen and national politicians with aplomb, and assured the new state favorable consideration in the nation's capital.

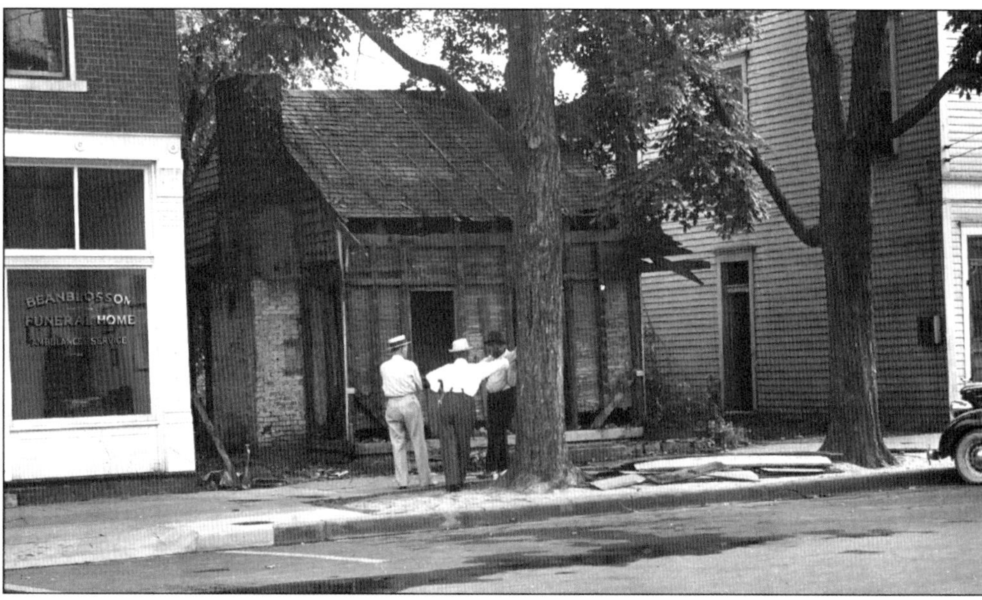

This tiny house on Chestnut Street in downtown was referred to as the "old Wiseman house," having been the property of the Wilford H. Wiseman family from 1851. It is thought, however, to have been built by John Tipton, sole surviving officer of the Corydon Yellow Jackets at the Battle of Tippecanoe, November 7, 1811. Tipton brought the survivors back home. He later served as county sheriff, and eventually became a United States senator from Indiana. He is thought to have built this house about 1816.

Two

The Square

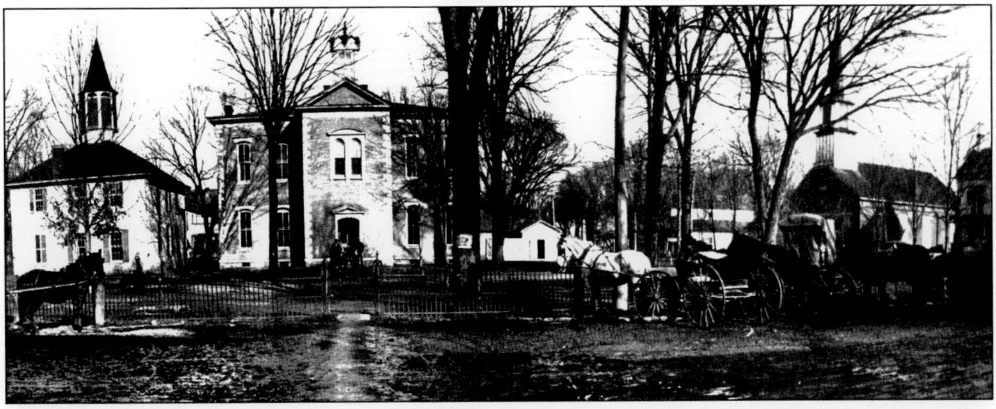

This panorama, probably taken in the 1880s, shows the Corydon Capitol, the county office building, and the Methodist church. The horses are tied to a special rail on the south side of the town square, where a wide pavement of bricks was put down so as to be easily washed. The small building just to the right of the office building provided public privies. Unpleasant, particularly on hot summer days, such structures were called the "necessary"—which they certainly were.

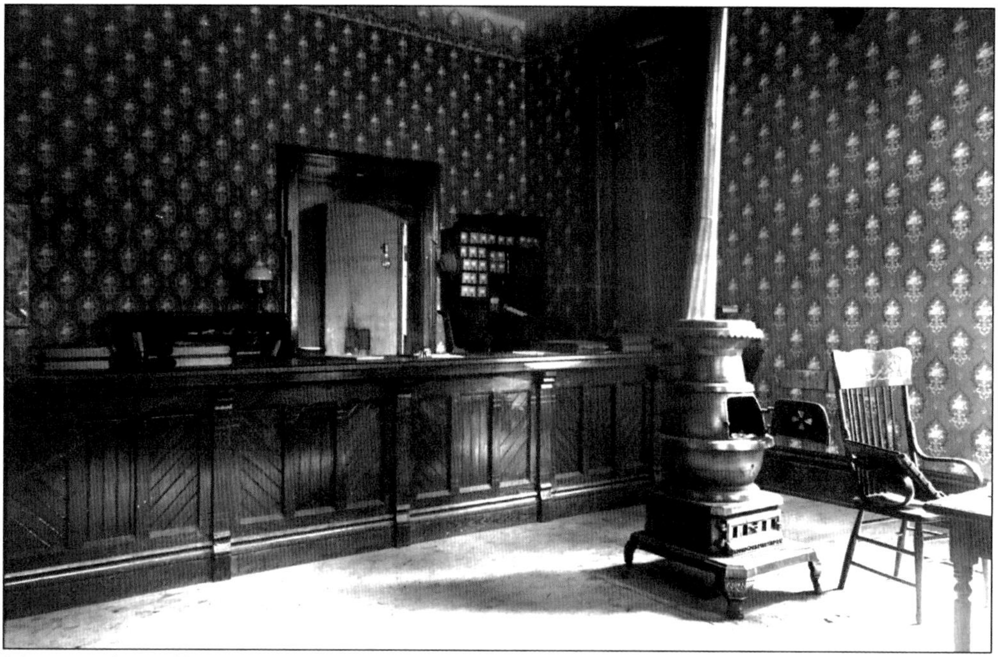

The recorder's office in the old county courthouse was well lit, on sunny days, anyway. At the time of this photograph, artificial light came from kerosene lamps. Heat came from coal stoves. Jef Wolfe, janitor for more than 30 years, started every winter workday by kindling 13 fires—15 when court was in session.

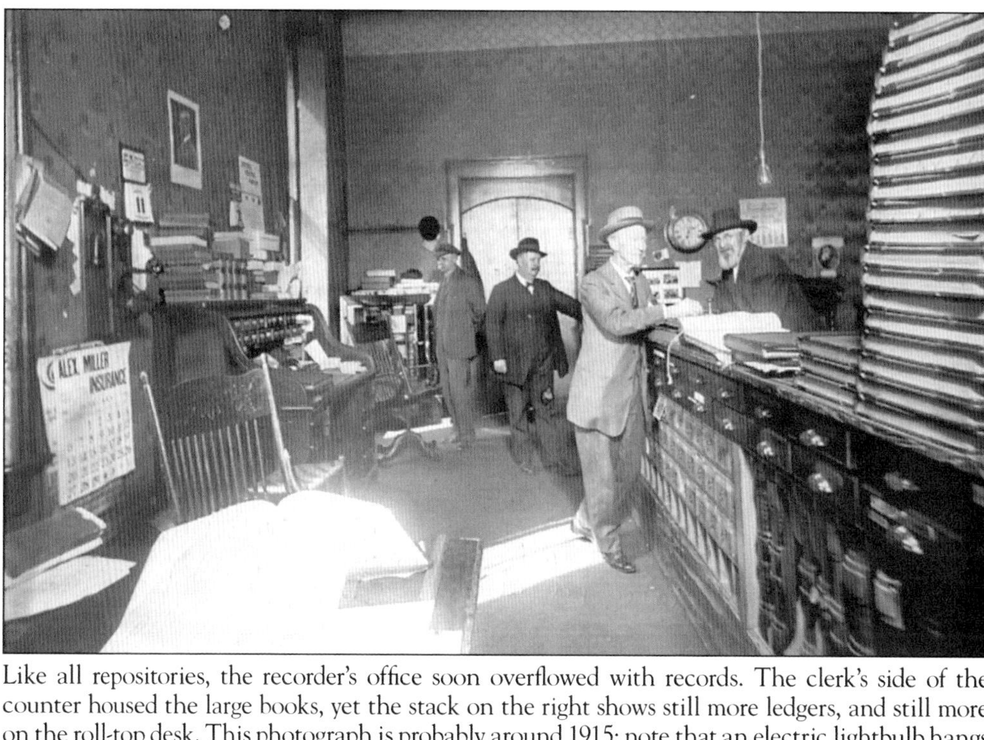

Like all repositories, the recorder's office soon overflowed with records. The clerk's side of the counter housed the large books, yet the stack on the right shows still more ledgers, and still more on the roll-top desk. This photograph is probably around 1915; note that an electric lightbulb hangs over the counter and no kerosene lamps are evident, yet the chairs seem not to have changed.

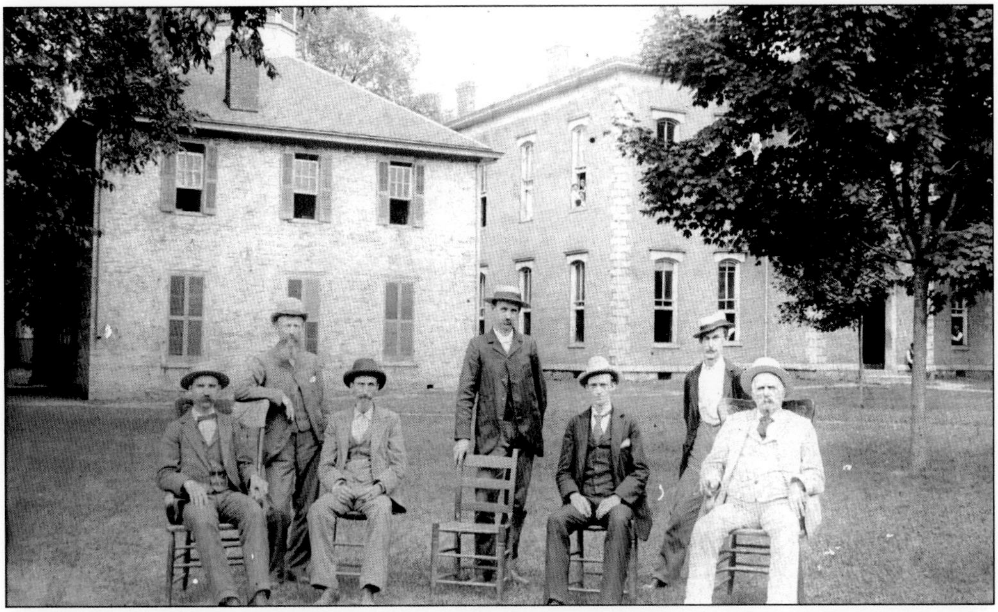

The gentlemen in this photograph are not identified, but the Corydon Capitol has taken up the purpose for which it was built—the Harrison County courthouse. The clerk's office was on the second floor, reached by an outside stairway on the north of the building. The brick county office building (to the right of the old capitol) was built in 1882 and stood until 1929.

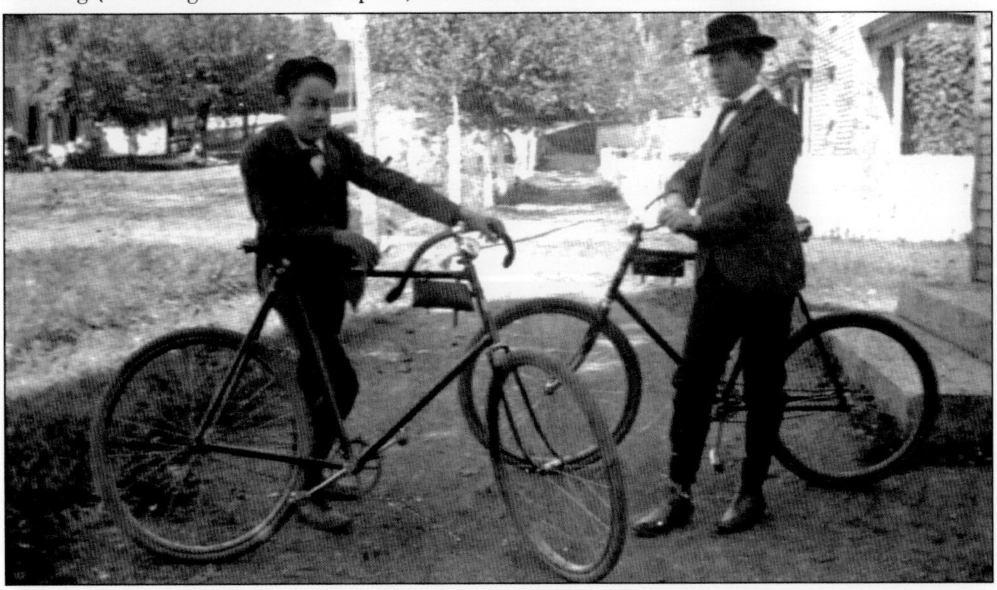

The first practical bicycle was the 1860s "bone shaker," a wooden contraption with iron-rimmed wheels and an iron strap to sit on. The high-wheeler became popular in the 1870s and 1880s. Both varieties were for young men only, requiring strength, daring, and a willingness to tumble heels-over-appetite. The modern bicycle, with chain mechanism and inflated tires, did not come until the 1890s. Popular among men of all ages, the bicycle was now acceptable for ladies too, offering healthful exercise in the out-of-doors. In these early days, roads were dirt, gravel, or stone paving. Tool kits such as those seen hanging from the handlebars came in handy. Cyclists pose in front of the Corydon Christian Church on Mulberry Street.

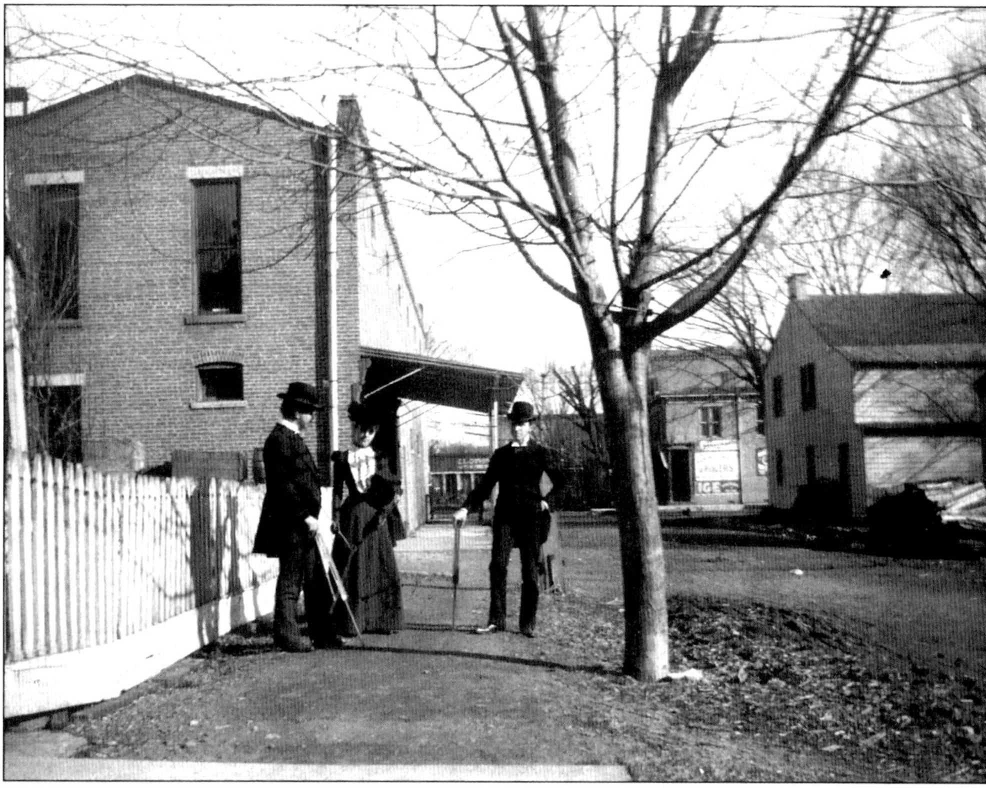

This early-1900s photograph was taken in front of present-day Beanblossom-Cesar Funeral Home and looks east on Beaver Street. The dirt sidewalk is beside the Town Square Gallery building (left). The wooden residence to the right was the Benjamin Aydelotte house. Aydelotte owned land in south Corydon, which, in 1860, was sold to the Harrison County Agricultural Society for the annual fairs. In 1910, this residence was replaced with a redbrick bank building. The building across the street was a grocery and then, for many years, Davis Drug Store.

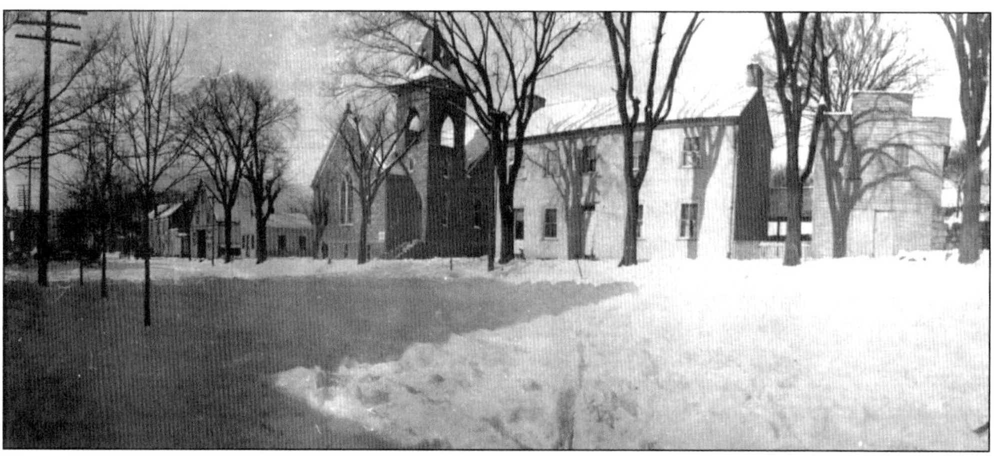

Here are the January 1910 snow-covered Walnut Street and Liken's Corner (far left), Liken's Stables (with the large door in front), a small frame building where the Star Cleaners building presently stands identified as Judge William A. Porter's law office, the Presbyterian church, the Porter-Griffin house, and the Porter woodshed.

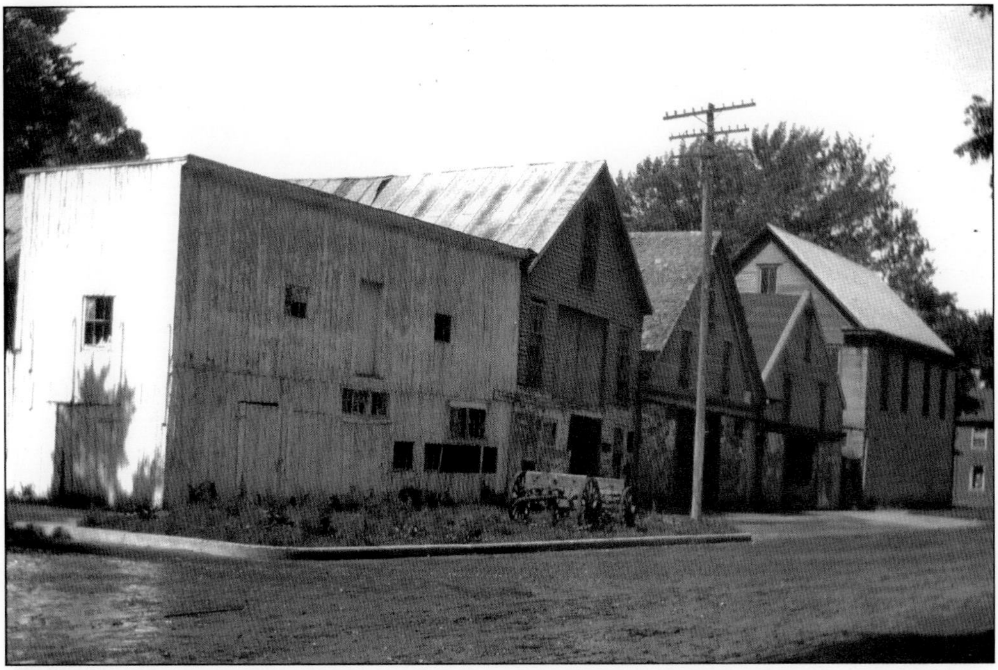

This 1912 photograph shows the site of the present Harrison County Courthouse. The large white building on the near corner is Bulleit's Blacksmith Shop. Amiel L. Bulleit established his business here and taught the trade to his son, John Bulleit. The two-story building on the far corner is the Dove's Nest. That establishment enjoyed the reputation of being a "notorious booze joint," but the name refers to the primary business of the "soiled doves," who plied their trade in the shadow of the courthouse. This entire block was cleared for the new courthouse in 1928.

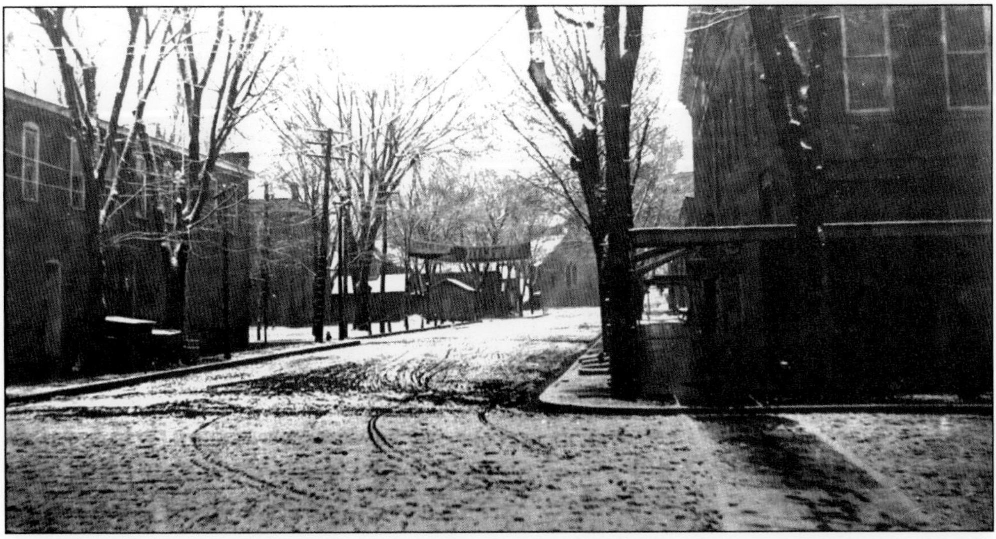

A dusting of snow, probably in the early 20th century, shows how welcome and practical sidewalk awnings were. The courthouse annex is visible to the left, and the Presbyterian church (now the Wright Interpretive Center) can be seen in the middle. The photograph looks north on Elm Street from Chestnut Street.

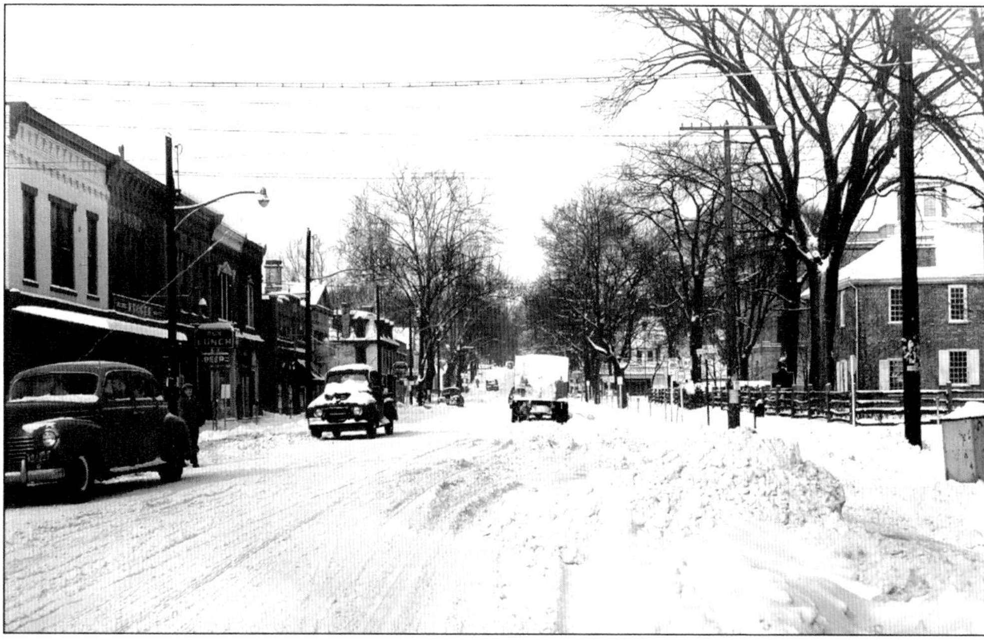

Although undated, this photograph probably shows the 14-inch snowfall of early February 1966. The restored Corydon Capitol is visible at the right, but Capitol Avenue is completely covered despite obvious traffic using it.

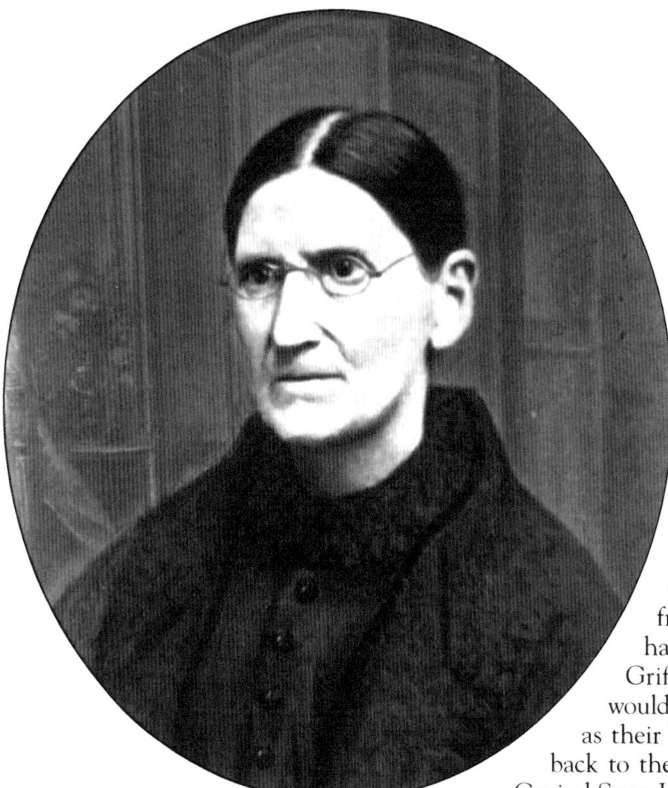

Judge William A. Porter and his wife, Elizabeth, lived in Gov. William Hendricks's house on the square. The judge's law office was a small frame building next door, which has been recreated. The Porter, Griffin, and Brewster families would keep the historic buildings as their homes until they were turned back to the state as part of the Corydon Capitol State Historic Site.

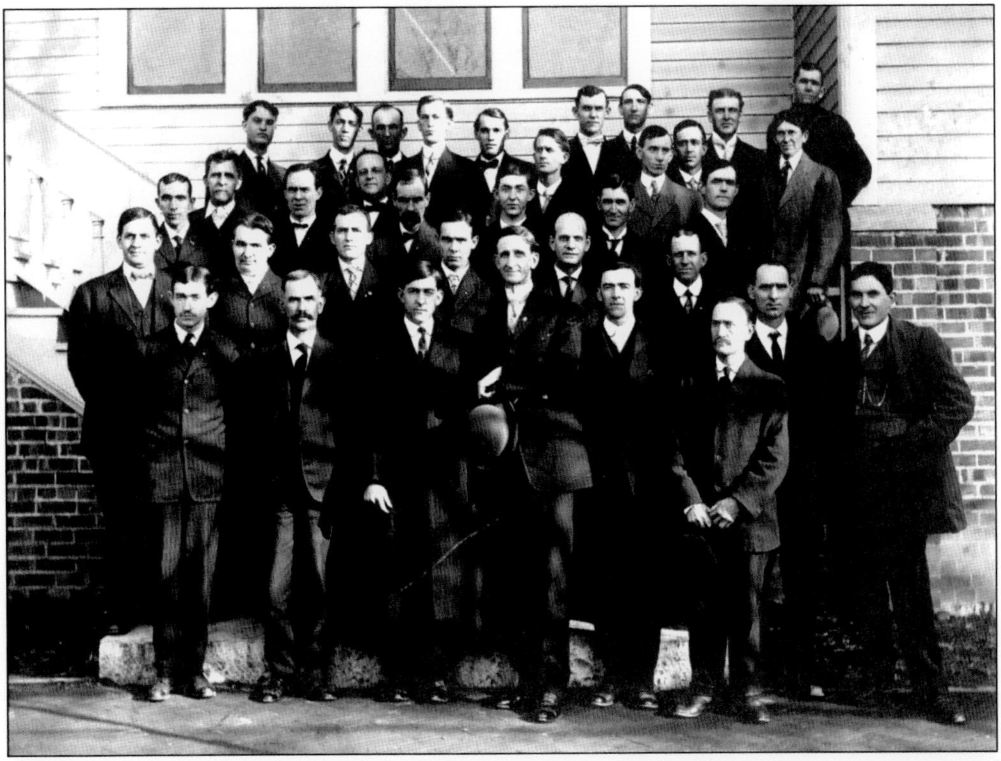

These churchmen posed on the steps, perhaps to mark a new building project or retirement of a debt.

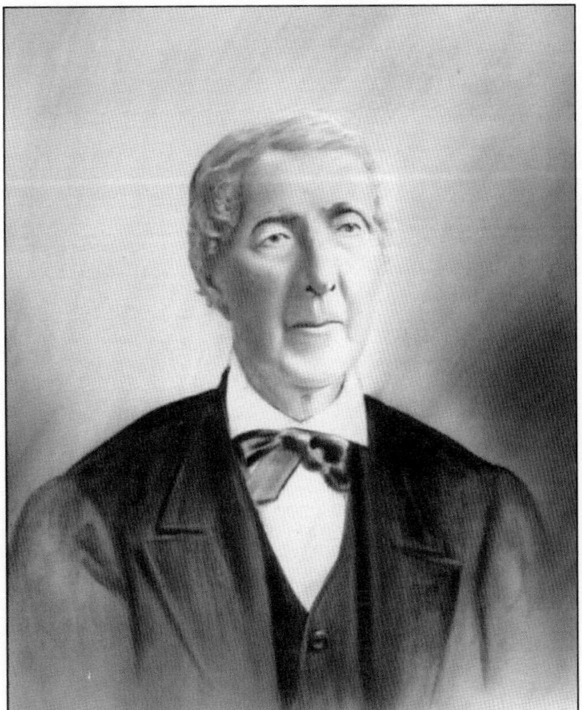

Judge William A. Porter purchased Gov. William Hendricks's house in 1841. His family lived there for 134 years. Porter was a renowned lawyer, staunch Whig, state legislature for many years, and Speaker of the House in 1849.

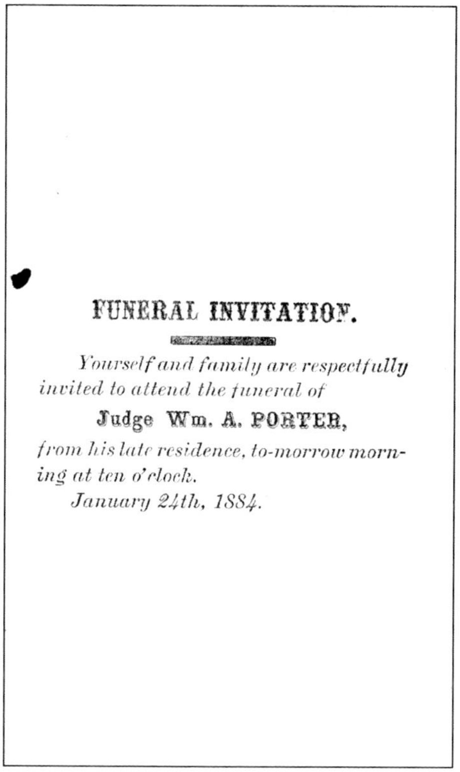

FUNERAL INVITATION.

Yourself and family are respectfully invited to attend the funeral of

Judge Wm. A. PORTER,

from his late residence, to-morrow morning at ten o'clock.

January 24th, 1884.

The funeral invitation for Judge William A. Porter is pictured. By the late 19th and into the early 20th century, funeral notices might be individually delivered to persons invited to attend, or they might be publicly posted, trusting that friends and family would know they were welcome to attend.

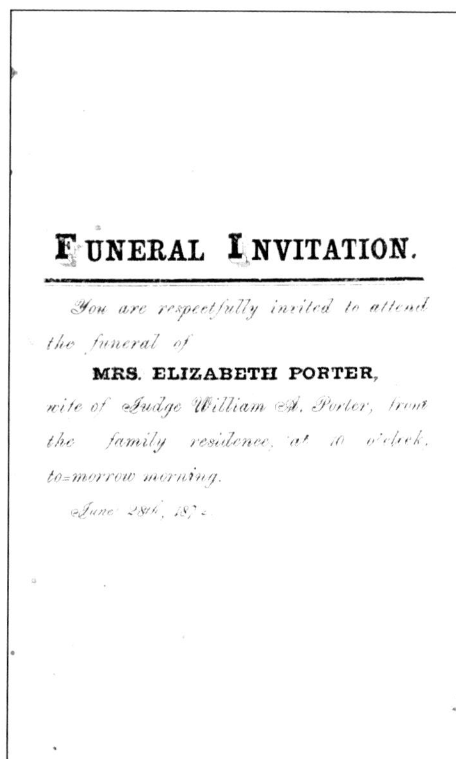

FUNERAL INVITATION.

You are respectfully invited to attend the funeral of

MRS. ELIZABETH PORTER,

wife of Judge William A. Porter, from the family residence, at 10 o'clock, to-morrow morning.

June 28th, 187[illegible]

This is the funeral invitation for Elizabeth Porter. In the 19th century, funerals were attended by invitation only. Weighty cards with engraved printing were usually hand delivered, and were kept as mementos of departed friends and loved ones.

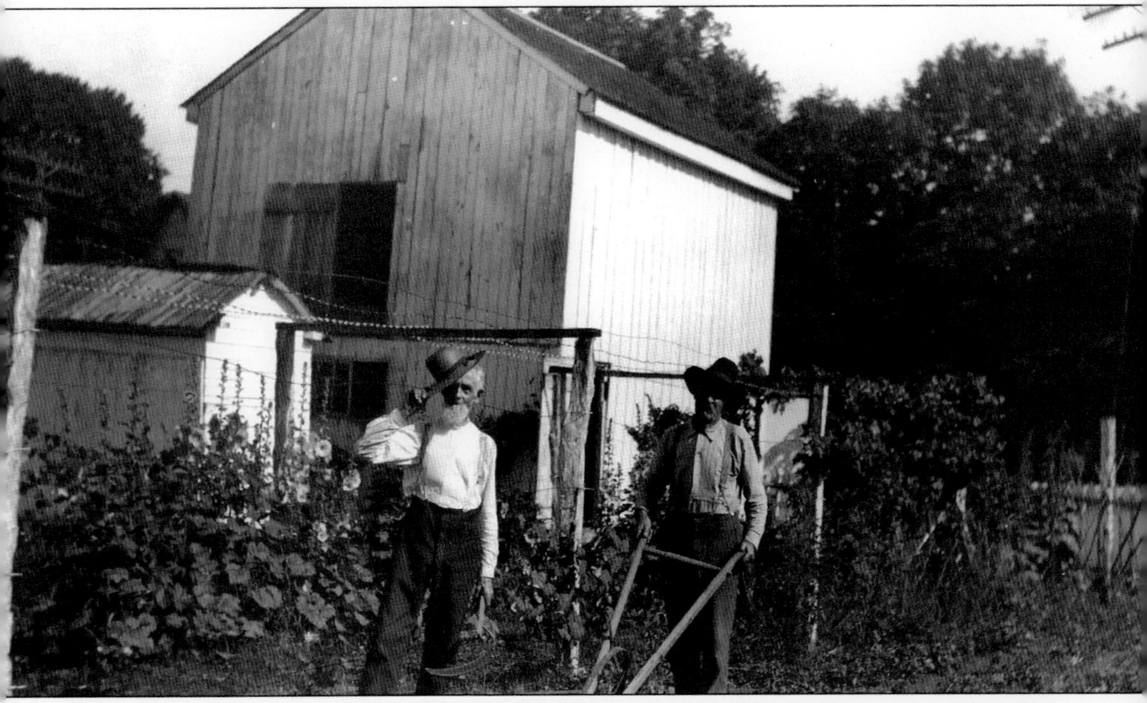

The heavy-timbered structure in the rear of this photograph had been a horse-powered carding mill operated by Thomas Paddox, but in later days it was the Porter-Griffin barn. It faced High Street. There was also a large stable nearby, surrounded by a large cow lot. The stable had stalls for the horse and cow on the ground floor and a hay loft on the second floor. Each spring, all outbuildings and wooden fences were whitewashed. Brothers-in-law Patrick Griffin (left) and Amzi W. Brewster (right) stand in front of the corncrib, grape arbor, and garden. Most town lots were large enough for a large vegetable garden and shelter for a family cow, which could be pastured on common lots. Flowers were also grown in profusion. Prized for color and fragrance, they were artfully incorporated into landscaping, cut for bouquets, and eagerly shared by means of seeds or slips, small sprouts pinched off and rooted for a new plant.

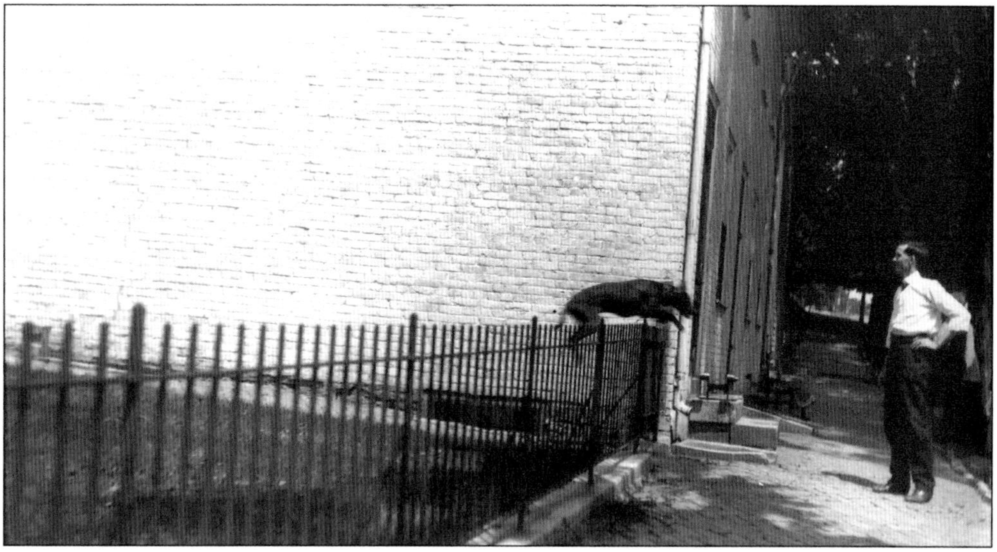

If this sturdy cast-iron fence was intended to keep in the Porter-Griffin family pets, it obviously did not work for John Henry. He jumps it in this 1908 photograph to join his master Maurice Griffin.

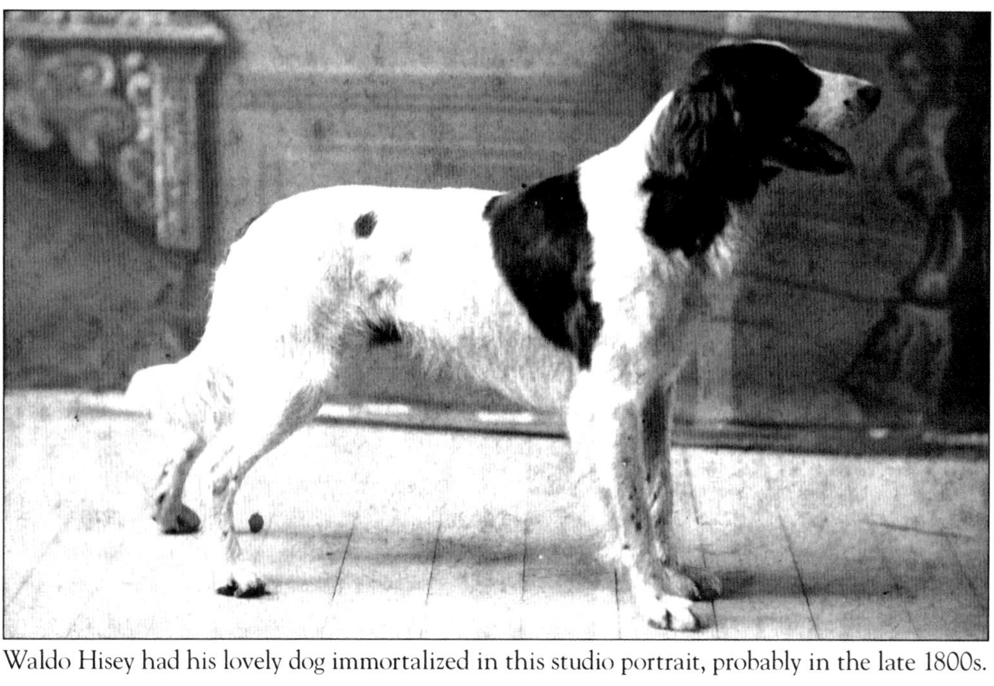

Waldo Hisey had his lovely dog immortalized in this studio portrait, probably in the late 1800s.

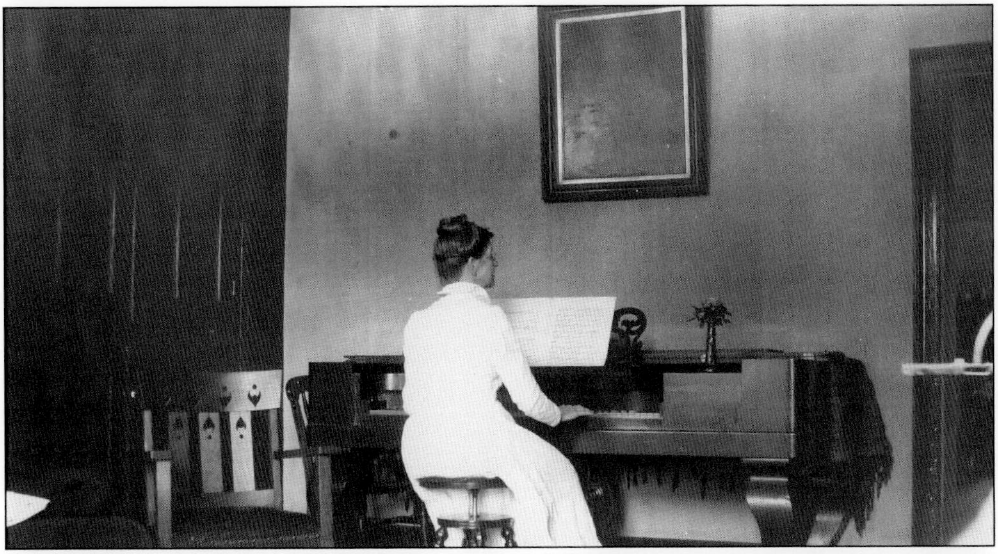

Judge William A. Porter purchased this piano in 1854 from Peters and Cragg of Louisville, Kentucky. Located on the Falls of the Ohio River, Louisville was a center of music publishing all through the middle of the 19th century. Composers, teachers, musicians, and instrument makers partnered and recombined through most of the century. They manufactured pianos and distributed for other firms. The judge's daughter, Helen Porter Griffin, plays the Peters and Cragg piano in this 1908 photograph. It was subsequently donated to the University of Louisville for display in the school of music.

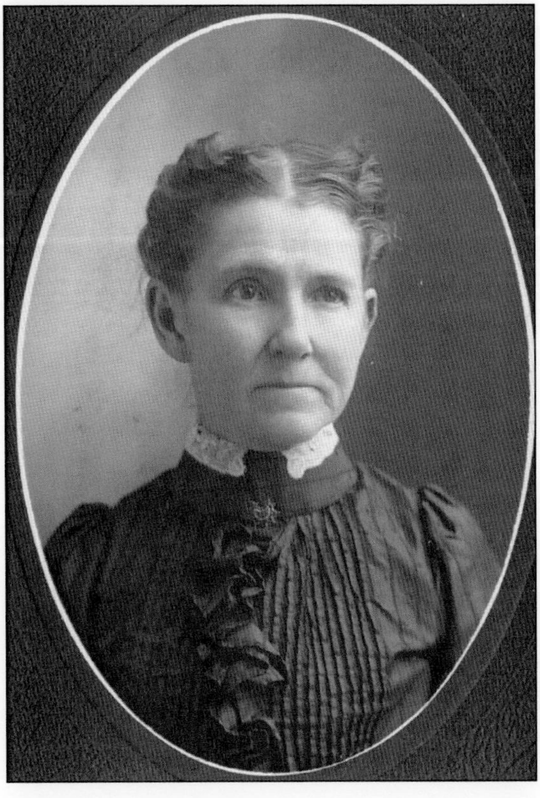

Helen Porter Griffin is seen in a studio portrait, probably taken in the 1890s. The daughter of Judge William A. Porter and his wife Elizabeth, Helen began the invaluable collections of photographs, clippings, and mementos, which her grandson Frederick Porter Griffin developed into the collection housed in the Griffin Center.

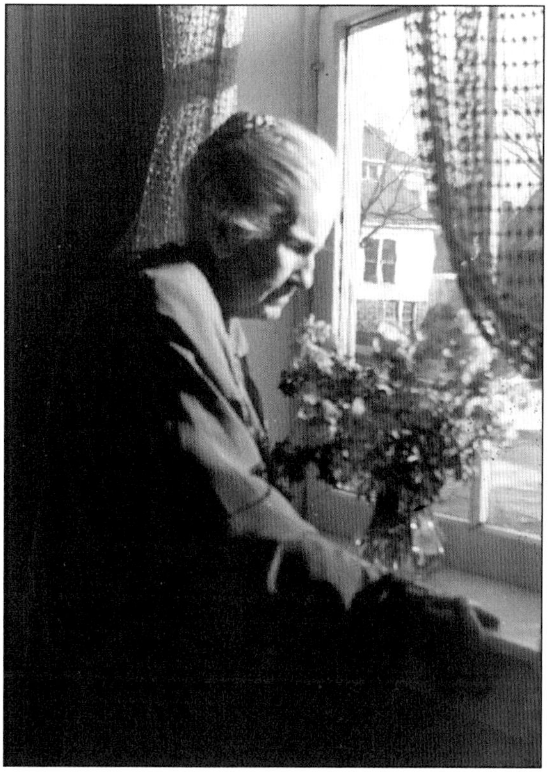

Helen Porter Griffin is seen at the window of the Porter-Griffin house (Gov. William Hendricks's house), where she was born and lived for 96 years. This photograph commemorates her birthday, December 1, 1939. Griffin died the following April. She was a girl of 20 when John Hunt Morgan galloped through Corydon.

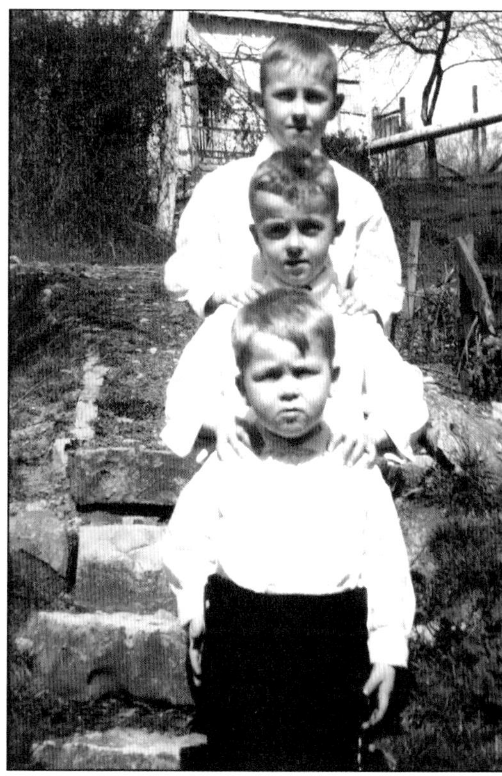

The Griffin brothers are seen on the steps leading up the hill to the wash house behind the Porter-Griffin house. On the top is Henry P. Griffin, then William "Tim" Griffin, and smallest Frederick P. Griffin, who would become Harrison County historian. The picture was taken in 1918, making Fred about three years old.

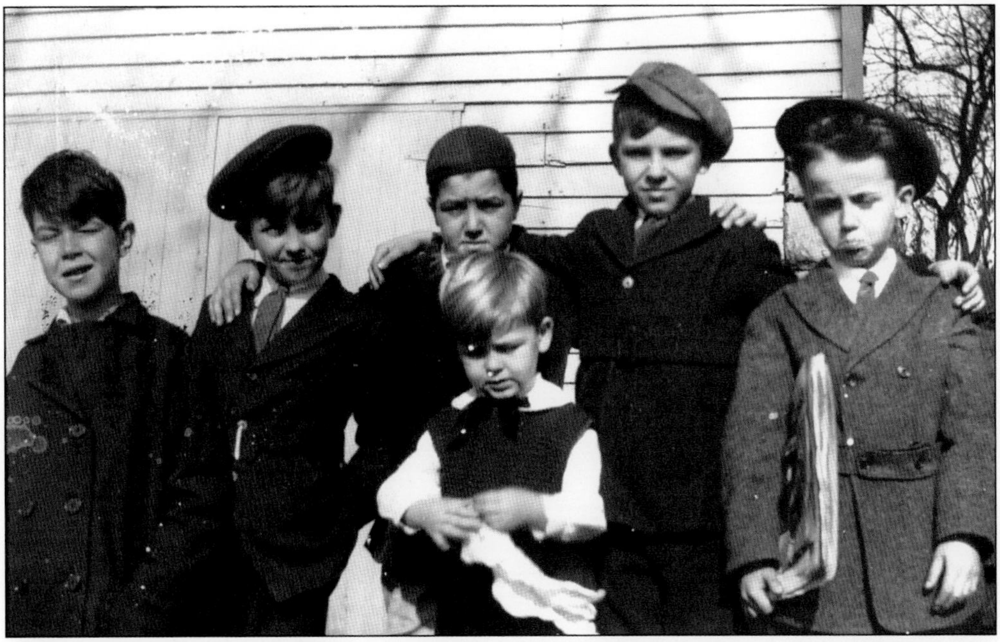

In the early 1920s, the Griffin brothers were joined by some cousins. Six boys appear in the photograph, but only five names are given: Dwight Brewster, Henry P. Griffin, Ben Brewster Sample, and William "Tim" Griffin. Fred Griffin stands in front.

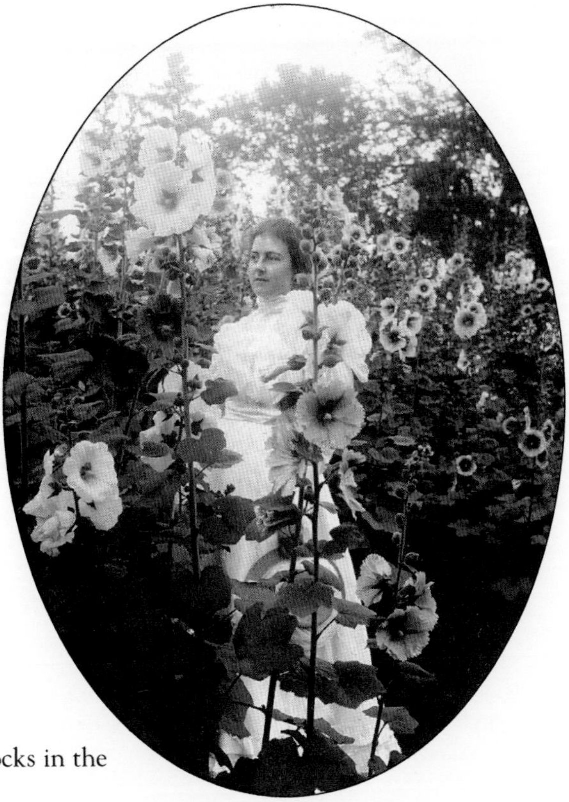

Annis Griffin stands among the hollyhocks in the Porter-Griffin house garden.

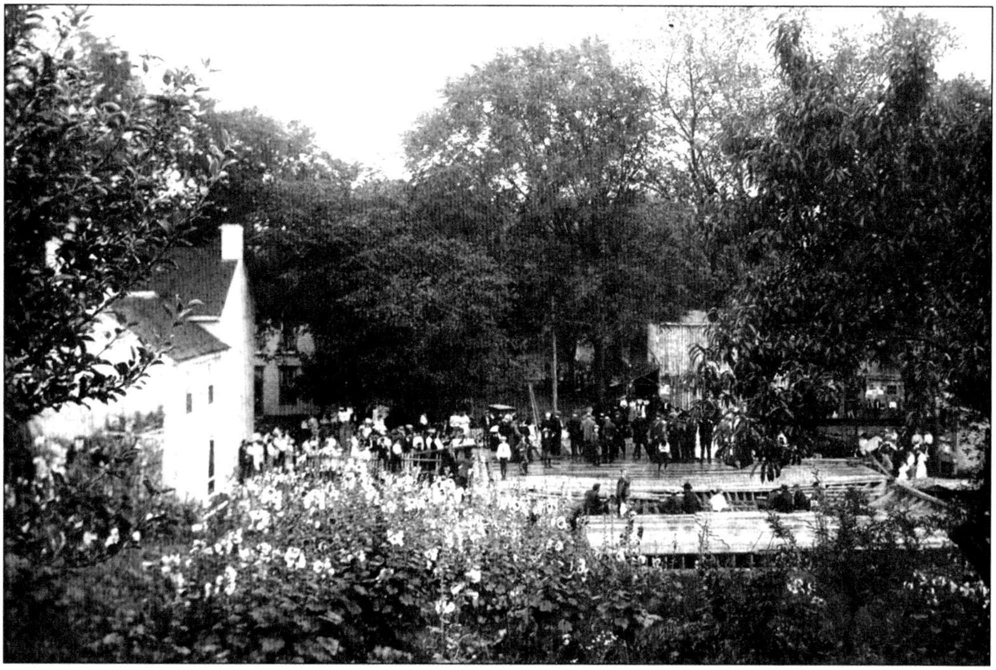

The photographer is on the hill above the Porter-Griffin house, the white structure on the left. Bulleit's Blacksmith Shop and Wagon Works (with awning) is seen behind the crowd. The occasion is the laying of the cornerstone of the Presbyterian church in 1906.

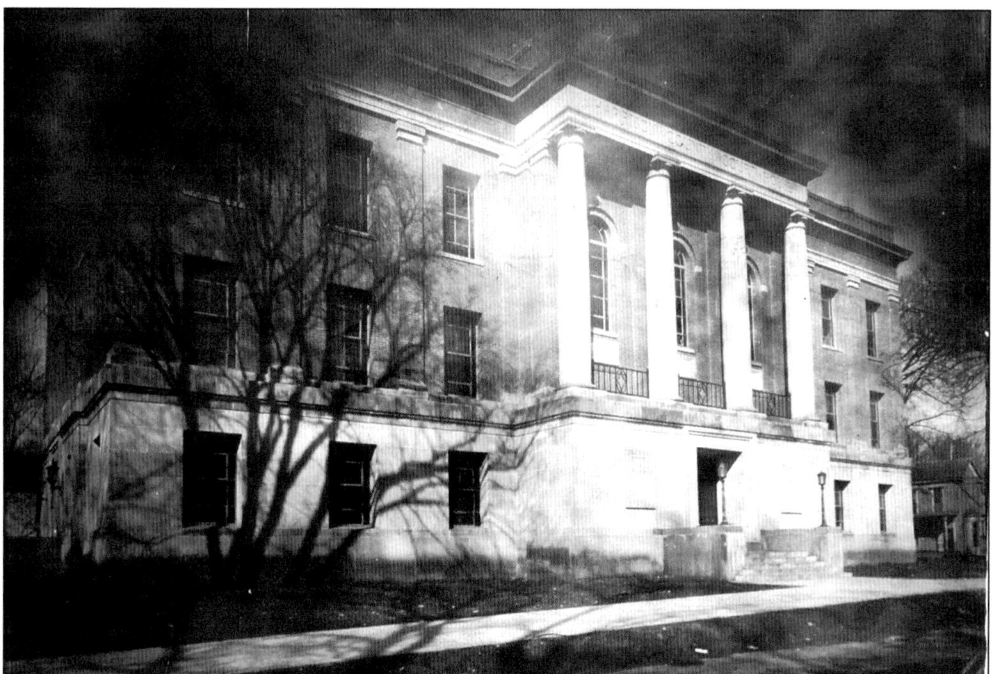

The completed courthouse is seen in 1928. Cherry Street was closed and transformed into the sidewalk, seen here, between the courthouse and the Corydon Capitol. The bond debt to finance the building was paid off in 1945.

Blaine Hayes Sr. was Corydon town attorney for 20 years in the 1920s and 1930s. A graduate of Corydon High School, Indiana University, and Indiana University Law School, Hayes was regarded as one of the finest attorneys in the state. In addition to his civic work, he was noted for breeding fine Guernsey cattle.

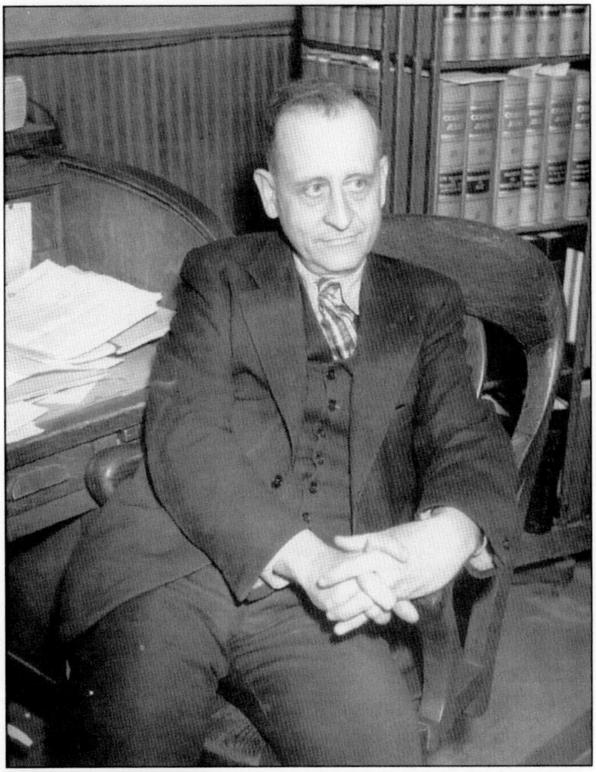

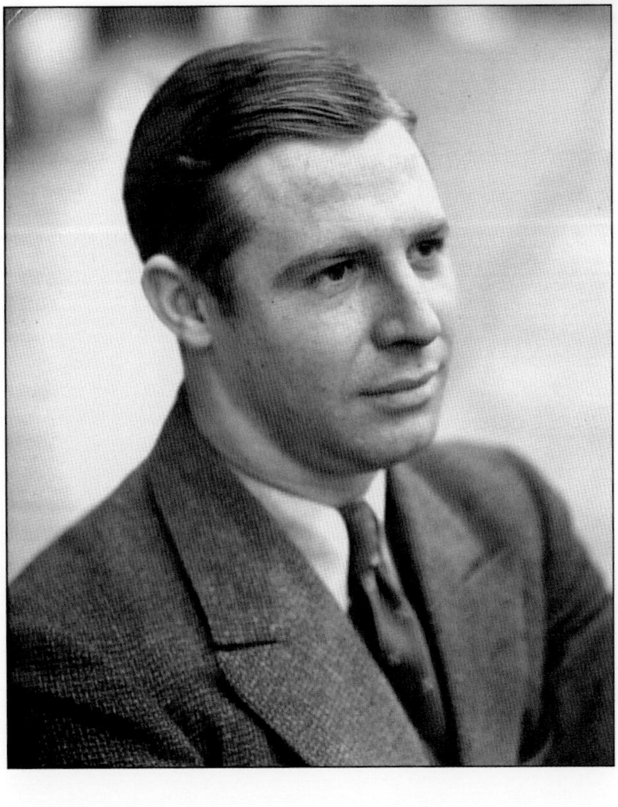

Another well-known native, Eugene "Shine" Feller was elected county prosecutor from 1949 to 1971. He continued in private practice still longer, maintaining a modest office on a side street. He earned a reputation as a formidable force in the courtroom and a thorough corporate litigator.

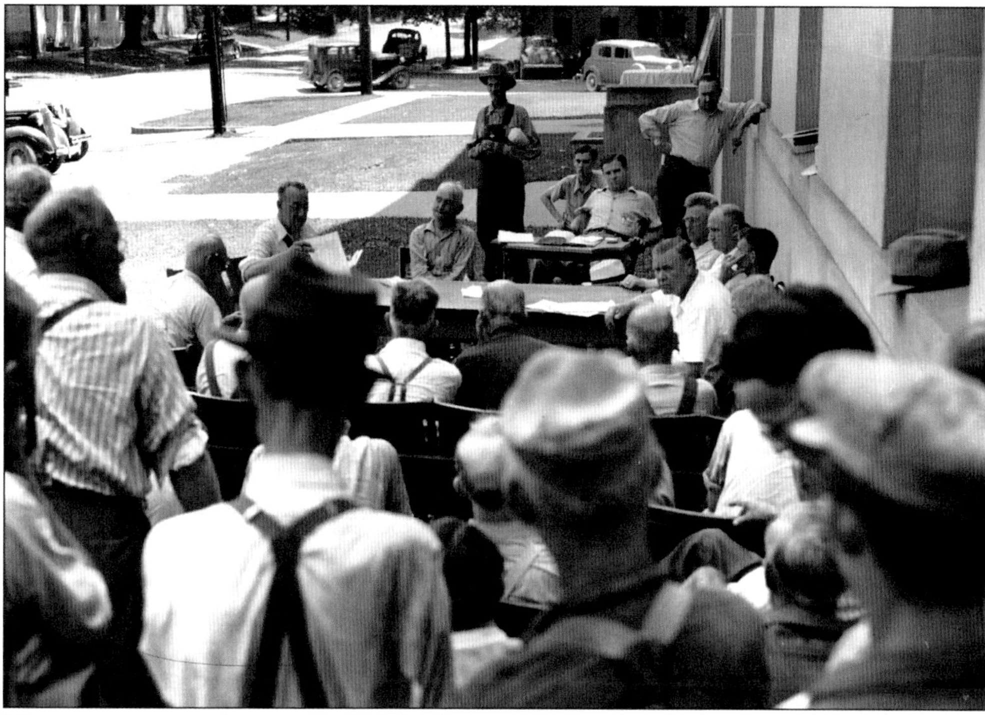

The new county courthouse was a sleek, bright art moderne structure, but modern conveniences did not yet include air conditioning. Here in the 1930s, court is convened outside to beat the heat.

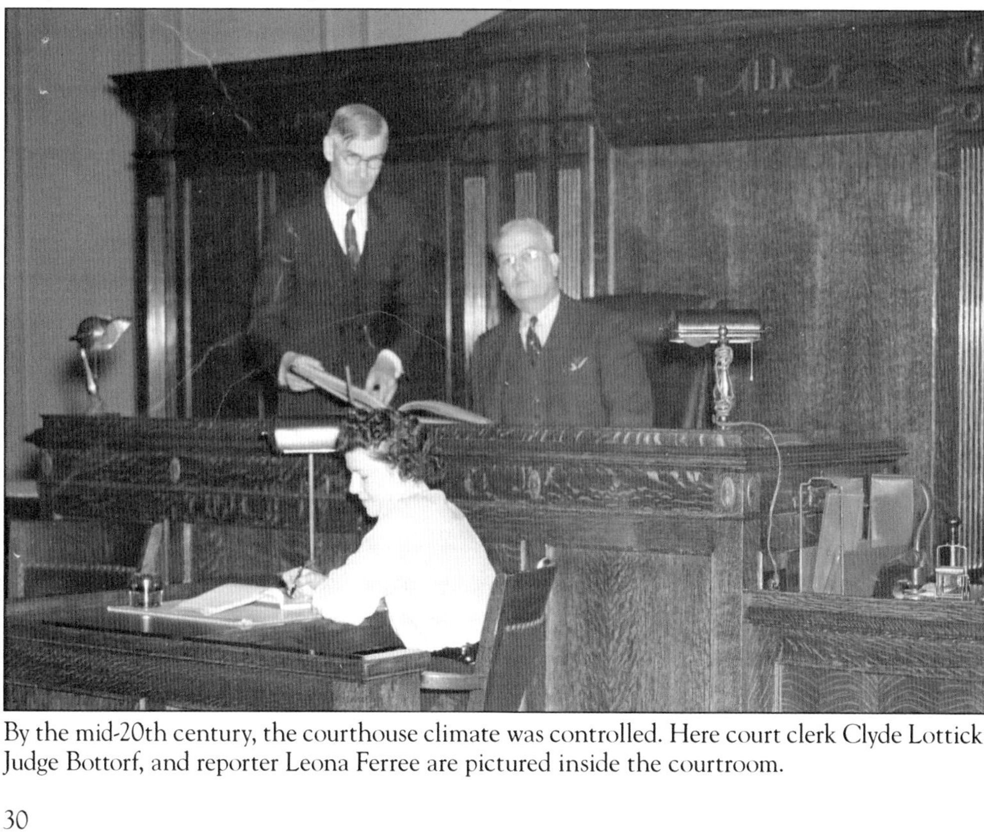

By the mid-20th century, the courthouse climate was controlled. Here court clerk Clyde Lottick, Judge Bottorf, and reporter Leona Ferree are pictured inside the courtroom.

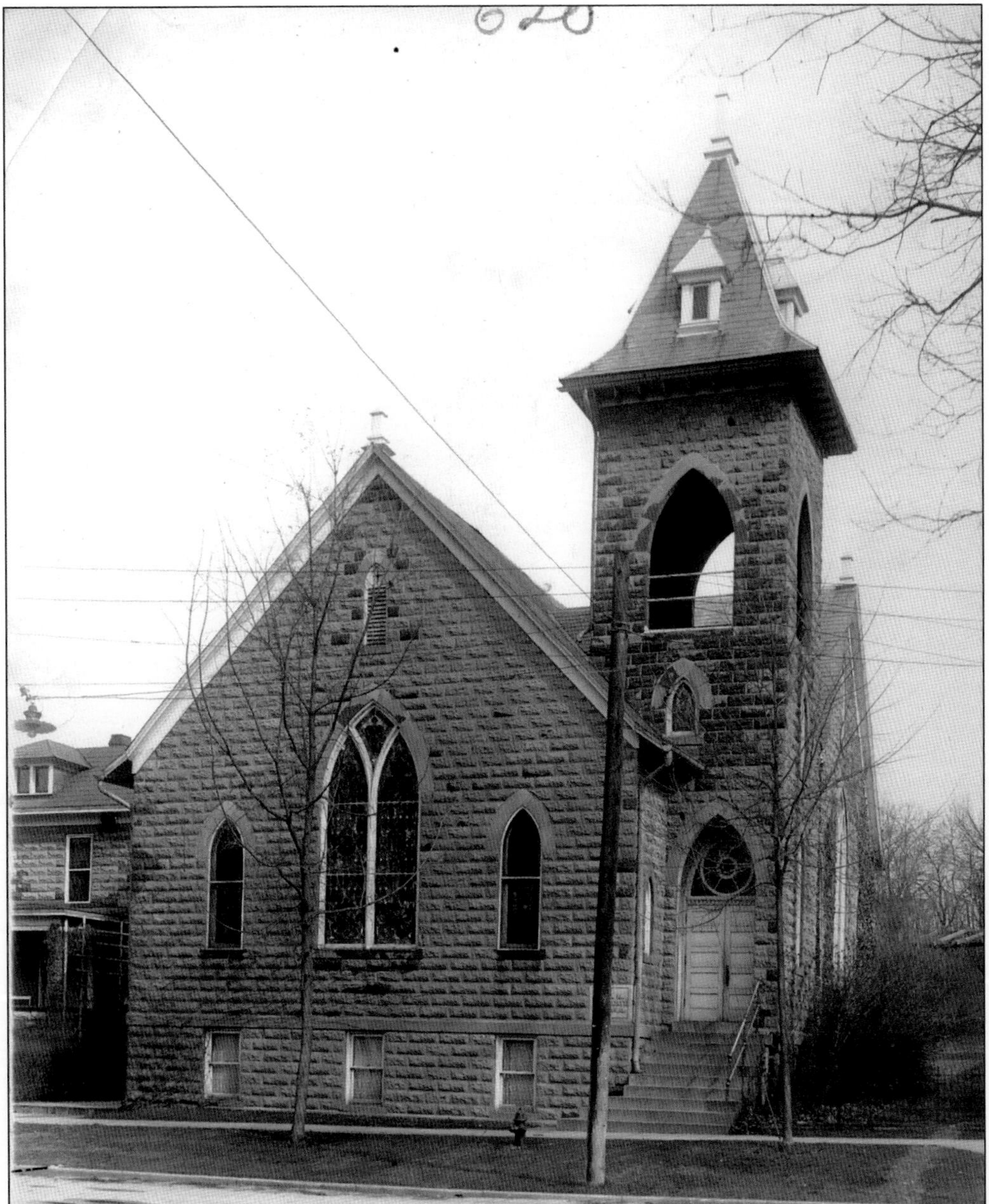

The Presbyterian church is now the Wright Interpretive Center, part of the Corydon Capitol State Historic Site. The Porter-Griffin house is to the right, out of the photograph. The stone house to the left is not the Presbyterian parsonage, but the home of Maurice Griffin and family.

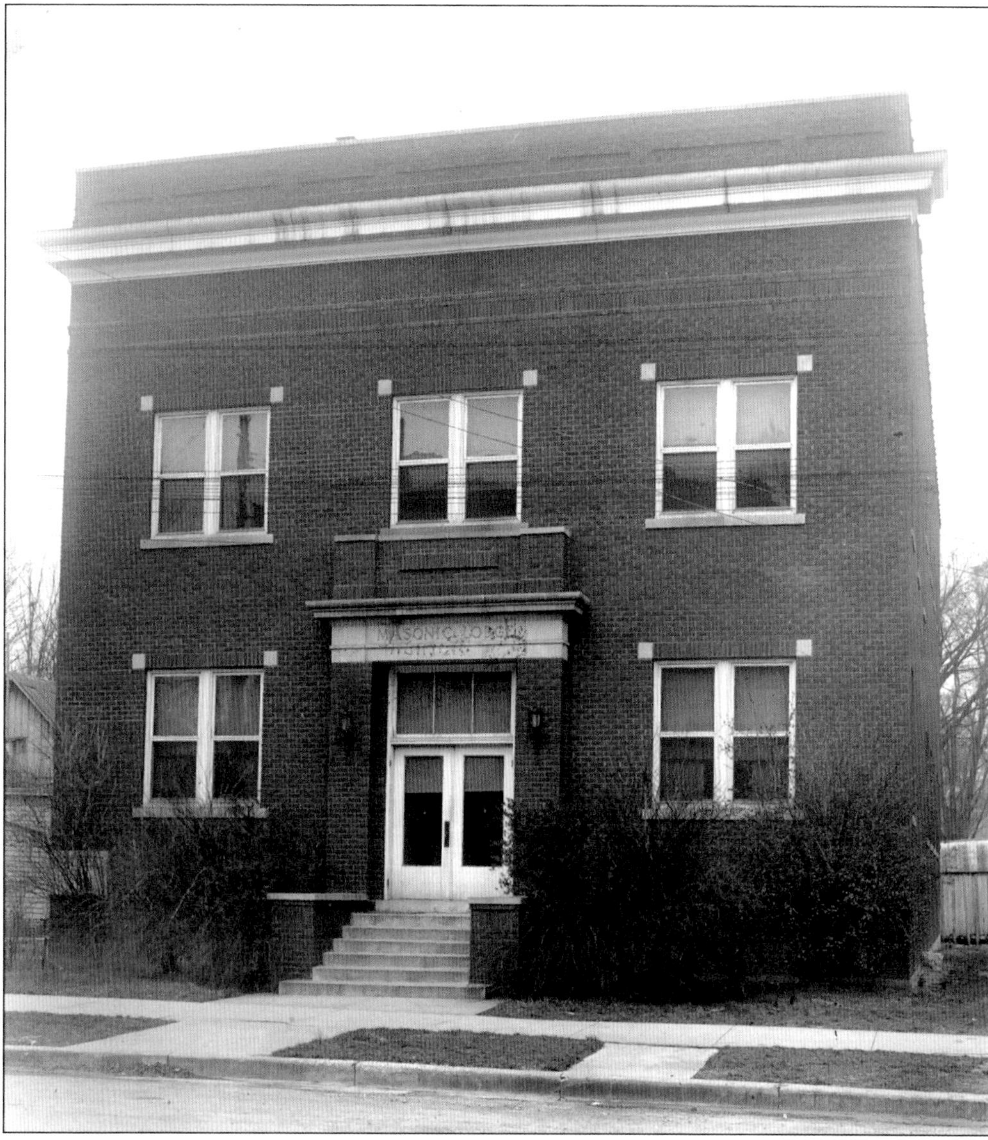

On May 26, 1817, Pisgah Lodge met for the first time and was constituted a Masonic Lodge under a dispensation granted by the Kentucky Grand Lodge. Many names from Corydon's founding and development appear on the membership rolls: Davis Floyd, Jonathan Jennings, Jacob W. Kinter, Walter Q. Gresham, Thomas McGrain, and many others. The lodge occupied several different quarters before settling into its own building in 1926.

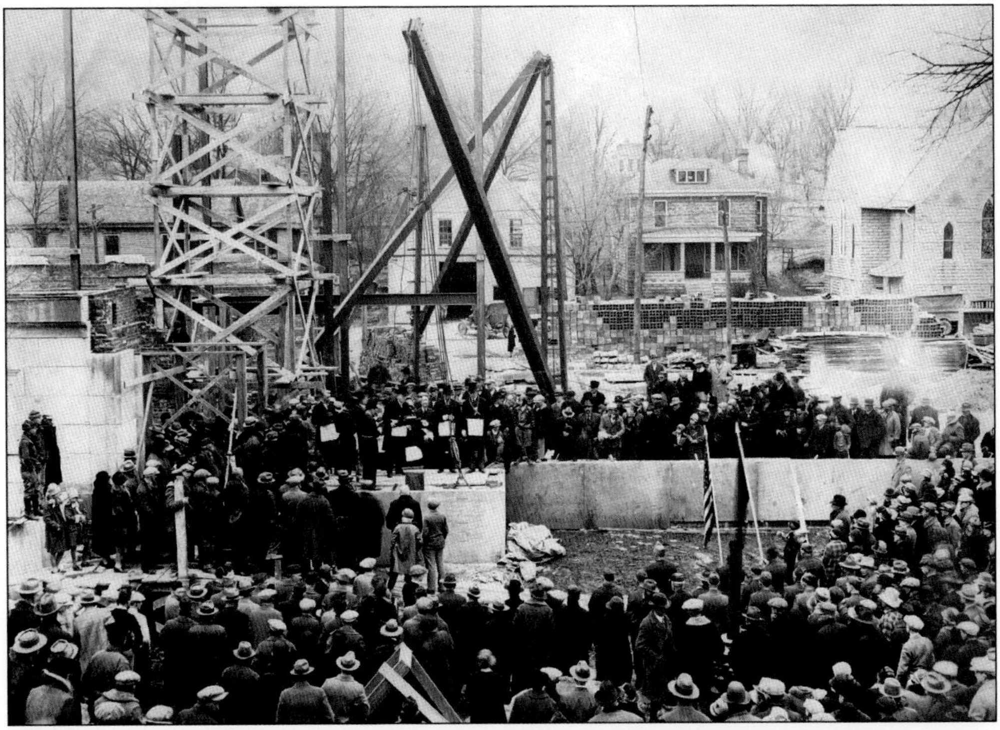

Grand officers of the Masonic Grand Lodge of Indiana came to Corydon to lay the cornerstone of the new Harrison County Courthouse on February 25, 1928. This photograph shows them putting the copper box into the stone. It contains lists of Indiana leaders, the act of the legislature legalizing the sale of the Corydon Capitol building and public square by Harrison County to the State of Indiana, an article about Martha Pennington Graham, daughter of Dennis and Elizabeth Pennington, and many other documents.

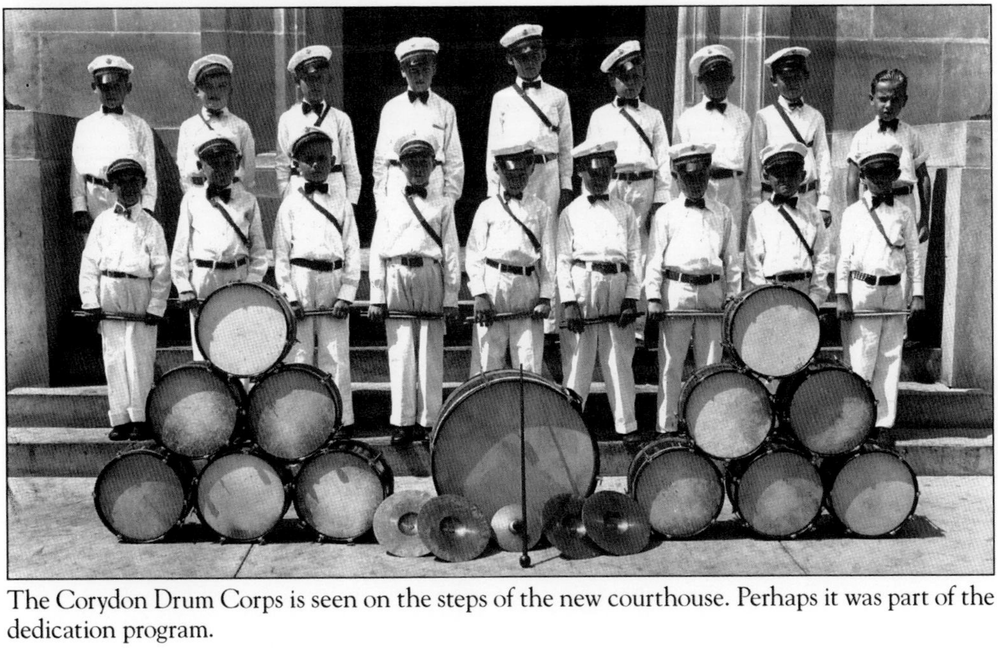

The Corydon Drum Corps is seen on the steps of the new courthouse. Perhaps it was part of the dedication program.

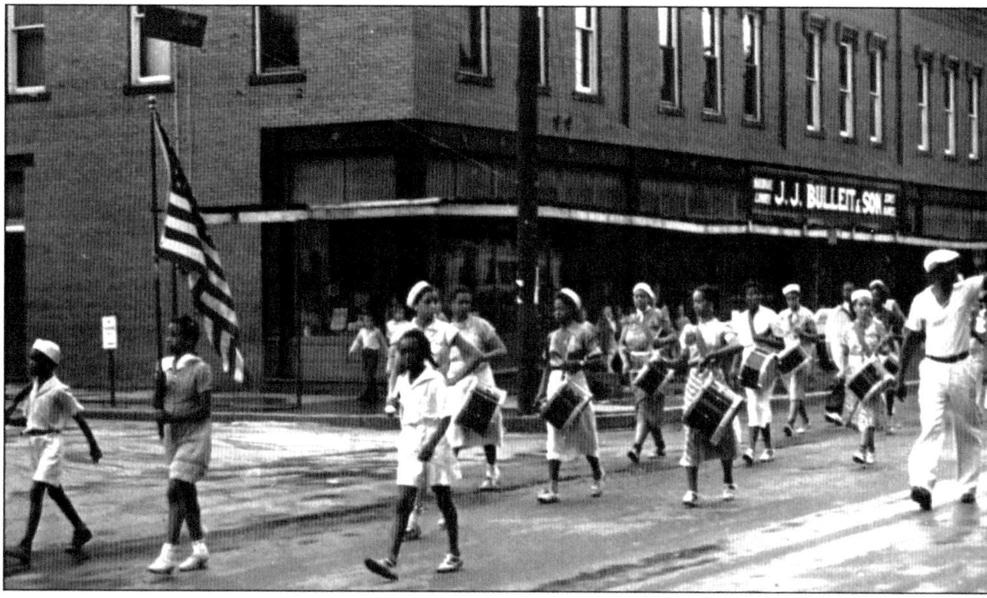

Corydon remained segregated for many years despite landmark decisions making Indiana a free state. This drum corps is exclusively African American. From the first settlement of the Northwest Territory, some whites feared that freed persons might become a financial burden on them. However, Paul Mitchem and his wife, Susanna, trekked from North Carolina to Indiana in 1814, bringing with them 107 enslaved people. They came specifically to free these people in a place where they would not be reenslaved after the Mitchems' deaths.

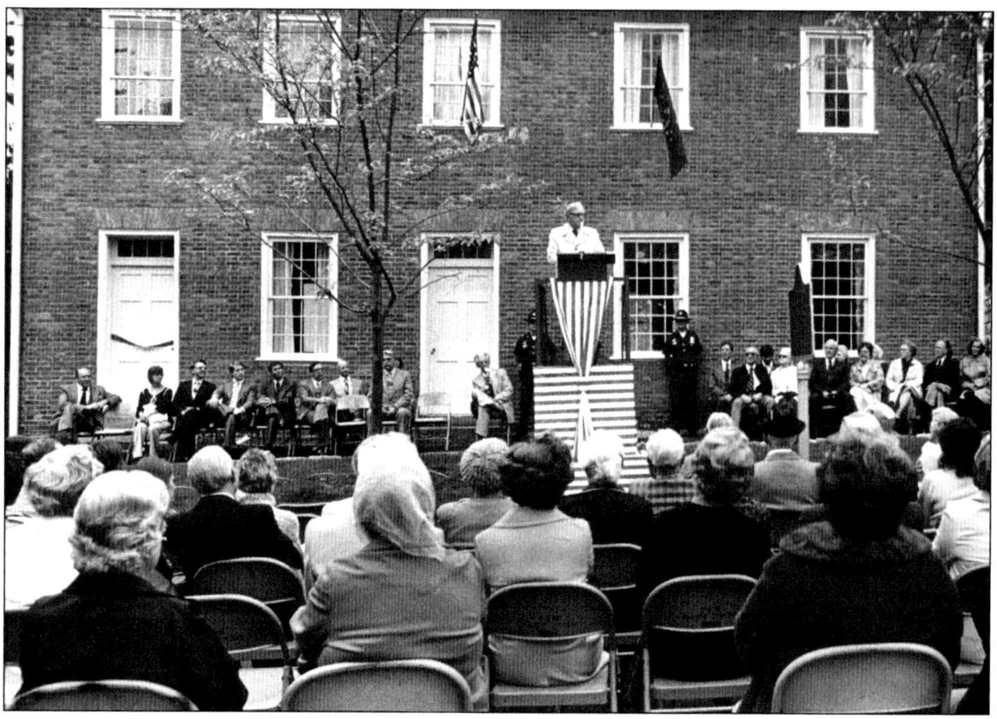

Gov. Otis Bowen dedicates the restored Gov. William Hendricks's house. It had remained in the Porter-Griffin family for 134 years before the state bought it in the late 20th century.

Three

Public Works

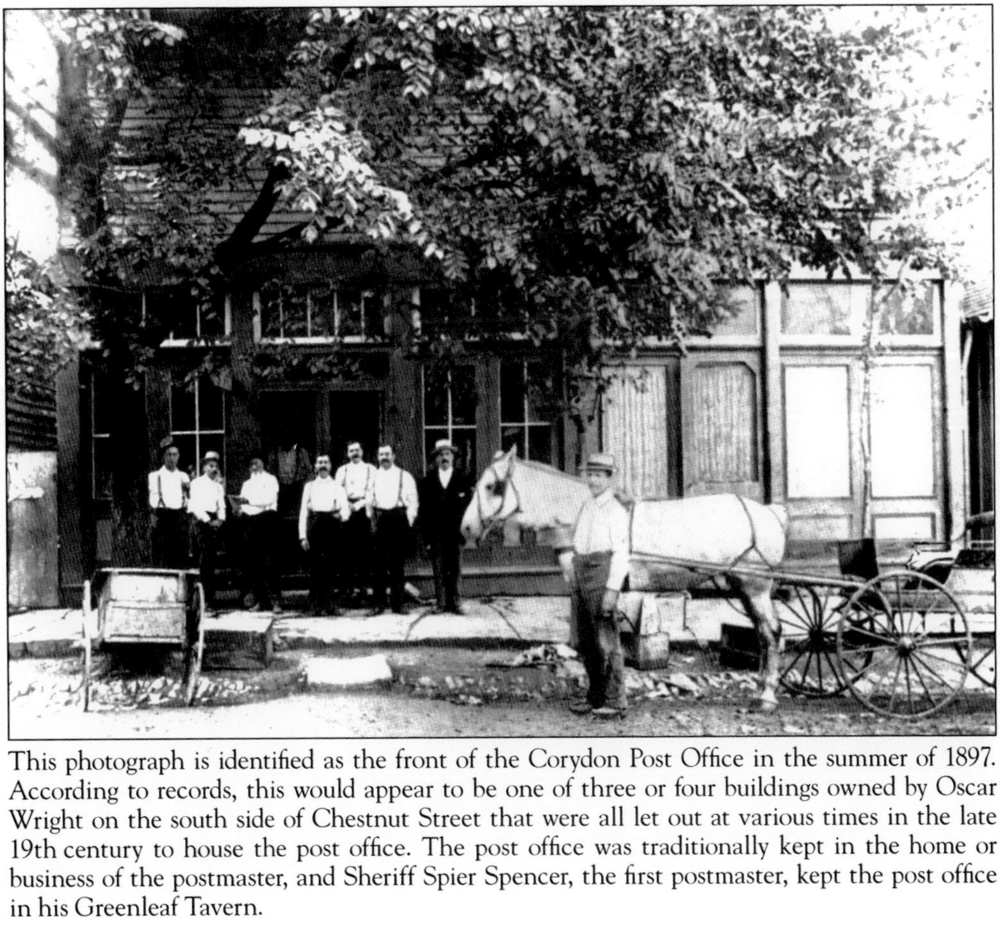

This photograph is identified as the front of the Corydon Post Office in the summer of 1897. According to records, this would appear to be one of three or four buildings owned by Oscar Wright on the south side of Chestnut Street that were all let out at various times in the late 19th century to house the post office. The post office was traditionally kept in the home or business of the postmaster, and Sheriff Spier Spencer, the first postmaster, kept the post office in his Greenleaf Tavern.

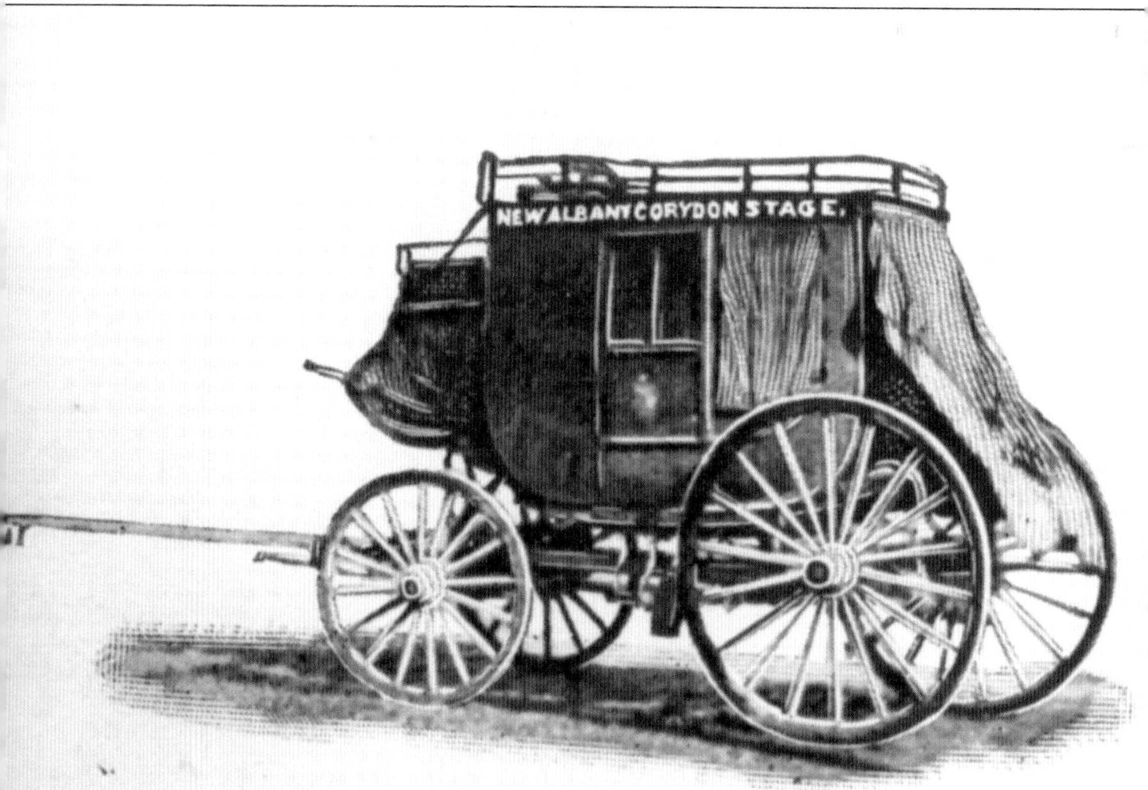

This is a depiction of the last stagecoach that carried passengers and mail over the plank road between Corydon and New Albany, prior to 1900. During the Civil War, the stagecoach brought news and mail every other day. About a mile outside of Corydon, the driver would quicken his horses. The sound of their iron shoes and the iron rims of the wheels clattering over the planks of the road announced his arrival early enough for the townsfolk to be gathered at the post office to receive news as soon as the coach pulled up.

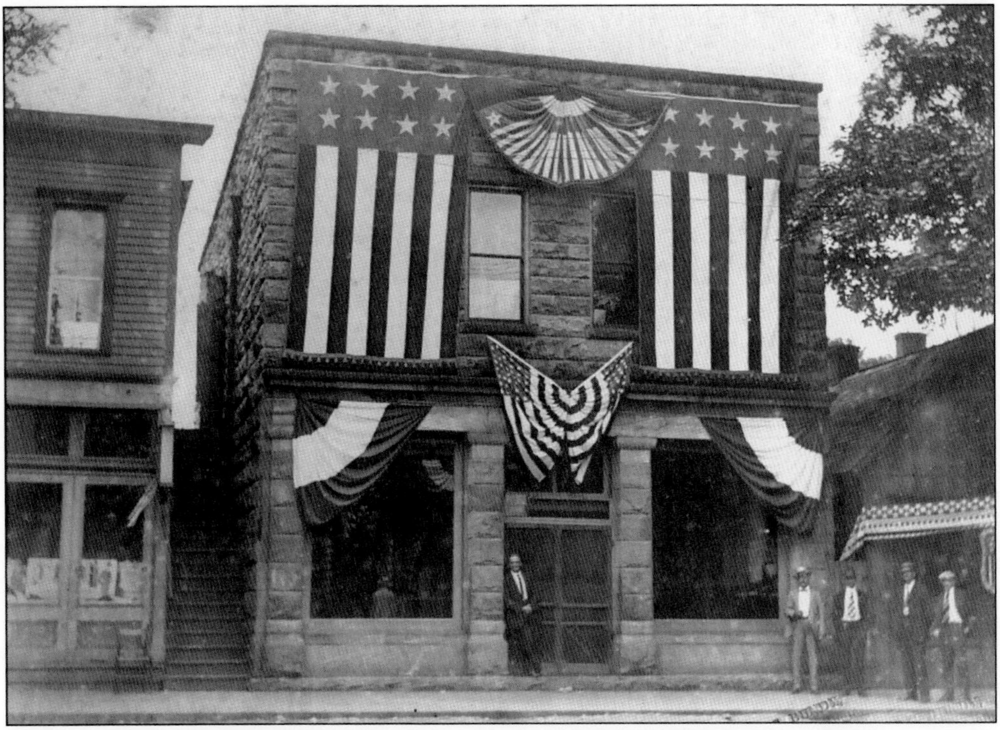

Between 1906 and 1910, Oscar Wright had this sandstone building constructed at 109 East Chestnut Street, specifically for use as a post office. The sandstone was quarried on top of Pilot Knob (west of Corydon), brought down by wagons, tooled, and laid by Robert Sims and Eck Brown. The post office was moved from next door and occupied the entire first floor of the new building, which still stands.

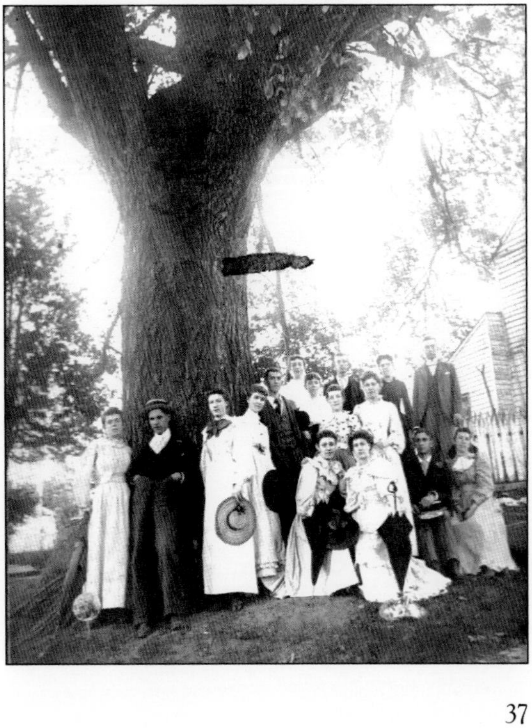

This photograph carries the enigmatic identification "Small Pox Crowd." It is unknown if these are survivors, nurses, or have some other connection. Seen beneath the Constitution Elm, they are Olive Griffin, Wilson Cook, Cad Shuck, Nellie Brewster, James Brewster, Maurice Griffin, Maggie Griffin, Nola Maxedou, Ed Keller, ? Brewster, Jennie Griffin, Hallie Mathes, John Denton, and Anne Allen.

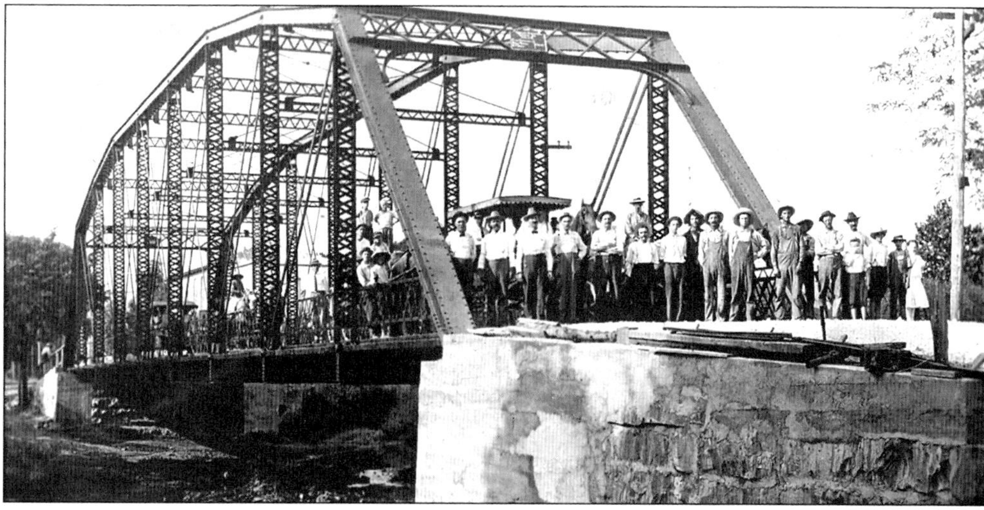

Workers and townsfolk gathered when this bridge over Little Indian Creek opened to travel on July 31, 1913. Harrison County limestone has long furnished solid foundations for many public structures. The riveted metal struts were the safest, longest-lasting building technique until modern concrete bridges were perfected.

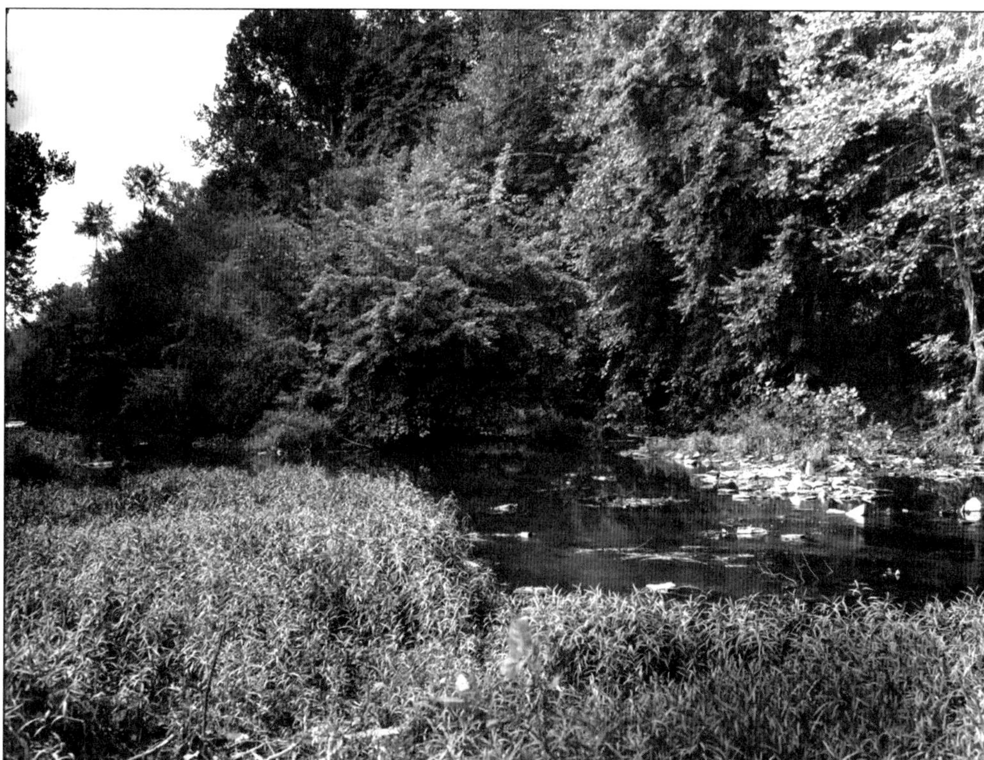

With Big and Little Indian Creeks meandering throughout Harrison County, Corydon is ringed with bridges. They have been important to thoroughfares throughout the county's history. This is a photograph of Indian Creek, which perhaps shows the 1913 bridge in the background.

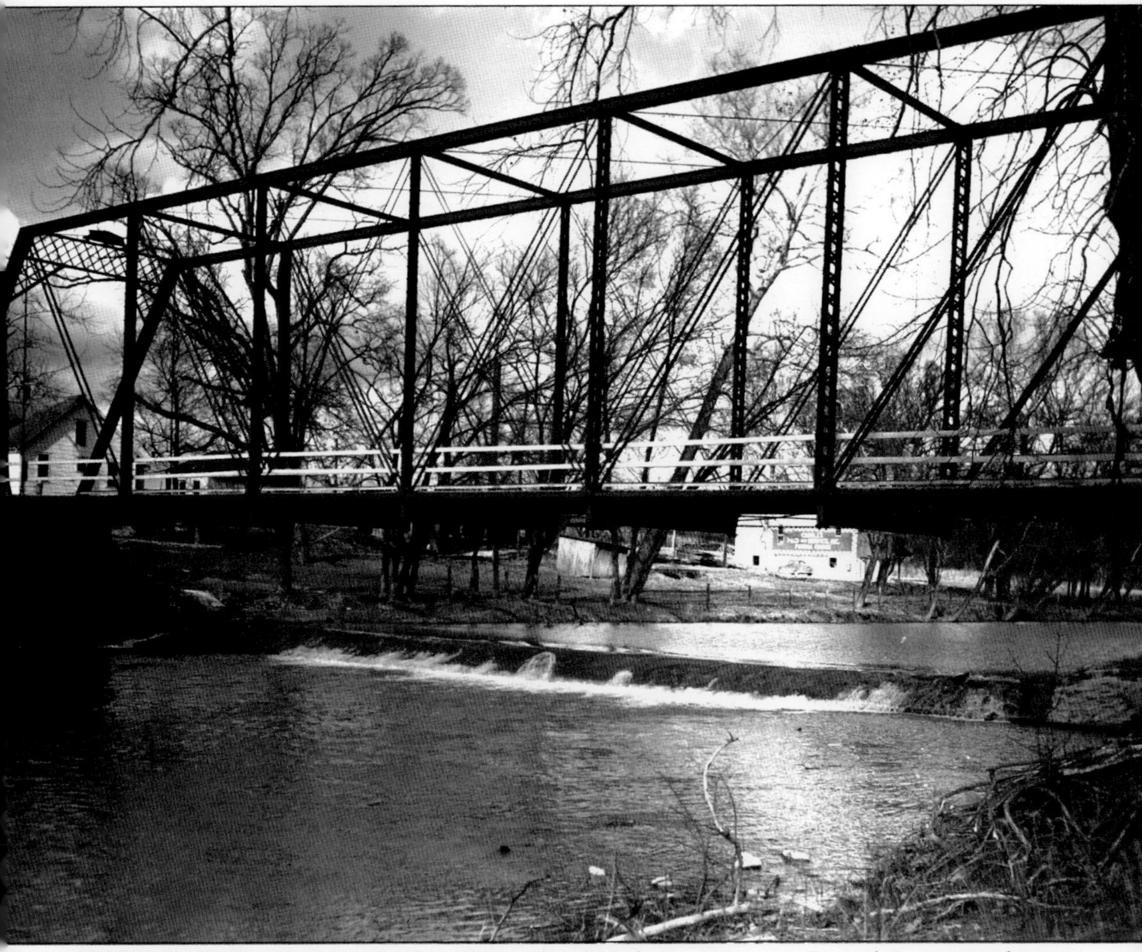

The North Bridge, photographed in 1954, carried Highway 135 on to Capitol Avenue and into downtown Corydon. The road was 32 to 36 feet wide. North Capitol Avenue is still lined with the elegant homes of the wealthy, but prior to the 1960 widening of the road to 44 feet, the street was lined with huge sycamore trees. They fell in April to make way for the new highway. The dam on the creek is still in place; it once powered a mill.

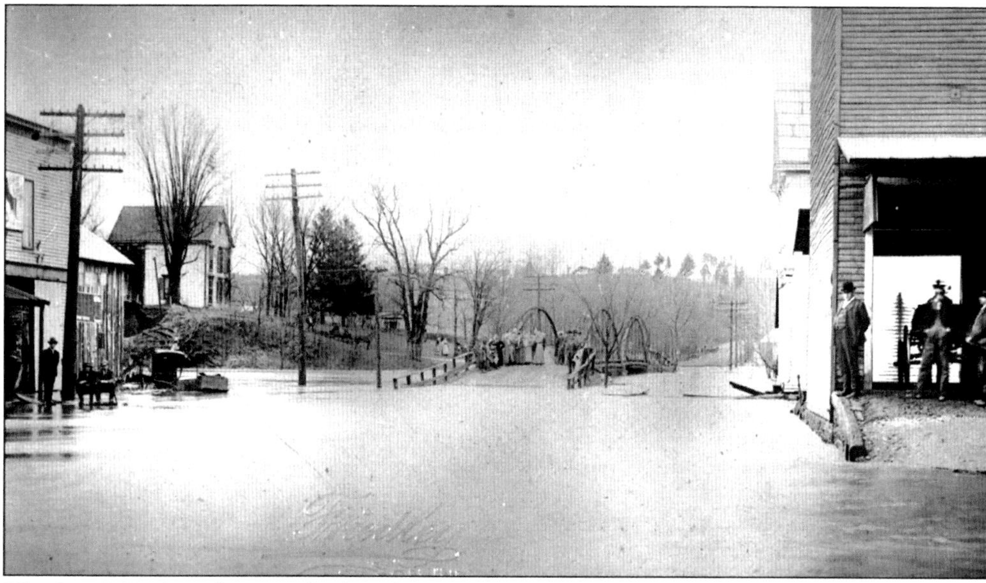

The South Bridge, photographed in the early 1900s, is seen apparently during high water. The south bridge is an especially low point, often flooded along with the surrounding buildings. The building on the rise to the left may be Mike Mitchum's Bakery. The wood frame Presbyterian church was also located to the left, before building the beautiful stone church beside the Porter-Griffin house.

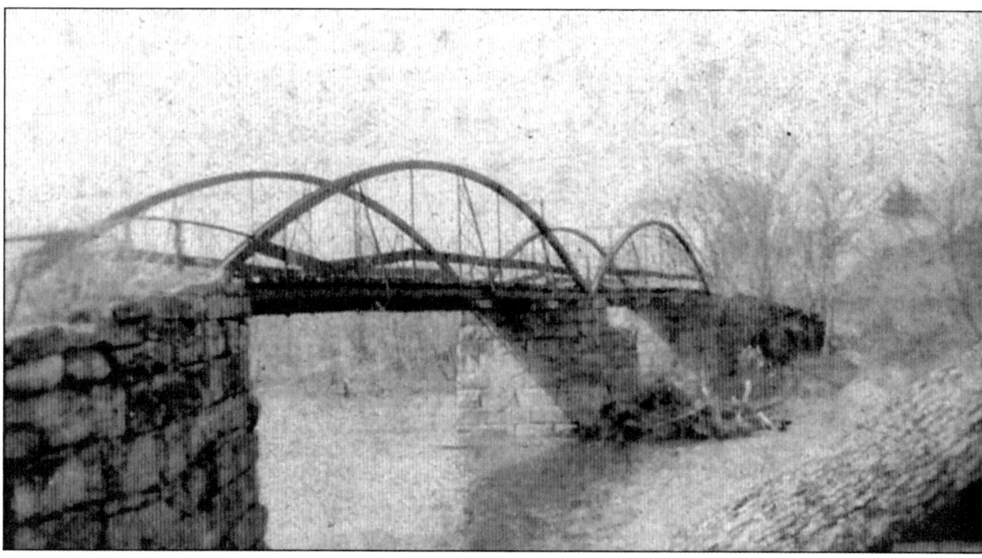

This is identified as the West Bridge. If so, it is the scene of one of the more brutal events in Corydon history. In 1873, a group emerged calling itself the Harrison County Regulators. It organized to hand out punishment to individuals who were considered to not live up to community standards. Targets were pulled from their beds in the middle of the night and flogged with switches. The men disguised themselves with hoods, earning the familiar name, White Caps. The intent was not to kill, but to make an example. James Devin and Charles Tennyson, however, attacked the Lemay family and shot two women in a botched robbery. At midnight on June 12, 1889, 150 White Caps took Devin and Tennyson out of the Corydon jail and lynched them from the middle of the West Bridge.

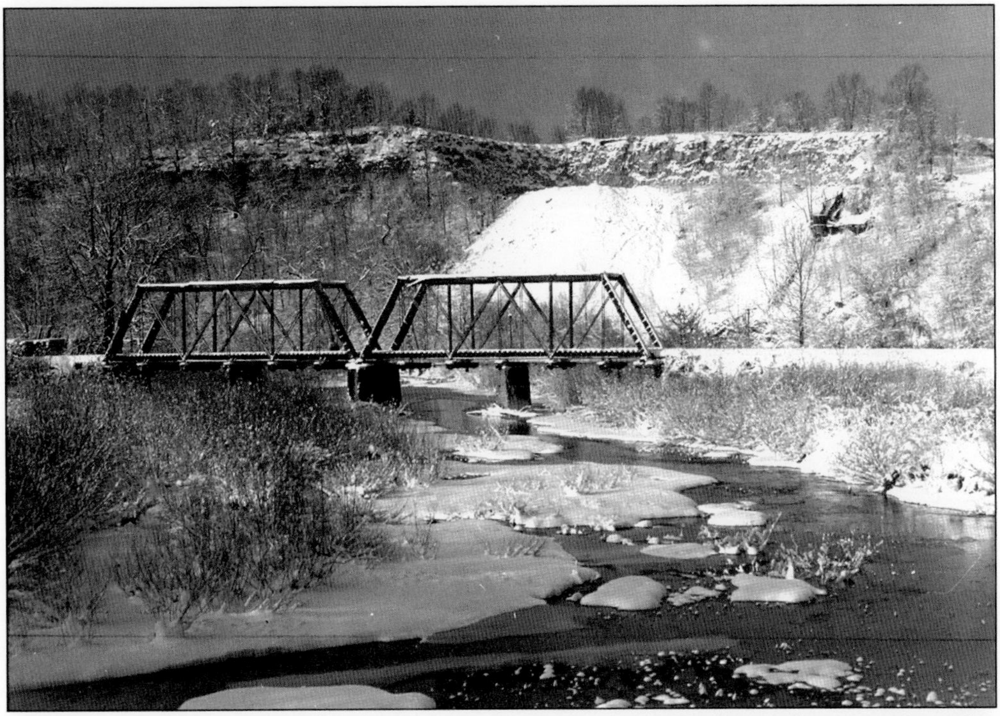

Seen here is the Louisville, New Albany and Corydon Railroad bridge north of Corydon. This railroad, as the name states, connected Corydon to the world beyond. People could go to the cities for the day and be home by evening.

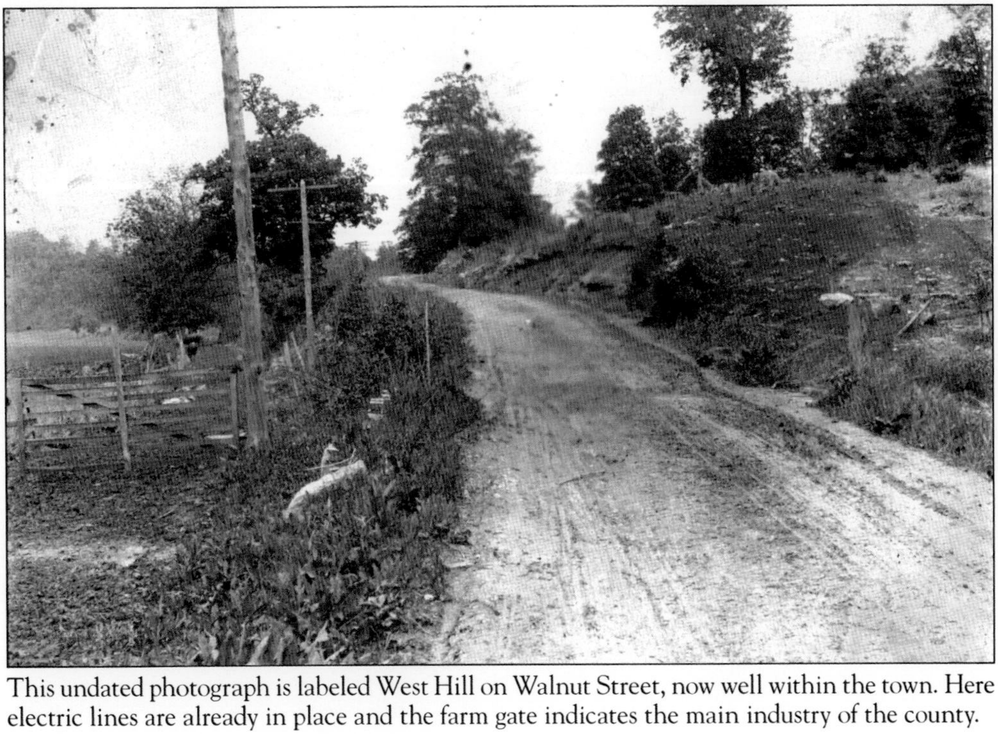

This undated photograph is labeled West Hill on Walnut Street, now well within the town. Here electric lines are already in place and the farm gate indicates the main industry of the county.

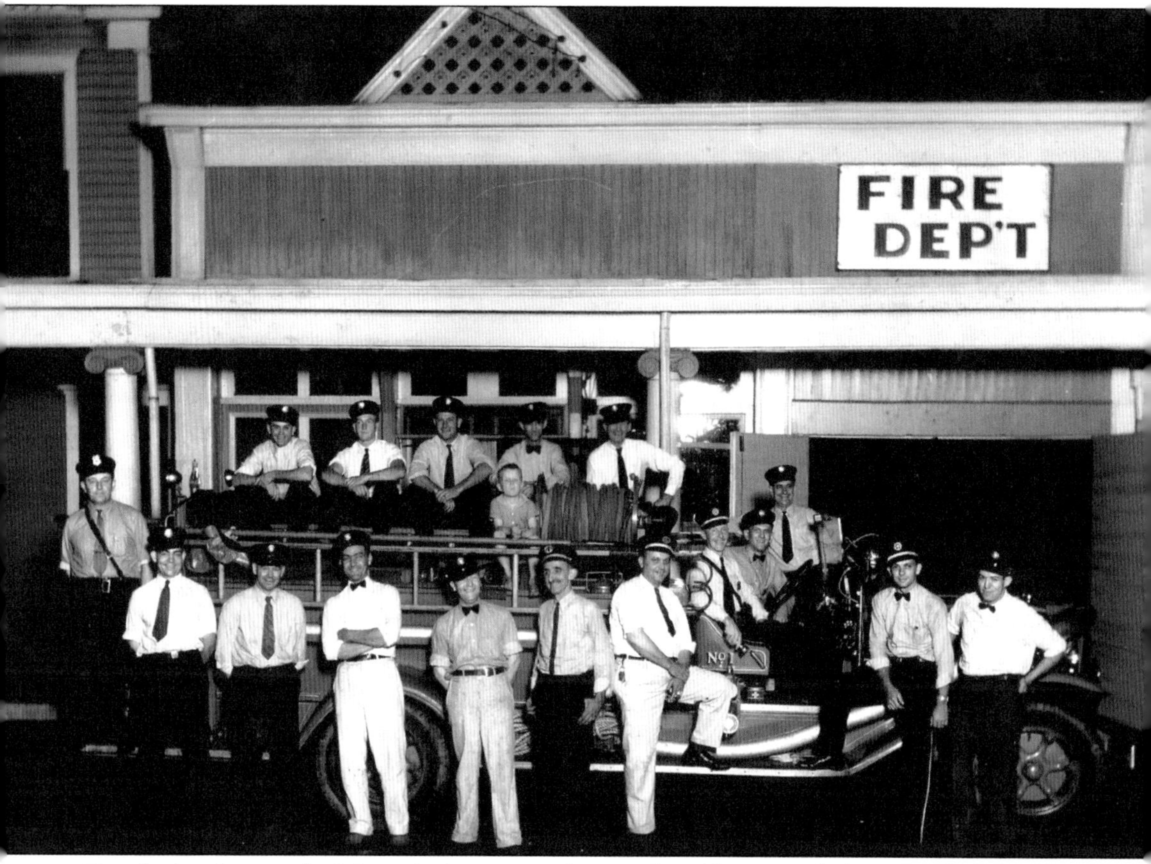

Corydon's volunteer firefighters had reason to be proud and happy with the arrival of the new 1933 Diamond T fire truck. The building in the back stood until 1978 when it fell to make way for the present town hall (1979). The volunteer firemen, standing from left to right, are (first row) Henry Able, Bill Dannenfelser, Jake Keller, Hugh Frederick, Cliff Hurst, Frank Dropsey, Chief Ollie Vaughn, Paul Quinn, and Cecil Rhodes; (second row) Claude Stonecipher, Mart Brown, Armen Best, Paul Saffer (child), Lewis Mauck, Harry Crosby, William Saffer (seated), Dusty Rhodes (seated), and Ray Clark.

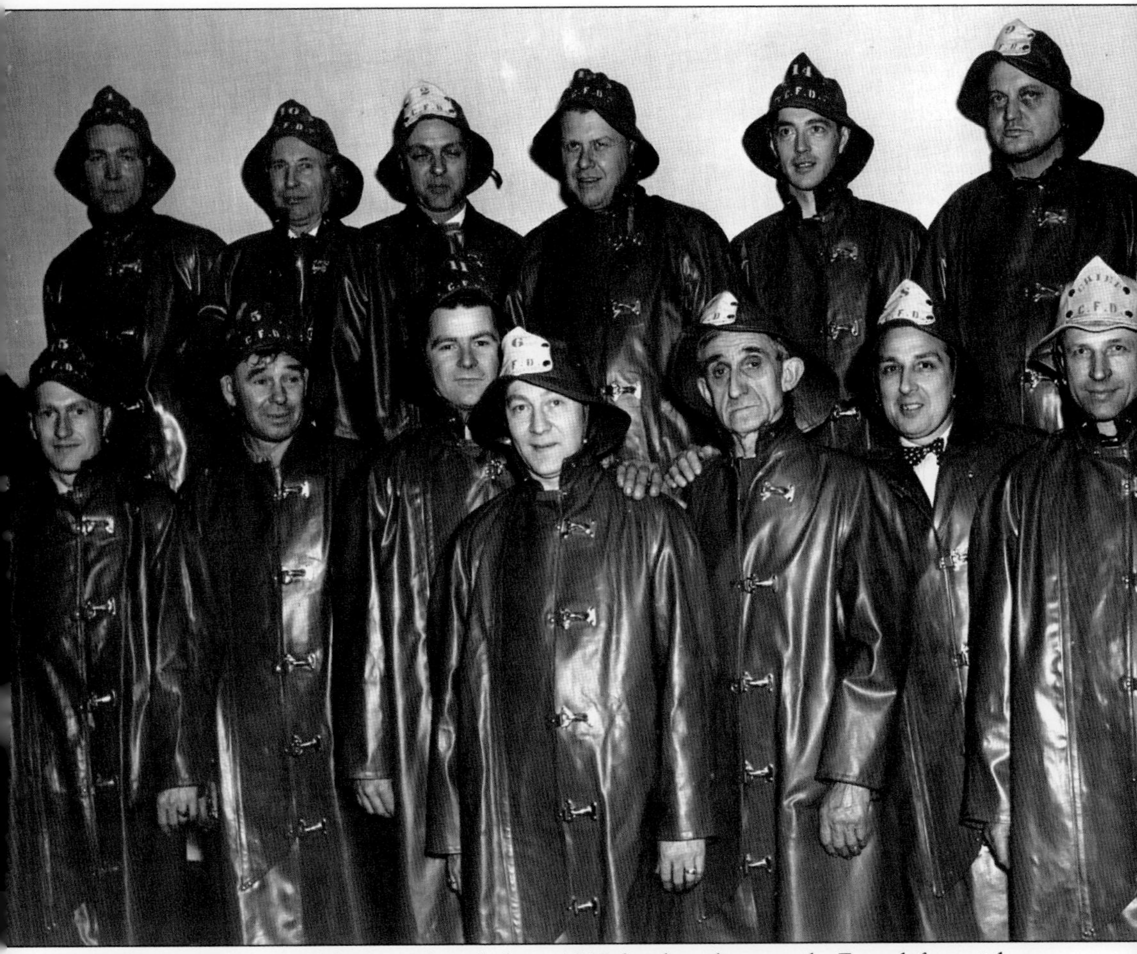

Corydon volunteer firefighters gathered about 1940 for this photograph. From left to right are (first row) Mike Schuppert (partly showing), George Kepner, Jake Keller, Jim Smith, Clifford Hurst, Frank Dropsey, Raymond "Babe" Emily, and Chief Perry Huntsinger; (second row) Hugh Frederick, Harry Crosby, Paul Quinn, Earl Orwick, Gordon Walts, and Ollie Vaughn. Note that the men wear rain hats with flexible insignias, not helmets.

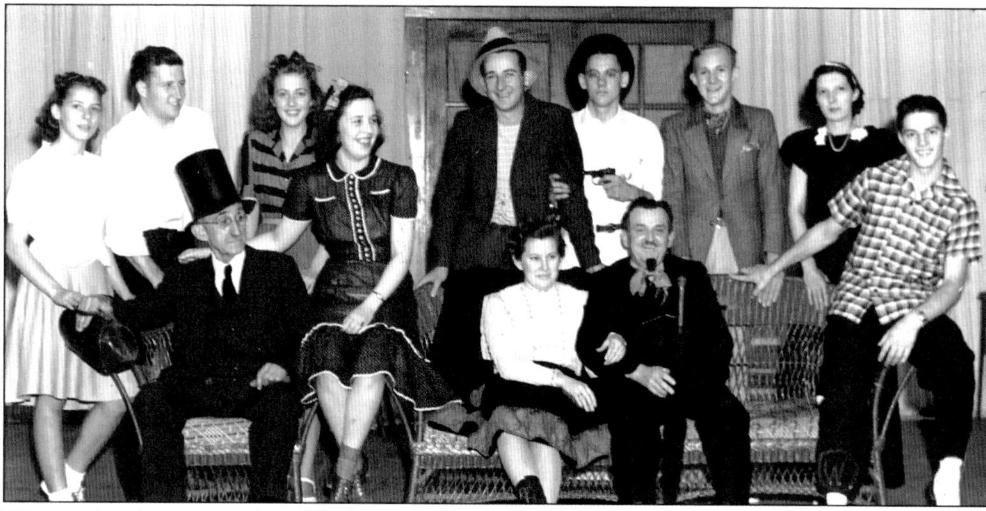

This undated photograph is labeled "*Mystery at Midnight*, Fire Men Play," at the old Corydon Grade School building. Perhaps this was a fund-raiser for some much-needed equipment. The "sheriff" is seen apprehending the criminal, or is himself the "murderer" about to dispatch his good-natured "victim."

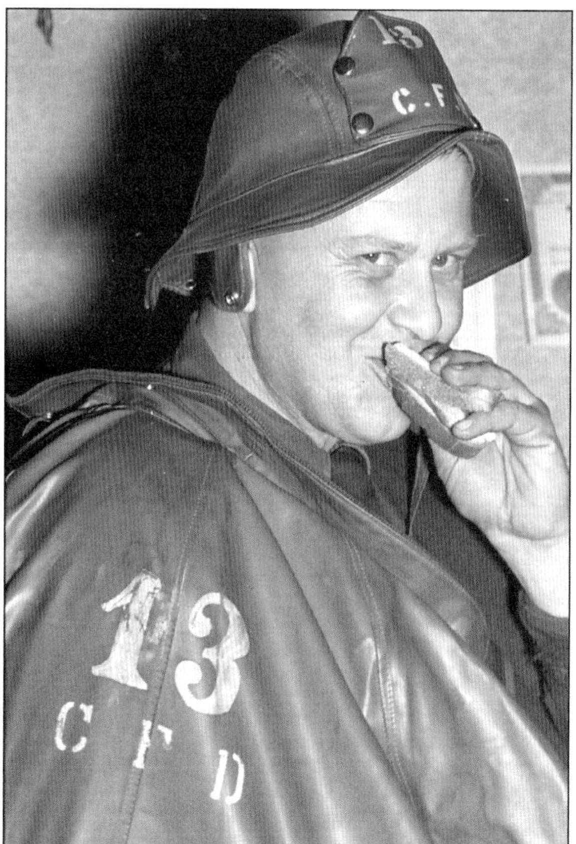

Earl Orwick, founder of Orwick Vault and Monument Company, was a well-known community leader, usually smiling and often snacking! Earl's father, Isaac Orwick, was sheriff of Harrison County from 1919 until 1923. Earl was sheriff from 1943 to 1947. A plaque in today's sheriff's office commemorates their service.

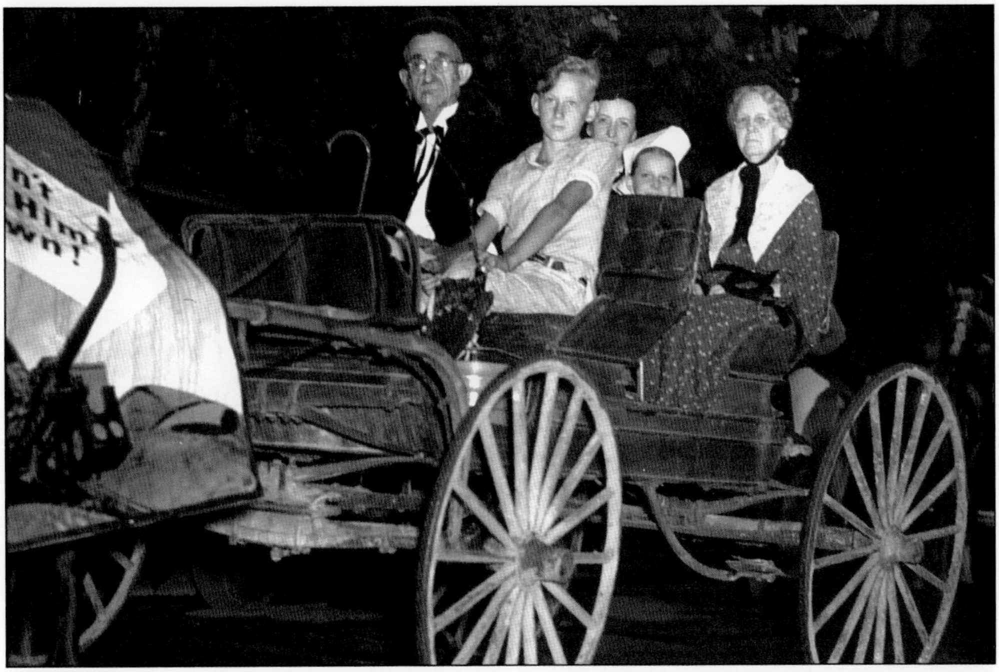

Frank Dropsey was always among the first at any fire from the time he moved to Corydon from Lanesville, in 1890. At that time, each volunteer grabbed his own bucket when the town fire bell clanged. The first piece of machinery for the Corydon Fire Department was a chassis on which William Mitchell constructed a hose reel. Dropsey served as chief of the department for a number of years, finally retiring in November 1946. He remained active in the community he loved and is seen here driving a buggy during one of Corydon's many celebrations.

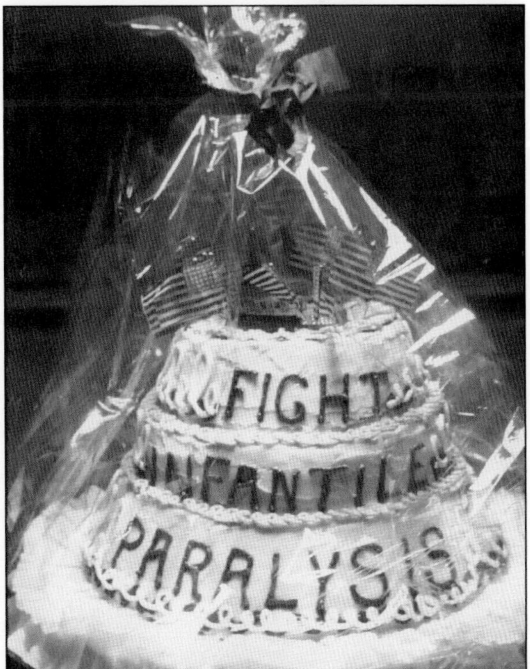

Before the Salk vaccine, each summer brought the fear of a polio outbreak. With miles of streams running all through the town, citizens knew that each swimming hole was a possible source of an epidemic. There were annual nationwide fund drives to pay for research to treat and prevent the disease. This cake would have been served at a fund-raiser kickoff.

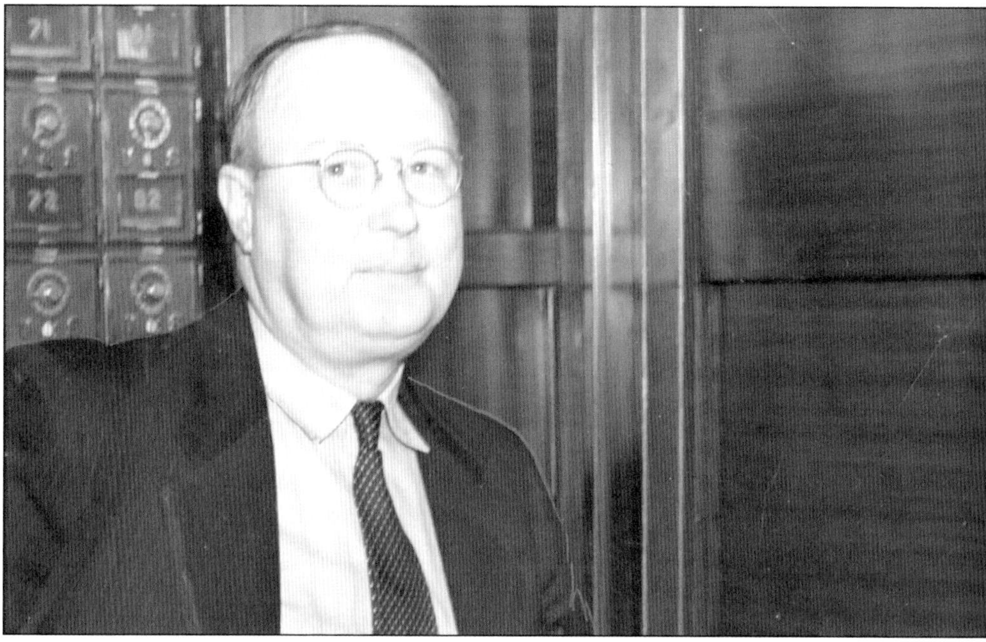

Henry W. Denbo worked in the Corydon post office for 26 years. He is shown here in the "new" building (see page 37), occupied in May 1925. It boasted 358 mailboxes made by the Keyless Lock Company of Indianapolis and installed by J. J. Driscol of Fanklin. Combination locks meant that no keys were required. Additionally, there were several windows for serving the public, large plate glass front windows and a skylight for brightness, and running water.

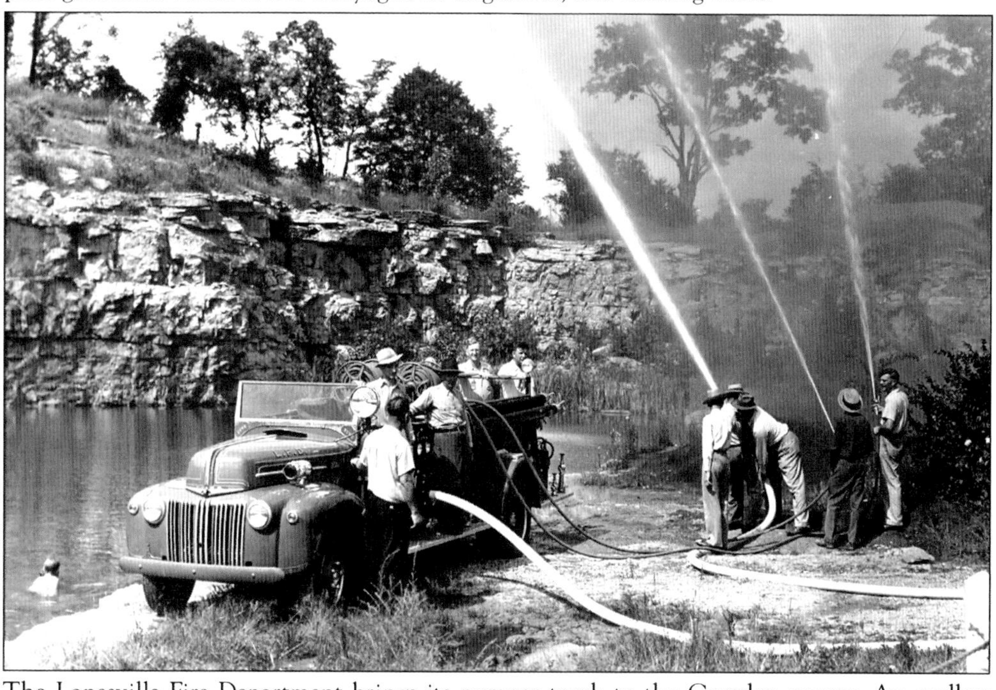

The Lanesville Fire Department brings its pumper truck to the Corydon quarry. An endless supply of water allows the men to test the equipment and learn to manage the force of the large hoses.

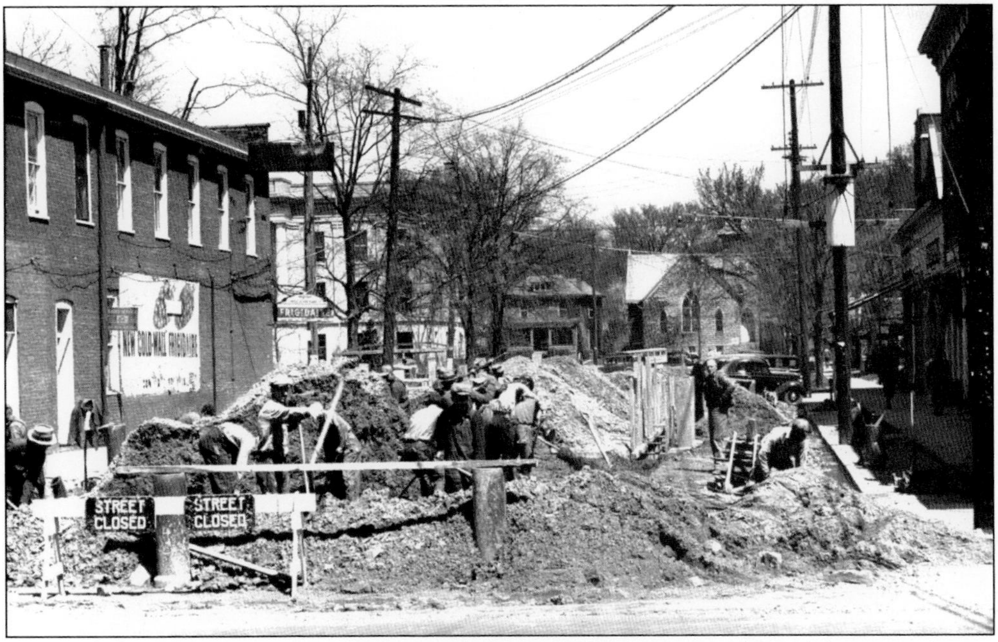

The Corydon sewer project, part of the Works Project Administration (WPA), began in August 1938 and was completed early in 1940. Costing less than $150,000, the project employed some 50 men to dig by hand with pick and shovel. This photograph was taken by Carl Rainbolt and shows work at Elm and Chestnut Streets. Looking north, the Presbyterian church and the home of Maurice Griffin are seen.

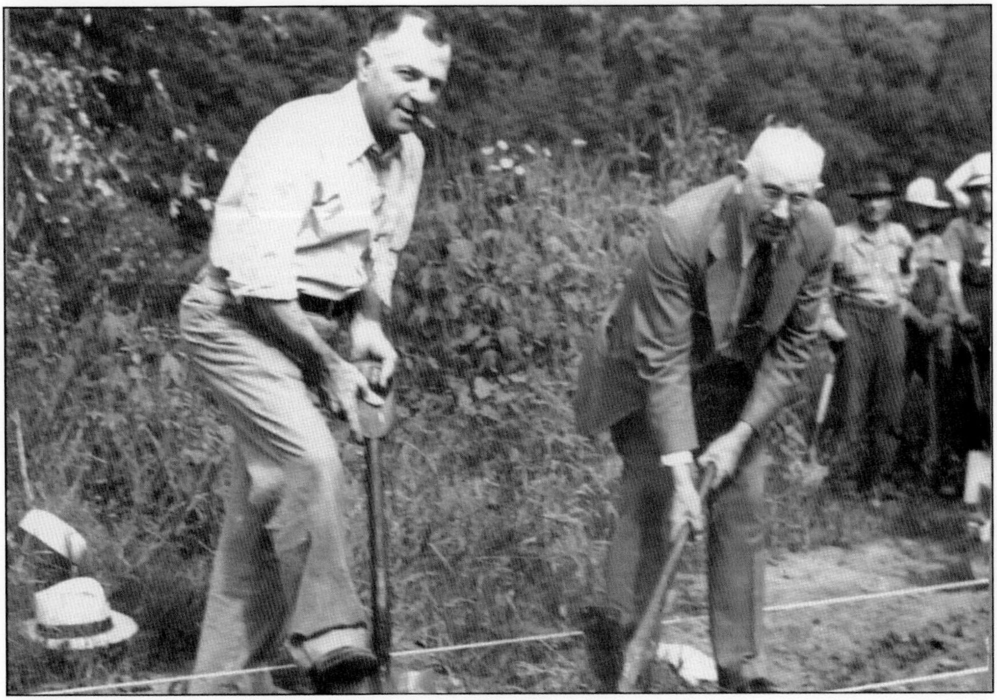

Clarence Kopp and Lew O'Bannon ceremonially break ground to commence Corydon's sewer project.

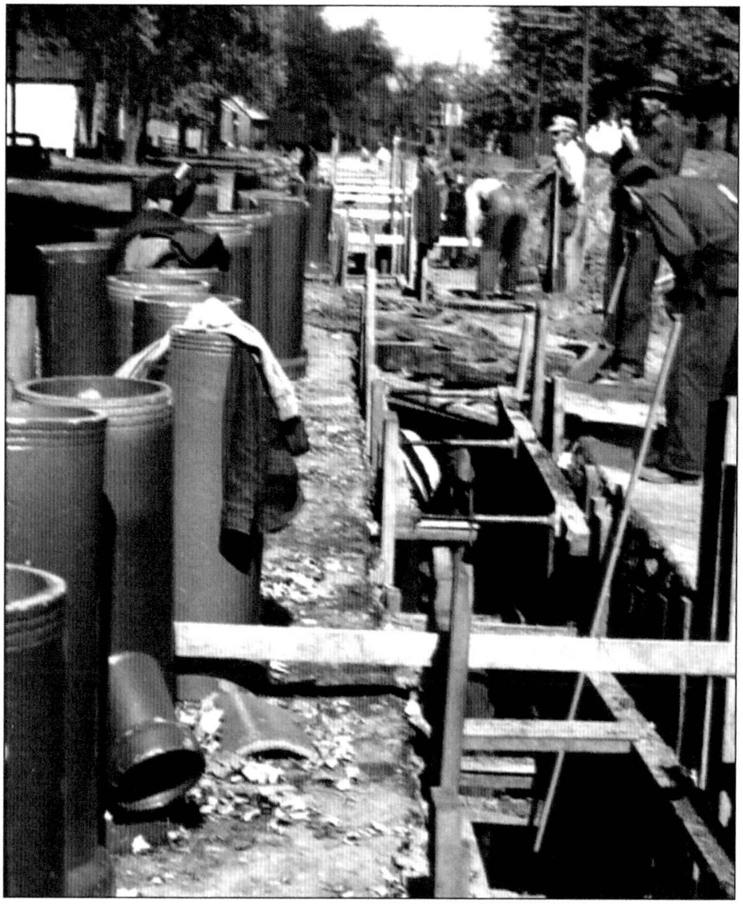

This view of the sewer project shows the shoring up carefully built into the hand-dug ditch, providing maximum safety for the men who would place the massive terra-cotta pipe by hand.

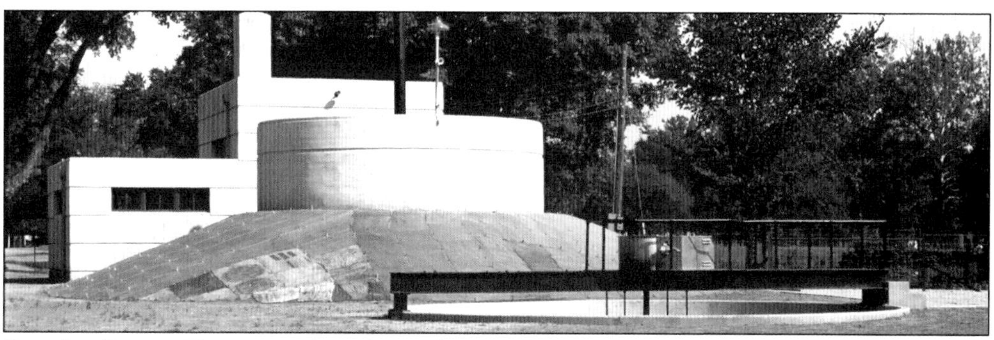

Corydon Sewage Treatment Plant, located on the bank of Big Indian Creek, was completed in the fall of 1939. The WPA sewer project included the treatment plant and a collection system. A 1993 update improved the plant's handling of ammonia and treated the water with ultraviolet light, instead of chlorine, eliminating the storage and handling of chlorine.

Claude Stonecipher worked with an acetylene torch on March 15, 1949, to free the sheriff and his deputy, who had been locked into the cell where William Dessie Messamore, a self-confessed bank robber, was being held.

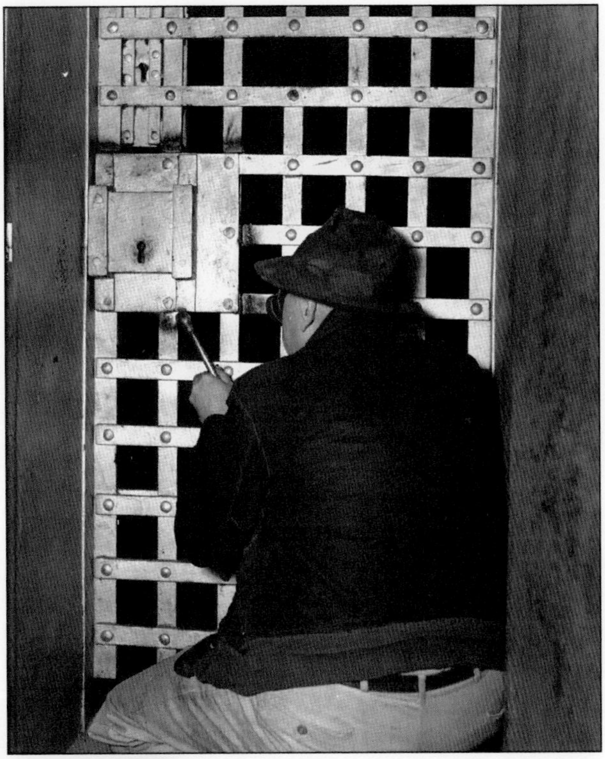

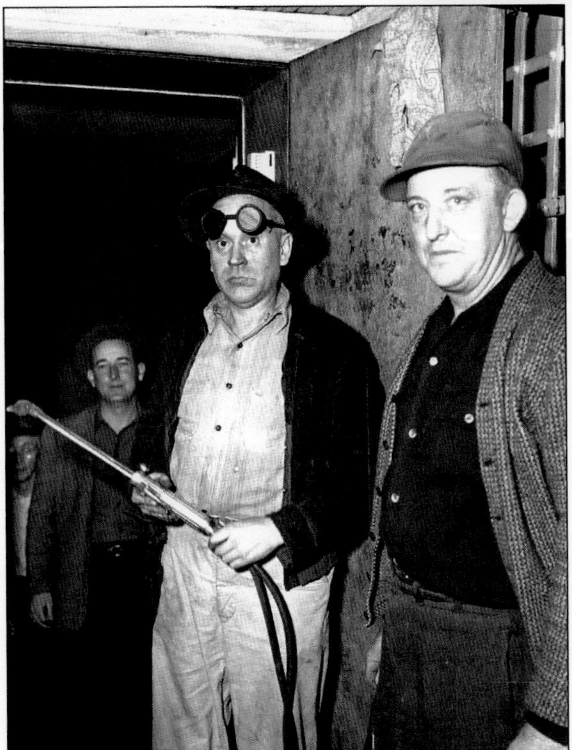

Deputy Sheriff Clarence Klee peers from the recesses of the cell where he and Sheriff Walter Baxley were locked by Messamore in order to escape. Stonecipher holds his acetylene torch; his helper, Dudley Cammack, stands on the right. Messamore was recaptured 22 hours later, in Brandenburg, Kentucky.

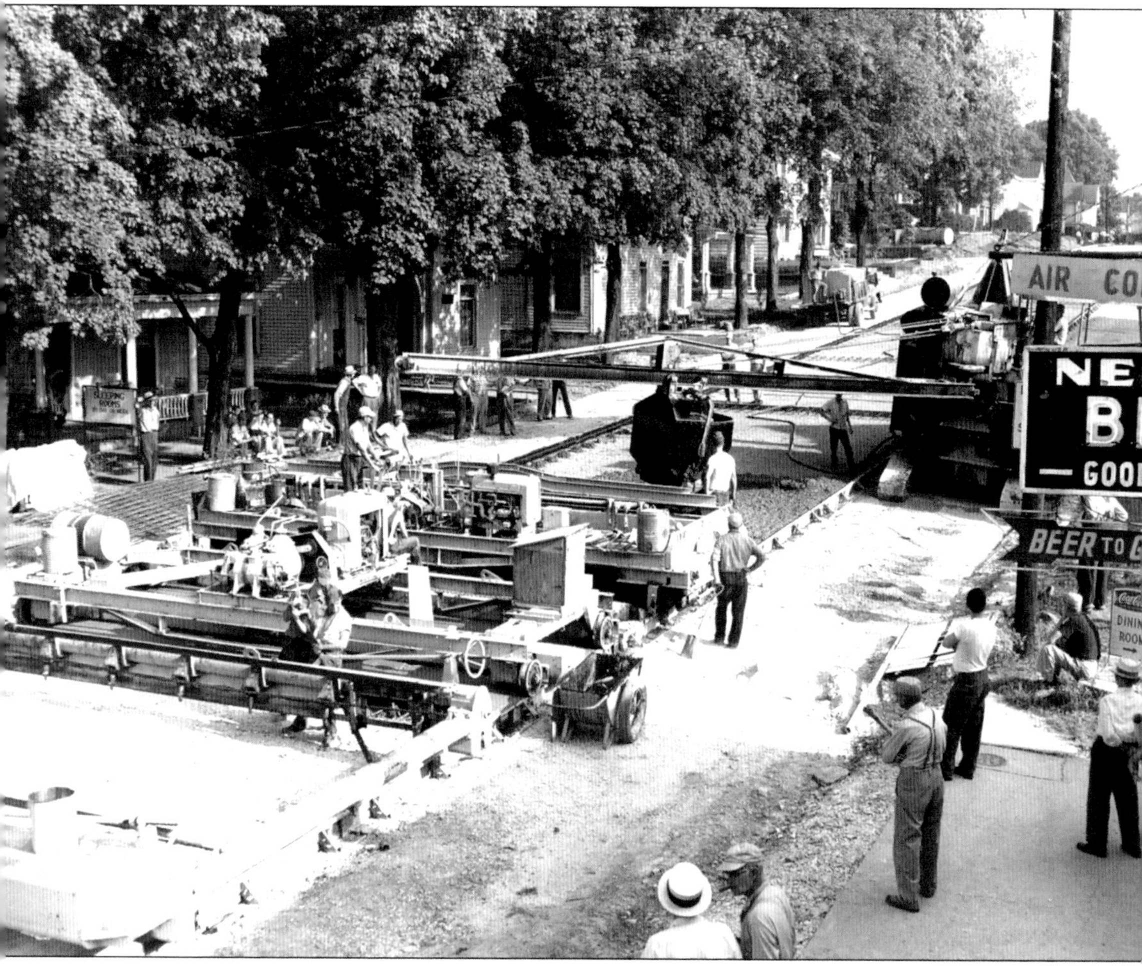

Constructing the new Highway 135 was a major project, involving widening, straightening, and smoothing. Better drainage also added years to the improved materials and construction of the roadbed. This is the 1960 highway project that claimed the big sycamore trees on North Capitol Avenue but still left many stately giants unharmed. Original plans called for leaving all the trees, but the pavement was only 32–36 feet wide. State regulations required that it be widened to 44 feet. It was a far cry from the first paving of Corydon roads, limestone quarried in Corydon, crushed, and spread on the streets ended the gluelike mud of rainy days and helped cut the dust of long summer droughts. Horses picked up shards of rock in their shoes, but alert drivers quickly stopped and flicked it out again. By 1960, automobiles were wider and faster and dictated smooth, wide roads of concrete and asphalt.

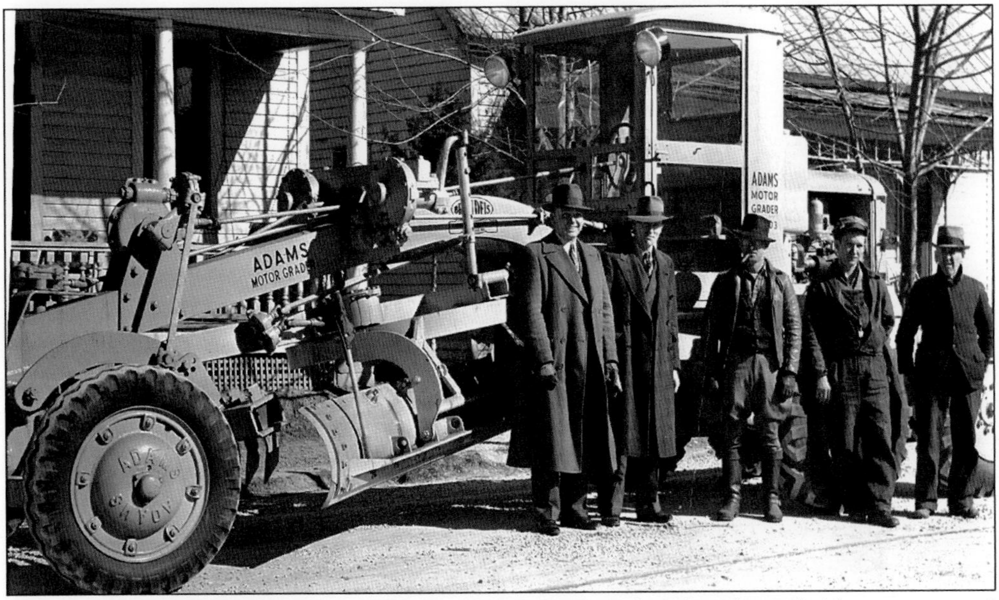

This photograph is undated, but the acquisition of a motorized road grader called for a ceremonial image with the new equipment.

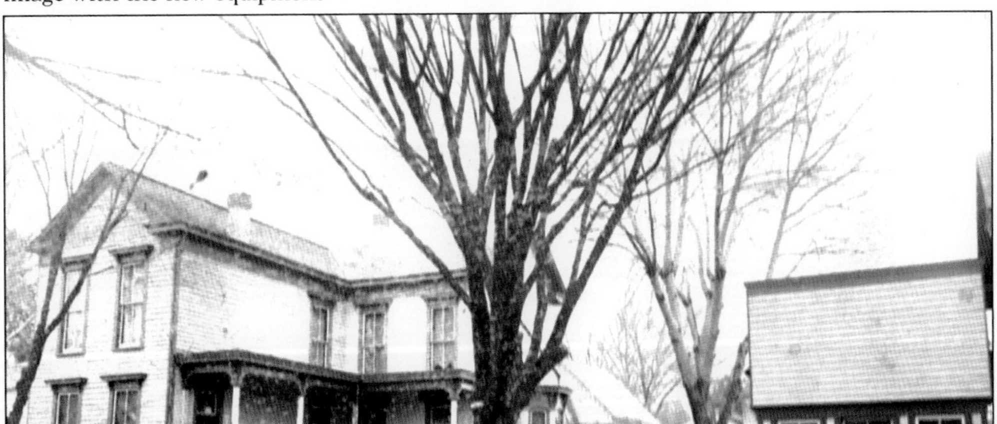

The rambling house of Strother Madison Stockslager stood at the corner of Elm and Walnut Streets. It had 11 outside doors. Stockslager was elected to Congress in the early 1800s and was appointed commissioner of the General Land Office in Washington, D.C., during the administration of Grover Cleveland. The Stockslagers' daughter Georgia Stockslager Fisher lived in the house until her death in 1967. Fisher was the librarian at the Corydon Public Library for many years. The small frame building on the right was the public library before 1914. The house and its appurtenances were purchased by the Harrison County Commissioners, who leveled the lot to build the present tourist information center.

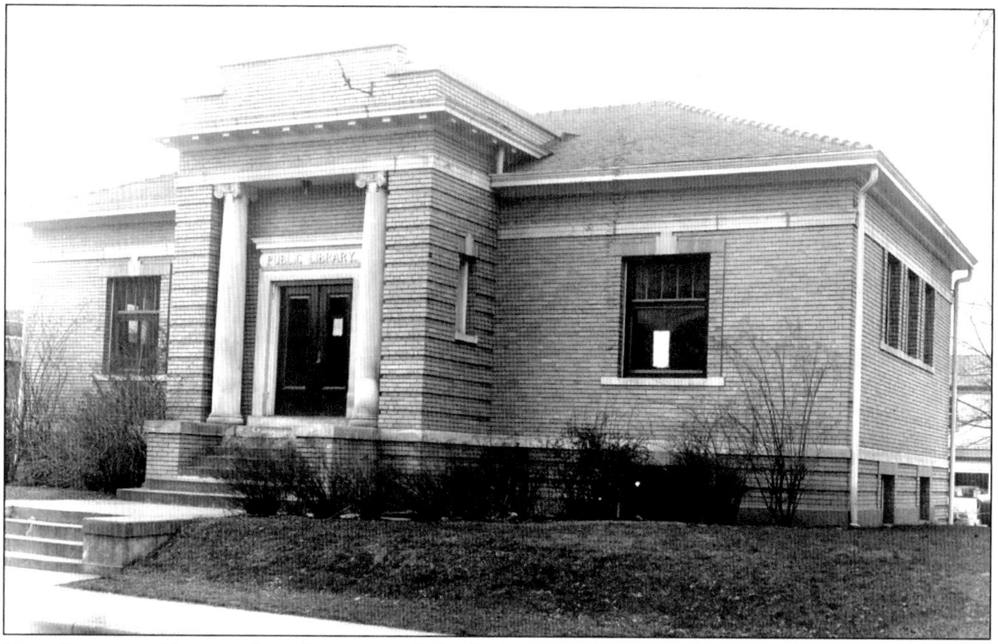

Corydon was able to take advantage of Andrew Carnegie's generosity in funding free public libraries and dedicated this building just before Christmas 1914. Like all Carnegie libraries, it was soundly and attractively constructed, with a comfortable, well-lit reading room to invite all persons to spend time reading. This building today houses the Frederick Porter Griffin Center for Local History and Genealogy.

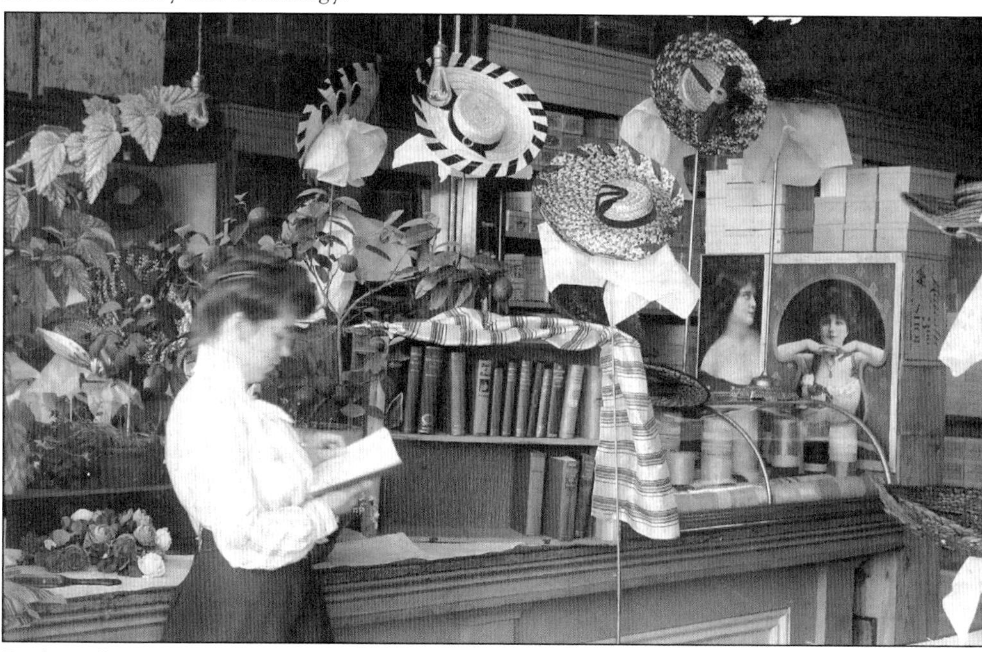

Fred Griffin's aunt Olive Griffin maintained a small lending library in the family store on the square. Around the dawn of the 20th century, she especially kept books for families, women, and children. She lent them gladly to friends and customers. She had no need of records—she knew exactly who had each book.

Four

BUSINESS

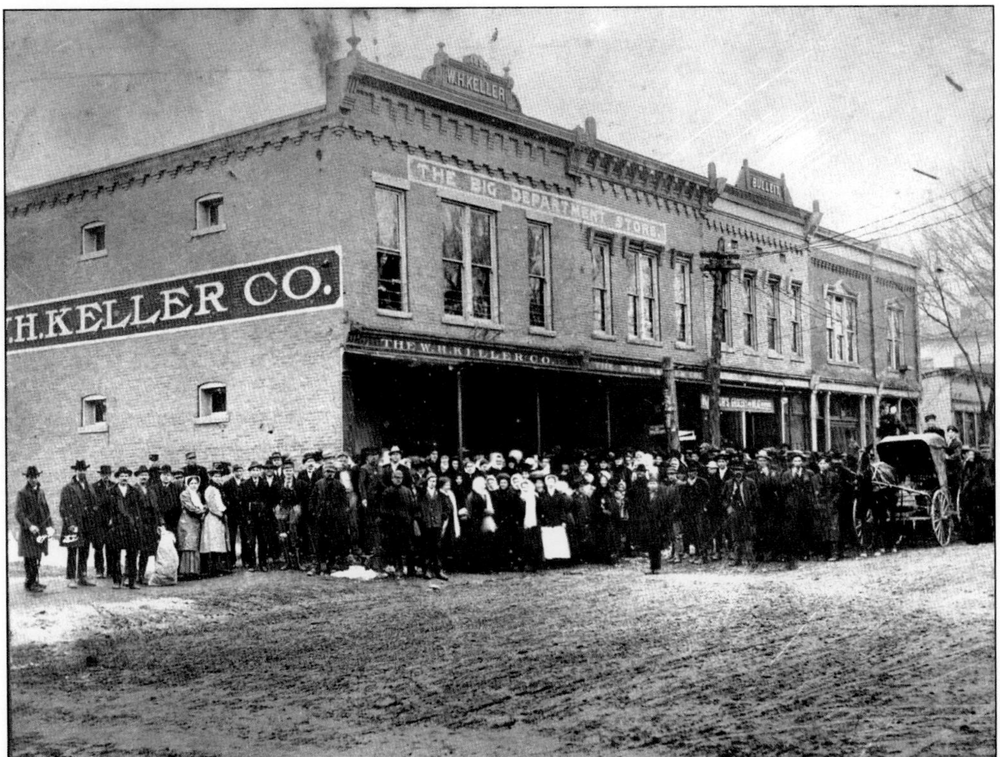

John Leonard Keller landed from Germany in New York in the fall of 1846. In his pocket, he had $1.10. By the spring of 1847, he was in Harrison County repairing and selling clocks. In 1866, he moved to Corydon and began a local business empire. Sons William H., Leonard C., and Edward G. Keller expanded the store into a department store and built Keller Manufacturing Company. This photograph was taken on February 23, 1910, celebrating a clock contest, reminiscent of John Keller's original trade.

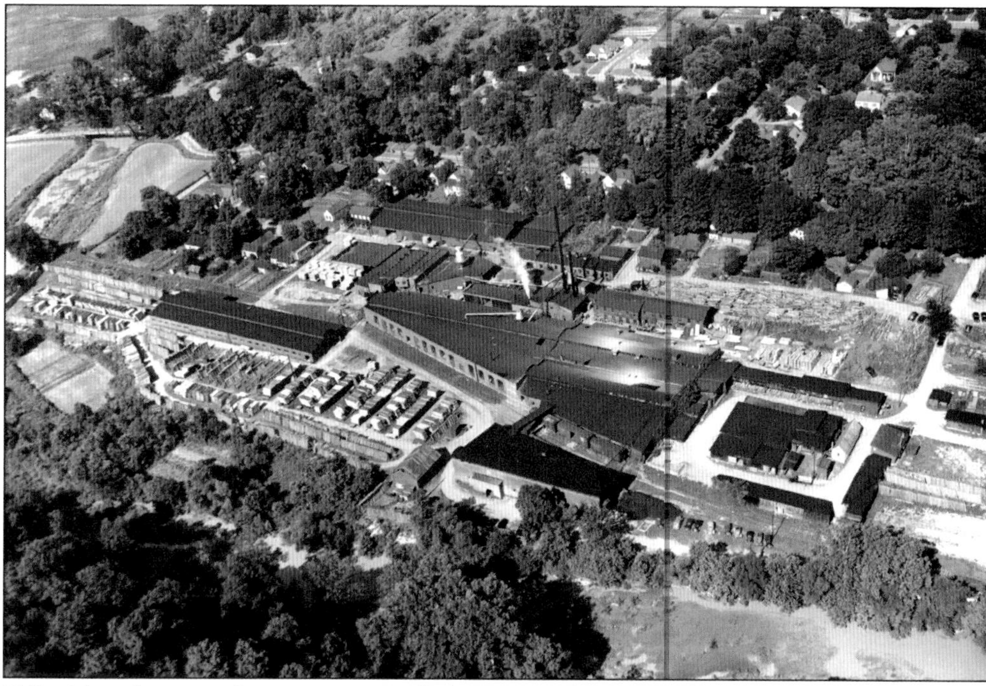

Keller Manufacturing Company occupied a large tract along Big Indian Creek and the Louisville, New Albany and Corydon Railroad. Organized in 1894 to manufacture wheel spokes and various other wagon parts, in 1900 the plant was enlarged to manufacture the Corydon wagon. Using oak and hickory from the local hardwood forests, the wood was aged in the large yard of the factory. As the wagon market became smaller, Keller Manufacturing developed a successful line of dinette sets, which were manufactured until near the end of the 20th century.

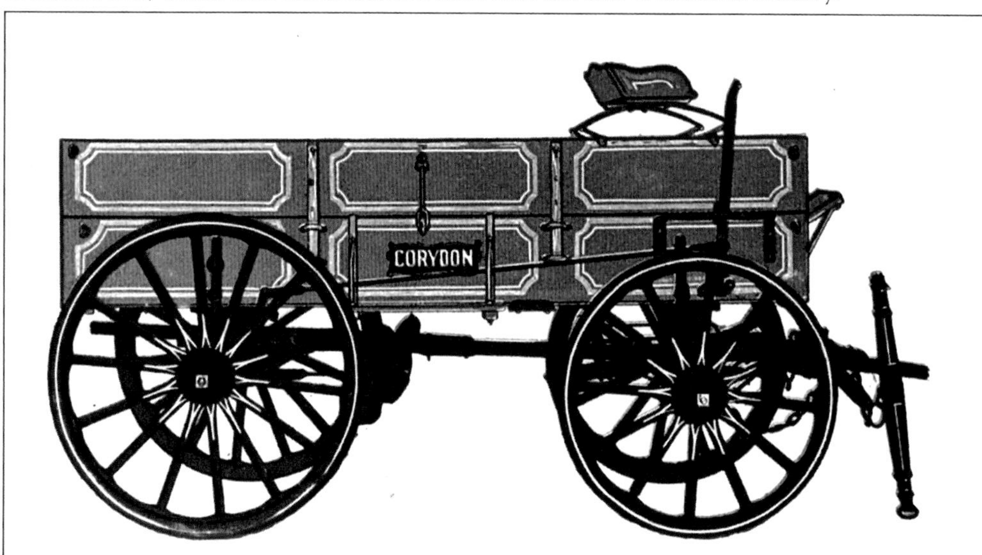

The Corydon wagon was a well-made medium-size wagon ideally suited to a family farm or to the subdivisions of large plantations. By the time the last wagon was shipped out in 1942, more than 296,000 Corydon wagons had been shipped to every section of the United States and to 10 foreign countries.

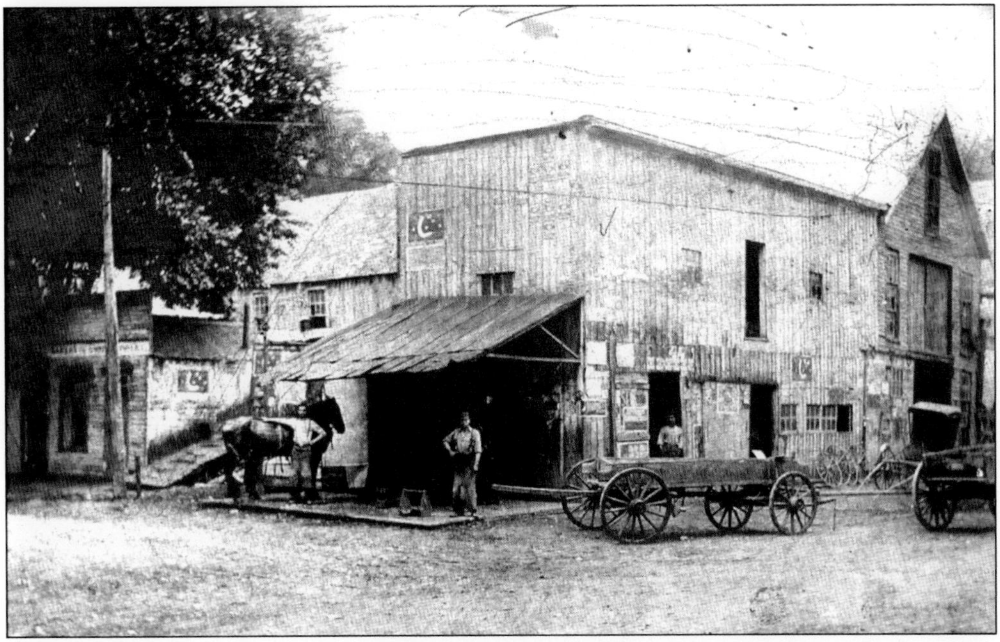

Amiel L. Bulleit and his son, John Bulleit, operated a blacksmith shop on the northeast corner of the town square. They were farriers, shoeing innumerable horses through the years. John even made shoes for Tom Mix's horse Tony. The Bulleits also built buggies, wagons, and farm implements in their shop, which occupied most of a city block.

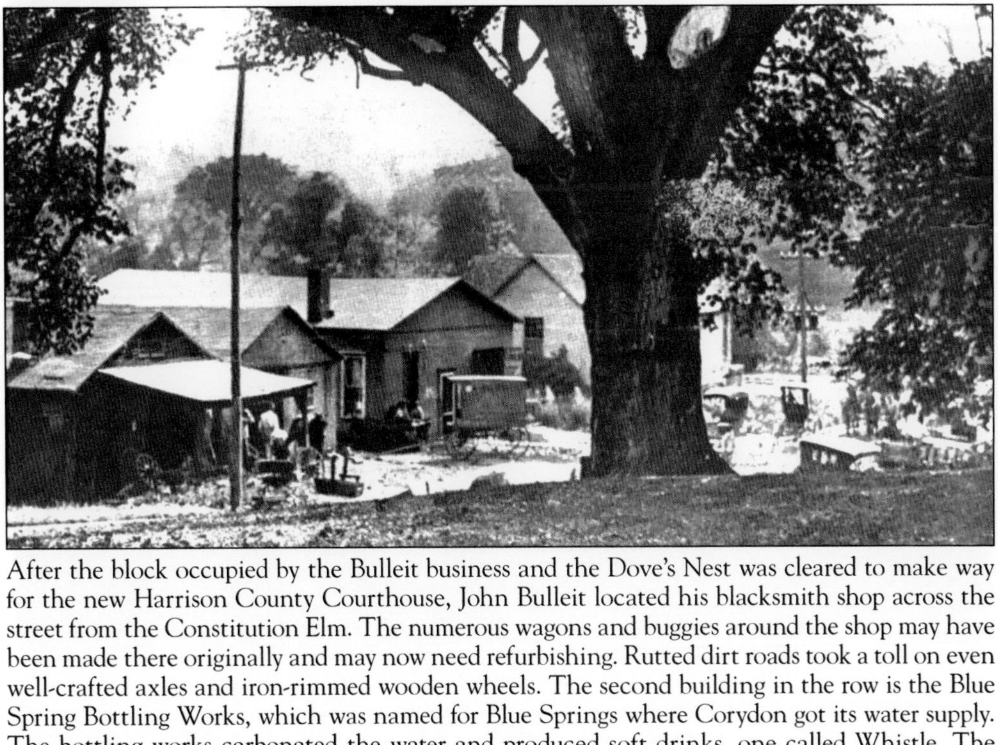

After the block occupied by the Bulleit business and the Dove's Nest was cleared to make way for the new Harrison County Courthouse, John Bulleit located his blacksmith shop across the street from the Constitution Elm. The numerous wagons and buggies around the shop may have been made there originally and may now need refurbishing. Rutted dirt roads took a toll on even well-crafted axles and iron-rimmed wooden wheels. The second building in the row is the Blue Spring Bottling Works, which was named for Blue Springs where Corydon got its water supply. The bottling works carbonated the water and produced soft drinks, one called Whistle. The third building is the freight station of the Louisville, New Albany and Corydon Railroad.

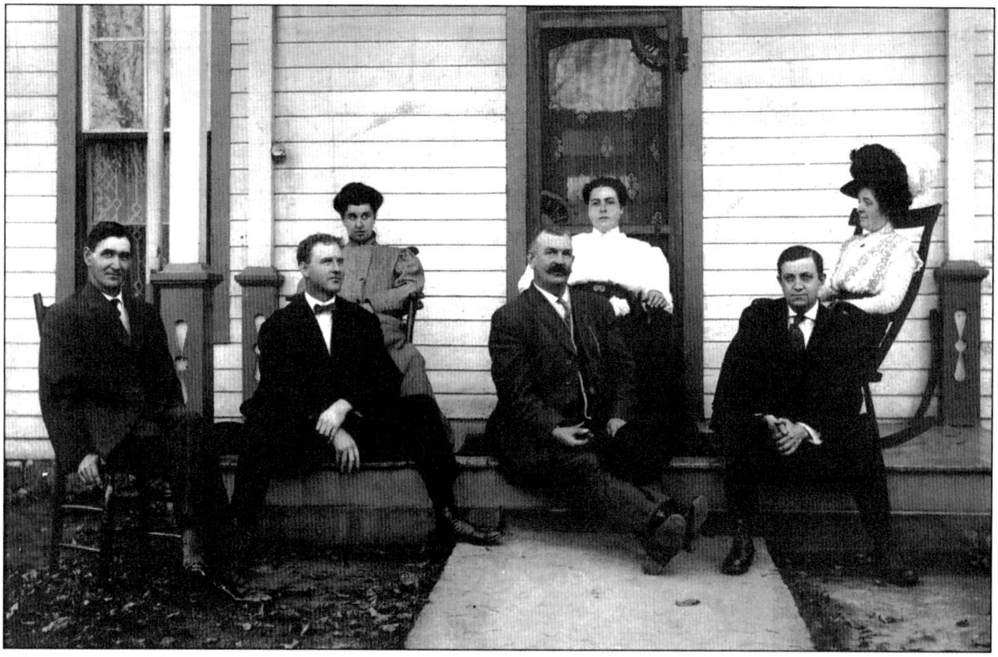

This *c.* 1909 photograph is captioned "Corydon businessmen on a Sunday afternoon." They are identified as Frank Wright, manager of a local electric plant; Chris Adams, field agent for Corydon Canning Company; David M. Rowland, salesman; and Victor Wright, assistant at Riely's Drug Store. The wives are Mary Rowland Adams; Verna Weathers Wright, Victor's wife; and Carrie Allen Wright, Frank's wife.

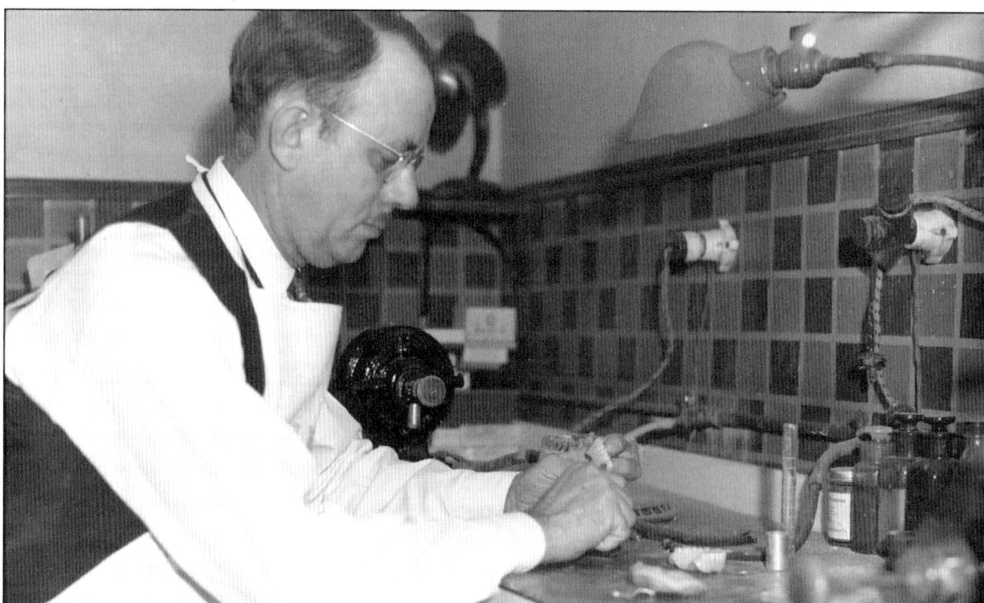

Dr. Lee B. Wolfe works on dentures in his office around 1922. Corydon had five dentists and as many doctors. The Porter-Griffin house is credited as the first hospital. For 15 years after the capital moved to Indianapolis, Dr. A. M. Jones practiced medicine in the downstairs west room (Gov. William Hendricks's office). Patients undergoing treatment stayed in rooms at the rear of the house.

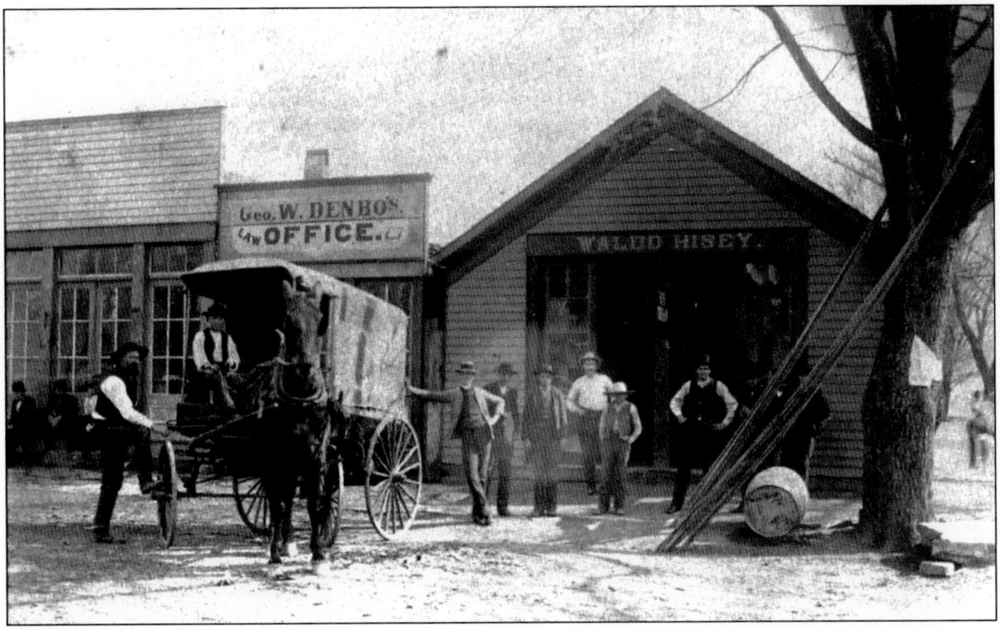

The tree located in front of Waldo Hisey's business may well be the "Wisdom Tree." Hisey's was located on the corner of Beaver Street and Capitol Avenue, where Davis Drug Store was in business for many years. The tree on this corner became a gathering place on the square, especially after benches were put around its trunk. Much wisdom was said to be shared in the shade of the tree. It stood until the 1920s.

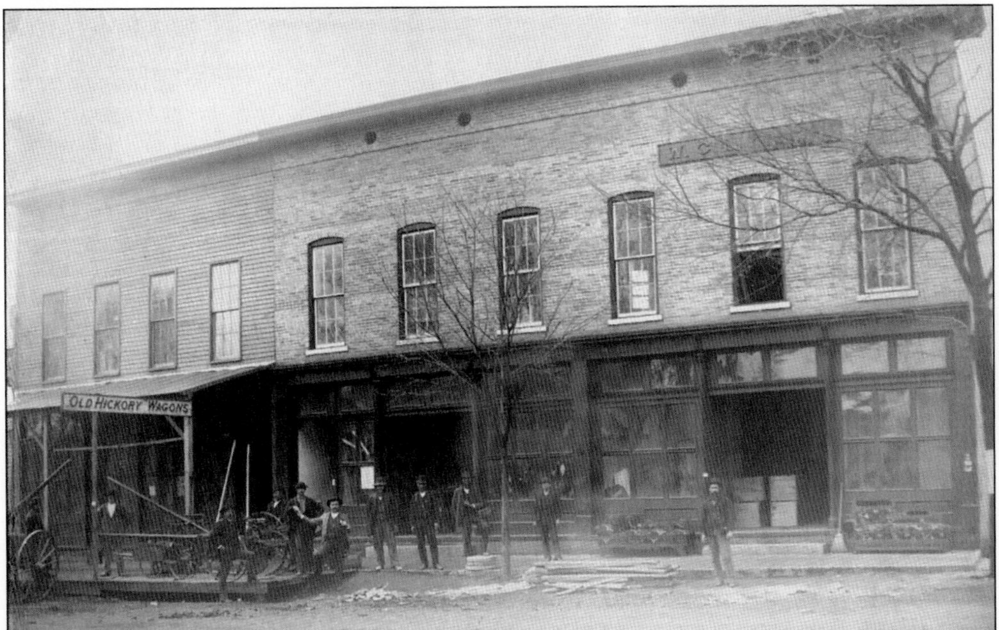

This store, located on the town square, sold hickory wagons. Southern Indiana's hardwood forests furnished material for strong, durable farm implements and household furnishings. Harnesses, farm equipment, heating stoves, cooking ranges, tinware, seeds, wheels, and springs were available on the first floor of hardware stores. The second floor might have furniture, clothing, and shoes.

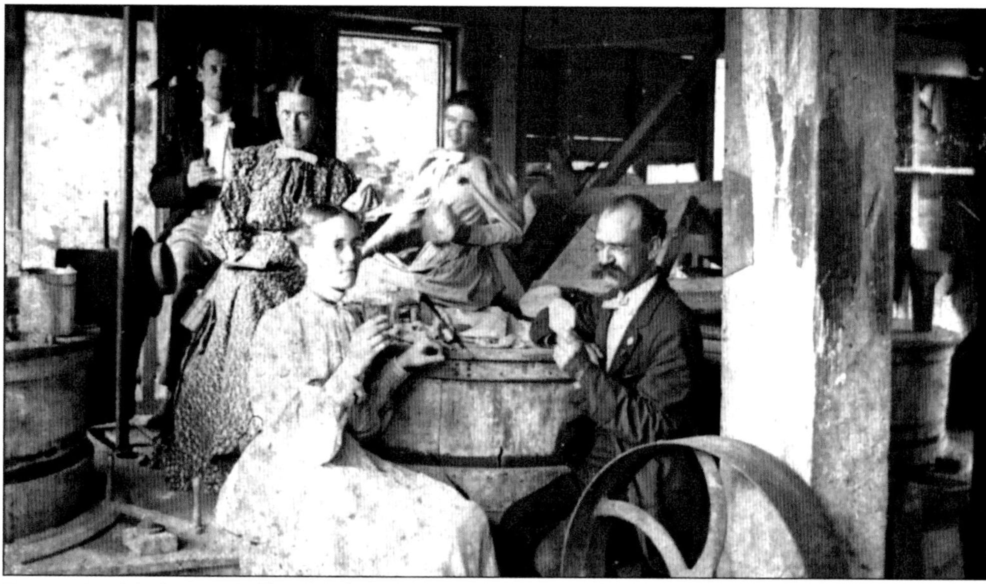

Pictured in McCarty's Mill around 1898 are a Mr. Winders in the back, Mrs. Lem Rowe and Laura Rowe Miller seated in the middle, and Mrs. Jess Singleton and Frank M. Singleton in the front. Milling was a major industry in Corydon. Big and Little Indian Creeks provided waterpower. In 1890, Charles Martin, Samuel Pfrimmer, and John Loweth organized the Corydon Milling Company, building a new mill, where they could use water or steam power, on the site of the White Mill. Lily White and Humpty Dumpty were popular brands of flour, but Gem brand was considered White Mill's best.

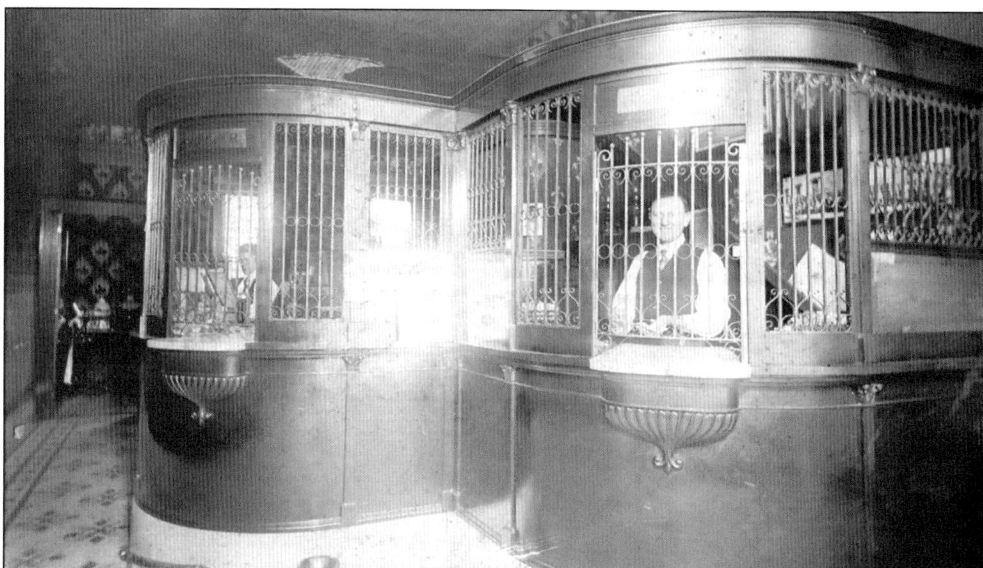

Will Huff mans the first teller's cage in the First National Bank, located at 209 North Capitol Avenue. Opened on April 2, 1903, First National prided itself on adhering to sound banking principles. Nevertheless, in July 1920 it folded into the Corydon National Bank, which opened in the 1880s under George W. Applegate Sr. and William B. Slemmons. Unfortunately, Corydon National Bank invested heavily in oil speculation in southern Illinois and was declared insolvent on February 20, 1922. Businesses and government entities throughout the county had funds in the bank.

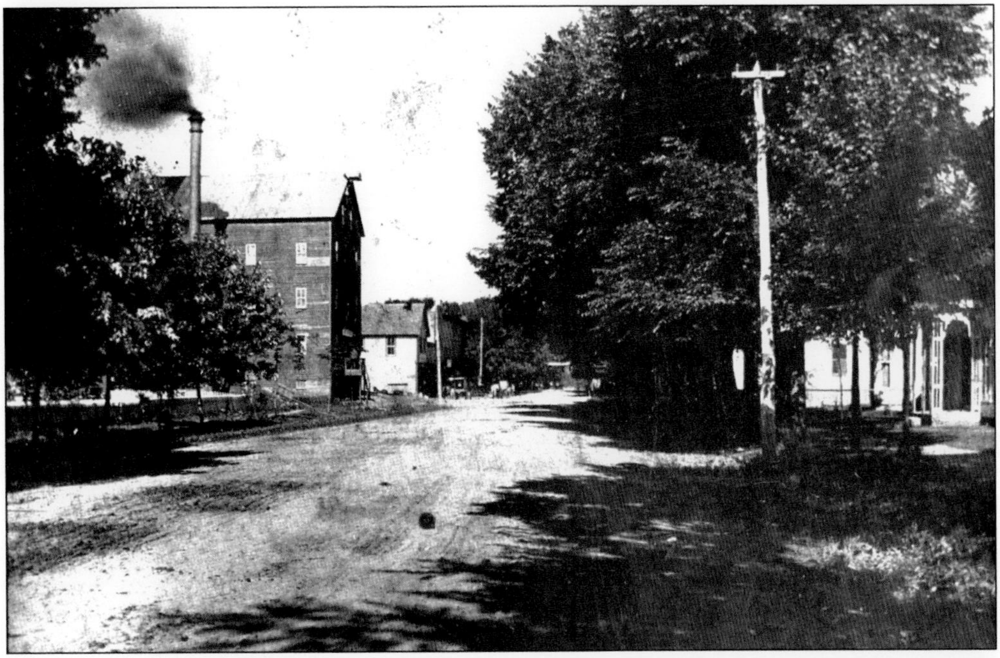

The Red Mill stood on Chestnut Street. Most of the mills throughout the county were water powered. The Red Mill, however, was steam powered. Built in 1833, the mill was once owned by Robert Leffler. According to town tradition, Leffler was in love with "a certain young lady" who returned his affection. Deferring to her father's wishes, however, she married another man. Although a great favorite in social circles, Leffler never married. The Red Mill was torn down in 1926.

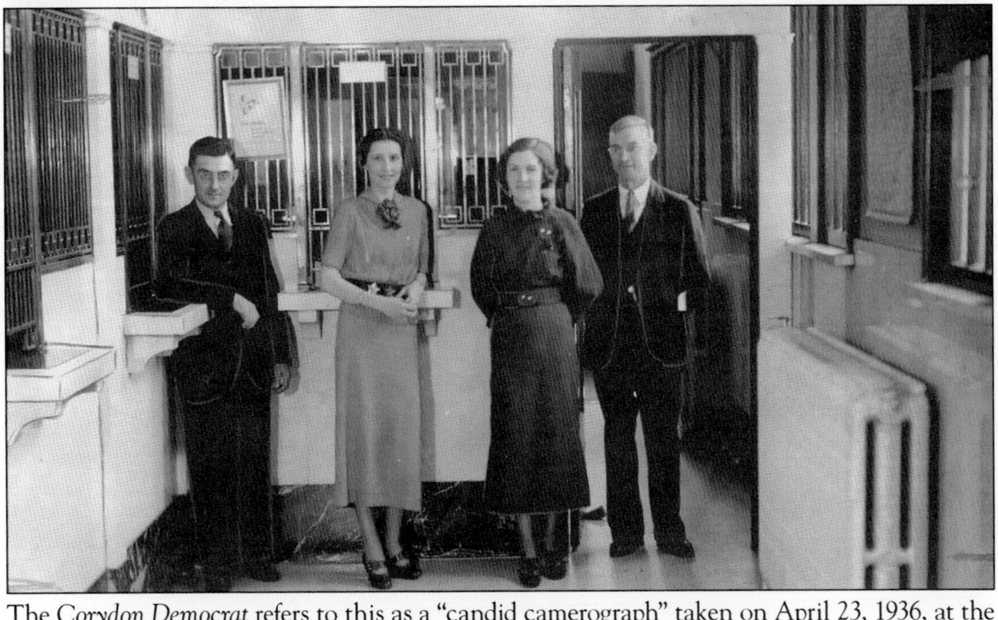

The *Corydon Democrat* refers to this as a "candid camerograph" taken on April 23, 1936, at the Corydon State Bank. From left to right are Willis Dome, secretary; Laura Frederick, assistant cashier; Margaret Hottell, bookkeeper; and Arthur B. Richert, head cashier. The Corydon State Bank was organized to recover from the shambles of the Corydon National Bank. The Corydon State Bank survived to be acquired by Liberty National Bank (now Chase) in December 1986.

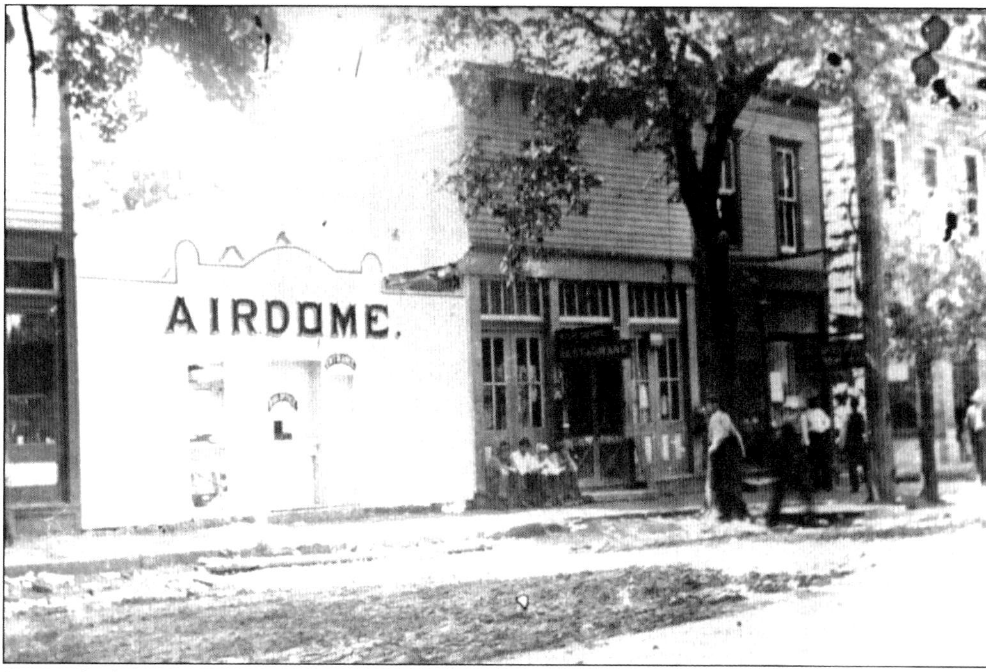

Located a few steps from the sandstone post office building on Chestnut Street, the Airdome was an outdoor movie theater, but predated drive-ins by many years. It was photographed in 1906.

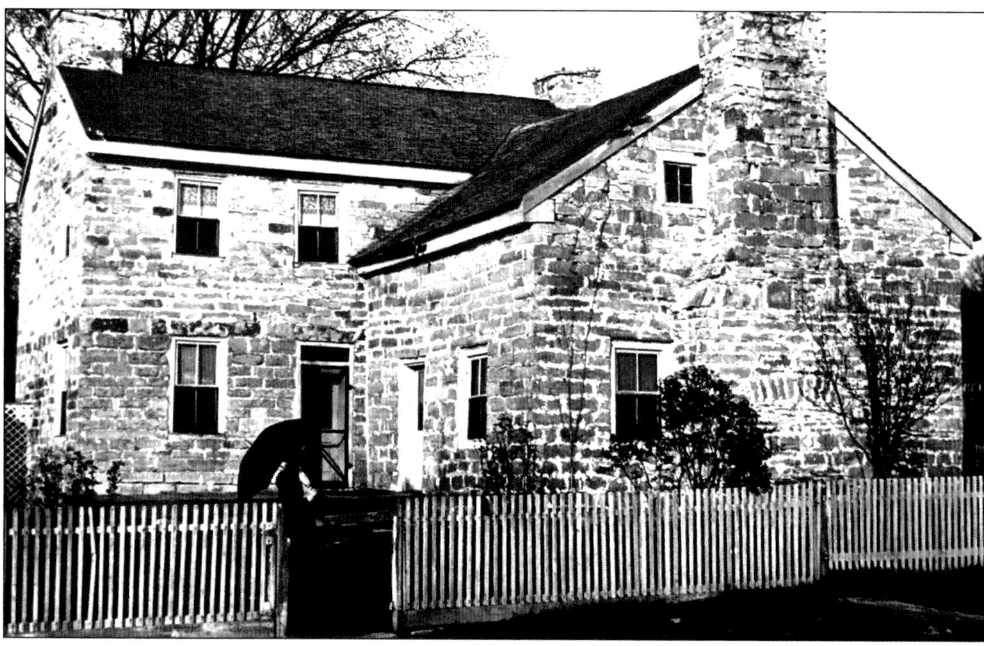

Intended to house those who came to the county seat for legal and political business, the Old Capitol Tavern was built in 1864 on State Route 62, about one mile east of town, to ensure adequate pasturage for travelers' horses. Also called Conrad Hotel, it was directly across the road from the present-day main entrance to the Corydon Country Club. The hotel burned down on March 15, 1921.

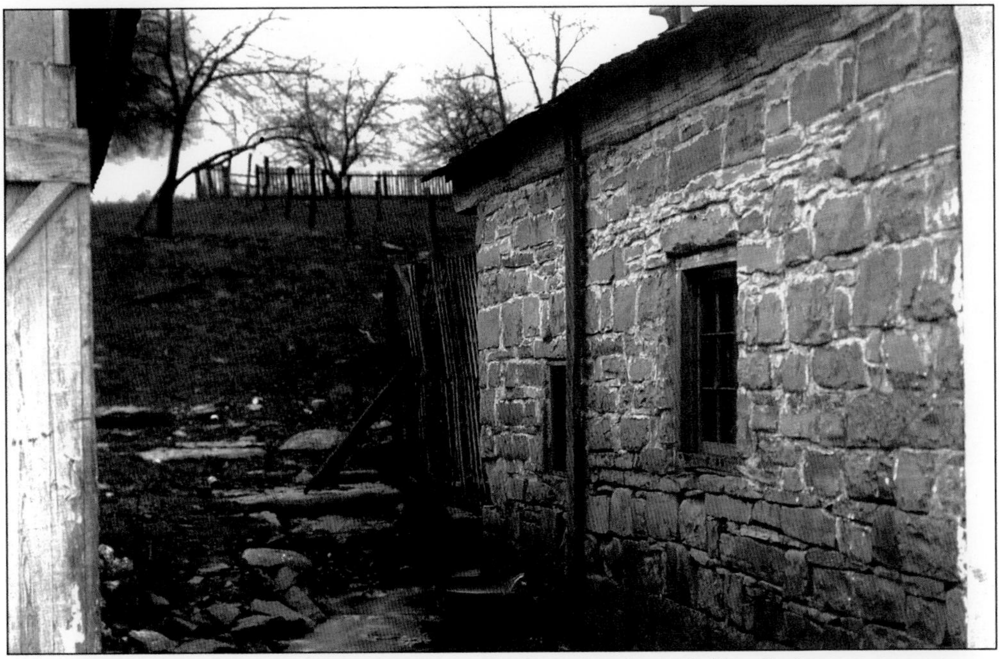

The springhouse at the Old Capitol Tavern was big enough to chill milk, butter, eggs, cream, and fresh fruit for discerning hotel guests. Harrison County is shot through with underground water, which is cool when it comes to the surface. Springhouses had a stone channel to contain the flowing water. Large crockery containers were then placed in this channel.

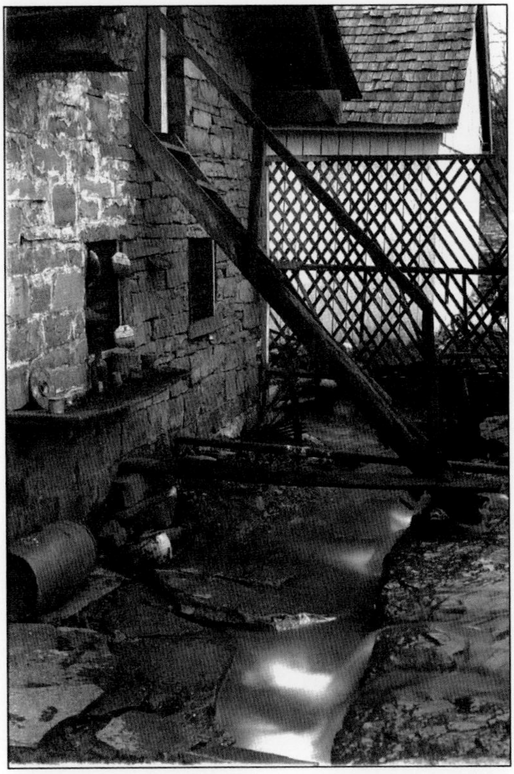

The upper story of the springhouse kept more fruit and root crops like turnips and potatoes to keep guests well satiated. The Old Capitol Tavern catered to the leaders, politicians, and lawyers who came to the county seat for sessions of court and government. They demanded the best in food and accommodations, and Corydon was more than ready to keep them happy.

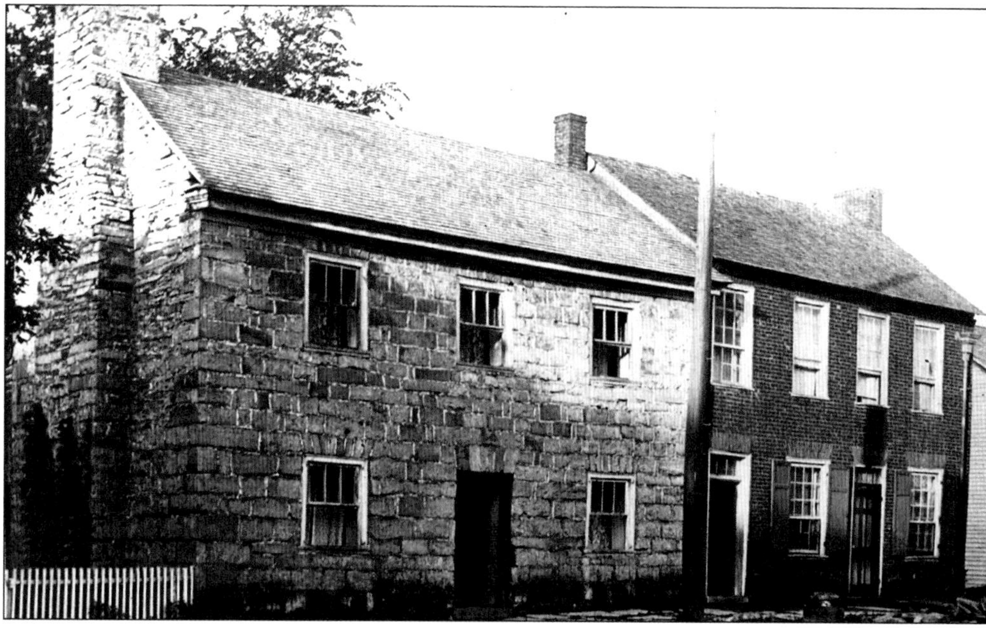

The Jack Jamison Tavern and the original Kintner House Hotel were located on the south side of Chestnut Street, at the foot of Oak Street.

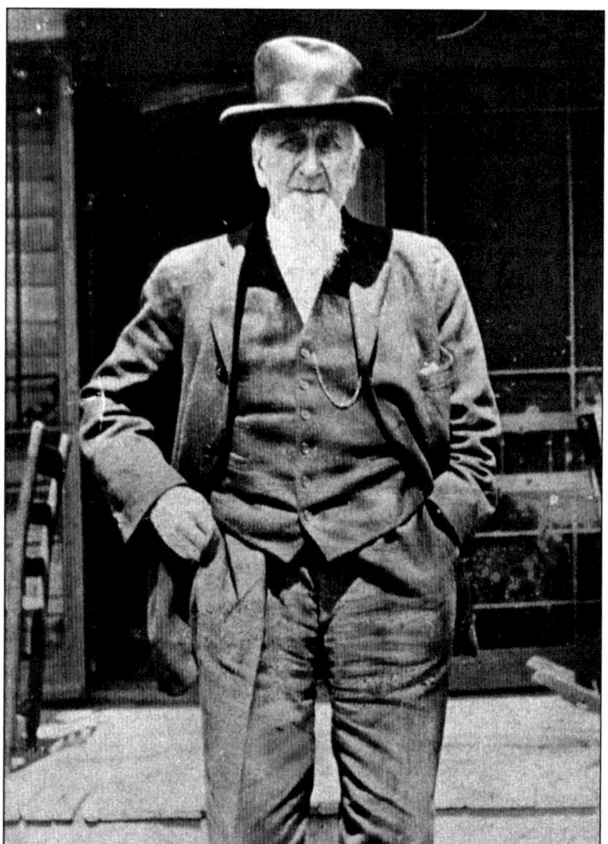

Levi "Dad" Blume, the "dad" of the hotel, was a Civil War veteran, although his dates of birth and death are not known. He must have been an outgoing, affable person. A story told in February 1912, reports that Blume had a rooster that crowed with gusto and without stop. During the cold, however, the rooster attempted to crow and the crow froze on his bill. Blume snapped off the crow, took it inside, and placed it behind the stove. As the crow thawed out, it sounded shrilly for quite some time, then trailed off softer and softer as it melted away.

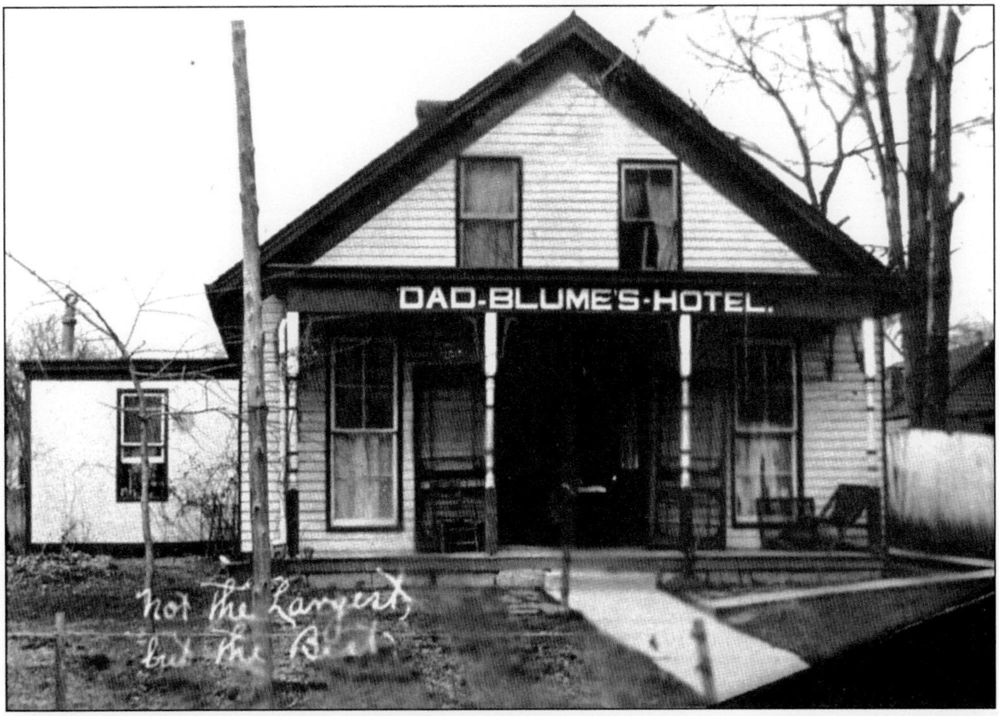

Dad Blume's Hotel was located at 112 West Walnut Street, which was near the railroad depot. Blume proclaimed his hotel, "Not the largest, but the best." Teresa Blume (1842–1914) was known for "setting a real good table," as Fred Griffin said.

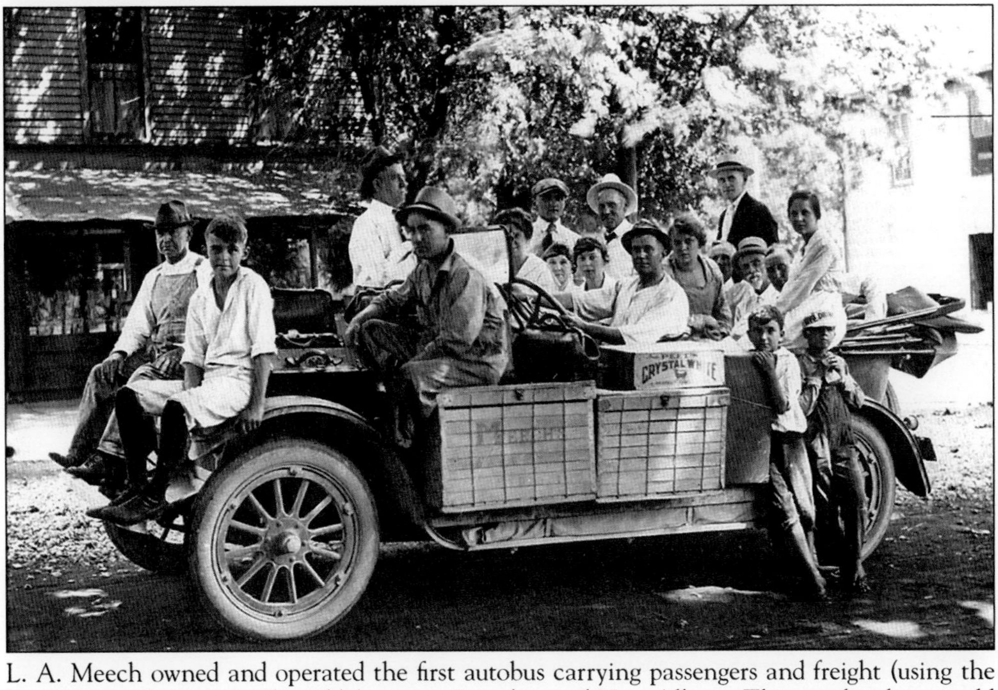

L. A. Meech owned and operated the first autobus carrying passengers and freight (using the hampers on the running boards) between Corydon and New Albany. This autobus line would continue serving Corydon until May 1972.

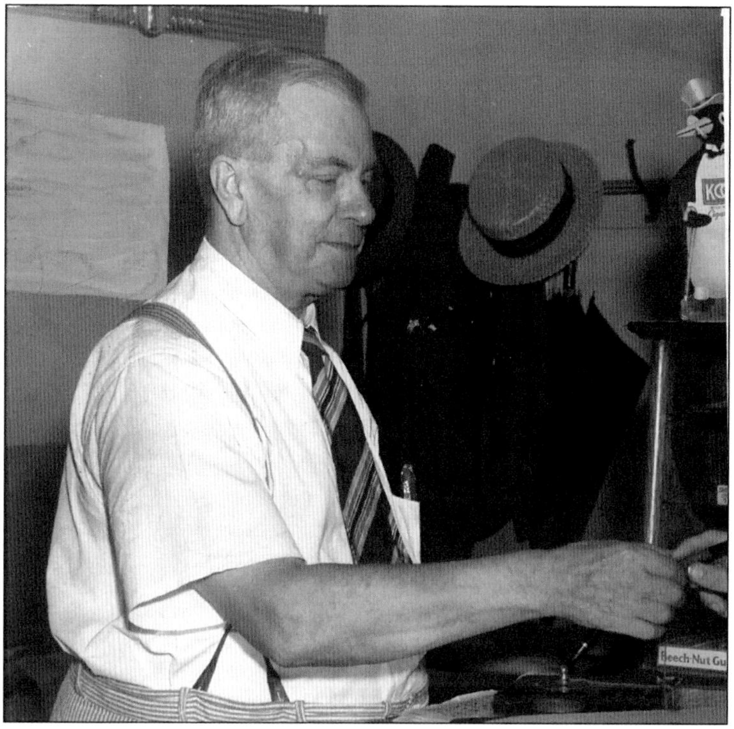

In 1927, L. A. Meech and Robert Sharp purchased half of the Posey House on Oak Street, tore it down, and built the Corydon Hotel. A grand opening was held on November 7, with dinner and music from the Corydon Orchestra. Each of the 26 guest rooms had running water; 14 had complete baths, the others only lavatories. Meech is shown here in the Corydon Hotel. The building still stands, but is no longer well appointed.

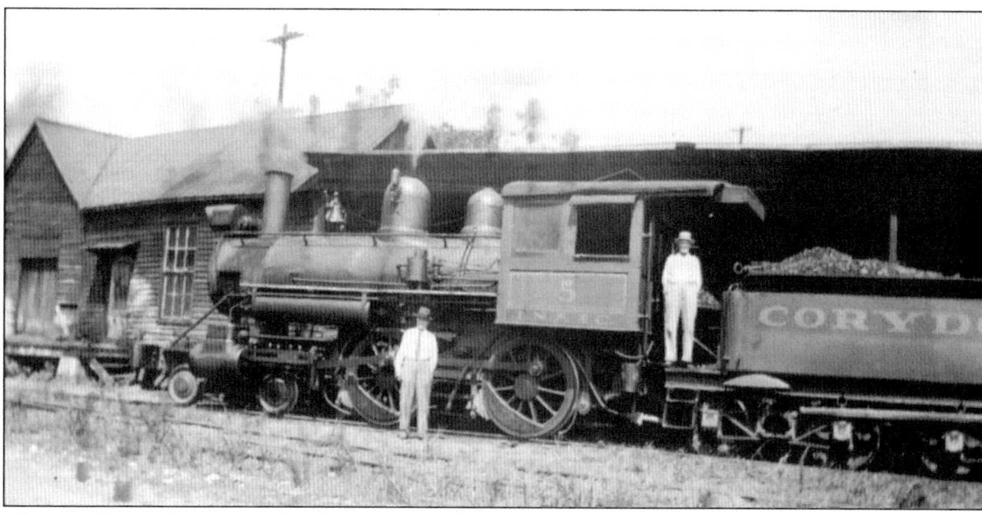

The hotels on the west side of town were located near the railroad station, which was—and still is—near the West Bridge. St. John Boyle, building the Louisville, Evansville and St. Louis Railroad, moved to Corydon in 1881 and began organizing the Louisville, New Albany and Corydon Railroad, the shortest in the state. The first train traveled in 1883. The early tenders, the car carrying the coal or wood immediately behind the locomotive, did not have brakes. They were slowed and stopped by means of a hand lever applied by a trainman. This usually resulted in freight, passengers, and crew arriving at the station in a jumbled chaos tossed to the forward end of each car.

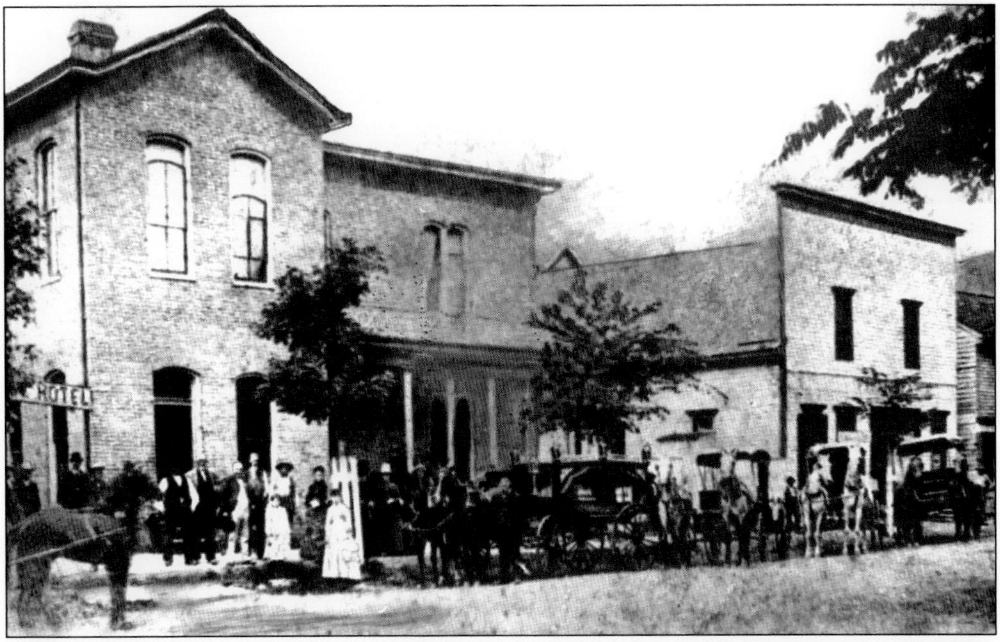

Tabler's Hotel (the brick structure) occupied the northeast corner of Capitol Avenue and Cherry Street. This block is now the site of the Harrison County Courthouse. For many years, the Tabler advertised itself as "the only hotel in Corydon with a bath." This photograph from the dawn of the 20th century promotes the William S. Shuck Livery (the frame building) rentals of hearses and carriages.

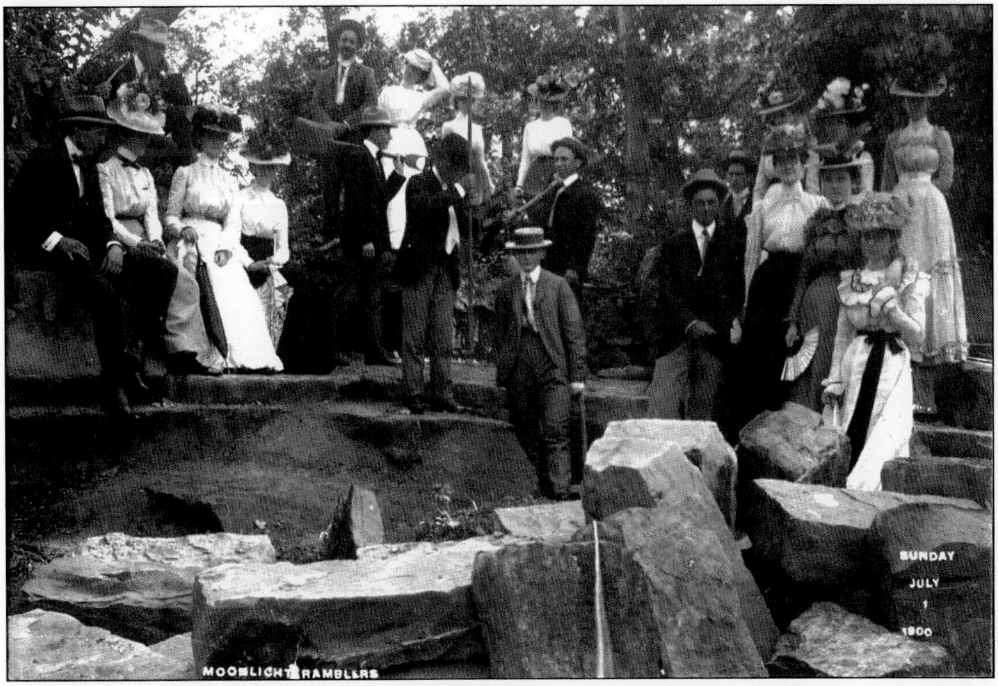

Stone Quarry, one of the earliest limestone quarries in Corydon, was located on the Cedar Glade farm. Corydon Crushed Stone operates today.

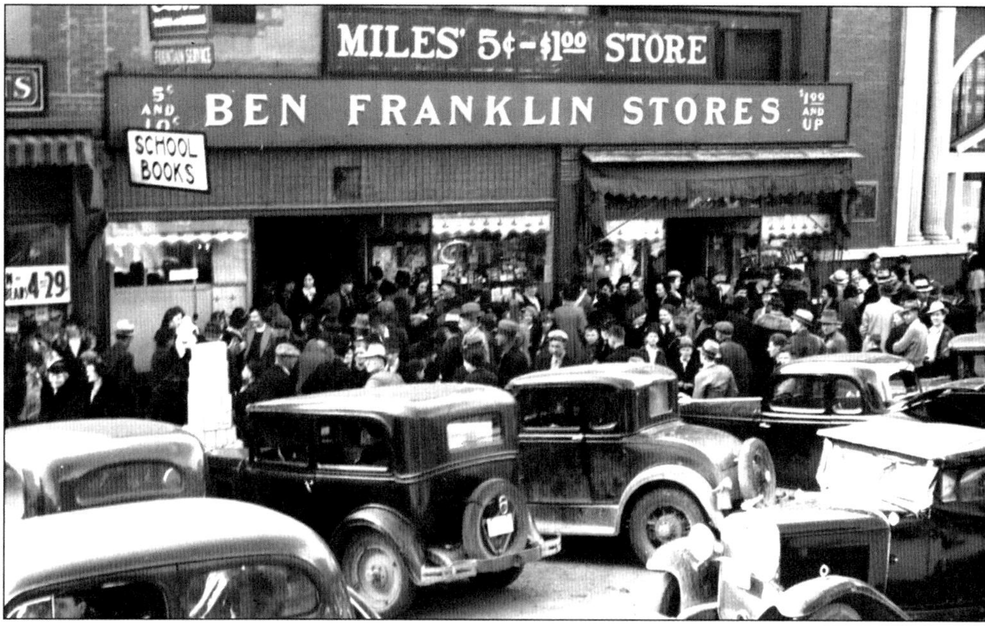

Saturday was the usual day to come to town. The square would be crowded with families shopping for groceries, clothing, household necessities, and farm equipment and supplies. It was also a chance to visit and catch up on news. It was a time for presenting programs and lectures, campaigning for office or public projects, and perhaps taking in a picture show (movie). Note the sign "School books." Books would be stored in various places during the summer. They might be taken to the schools in time for the first day, or students might have to buy some of their books.

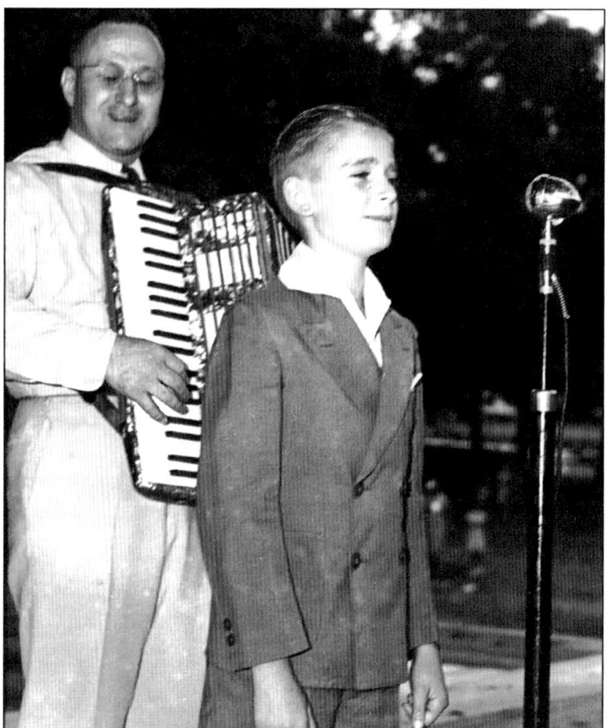

Hurley D. Conrad (left) spent a lifetime performing music, writing music, teaching music, and instilling a love of music in all those around him. The bandstand presently on the town square is named in his honor. Here he accompanies Chesney Davis.

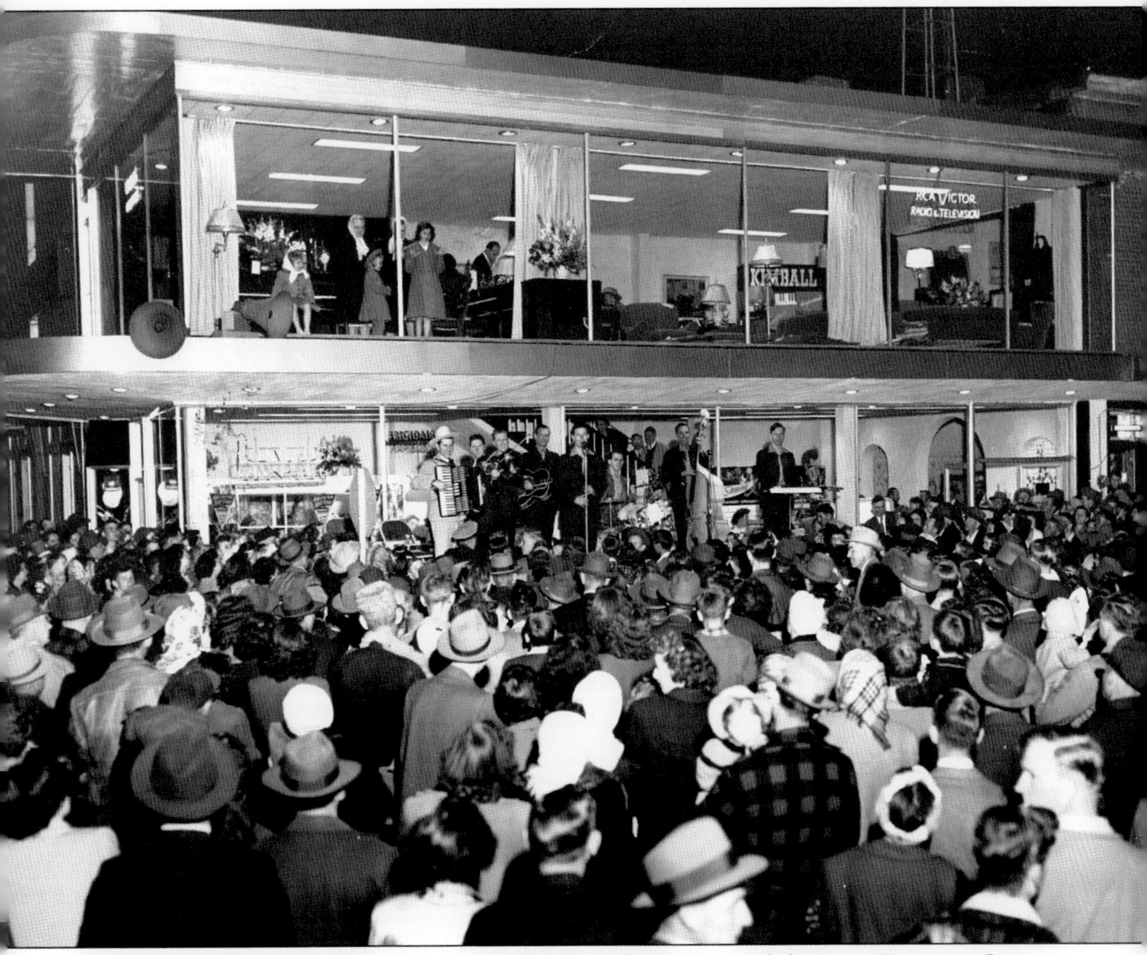

The history of Conrad's Music Store goes back to C. W. Conrad, born in Harrison County in 1857. He began his education in the county public schools and went on to the American Conservatory of Music in Chicago. He taught vocal music in county churches, but preferred traveling and conducting musical conventions in Indiana and adjoining states. He began selling pianos and organs in 1888 and broke the record of any salesman in the central states. In 1904, his son Claude H. Conrad graduated as a piano tuner, and on September 1, 1905, the firm was organized as C. W. Conrad and Son Music Company. Younger son Hurley D. Conrad continued to operate the family business at Beaver and Elm Streets. The grand opening of Conrad's Music Store in April 1949 brought out many of the townspeople. The modern building was almost entirely fronted with windows. Conrad's store occupied the first floor; the local radio station was on the second floor. The building still overlooks the square.

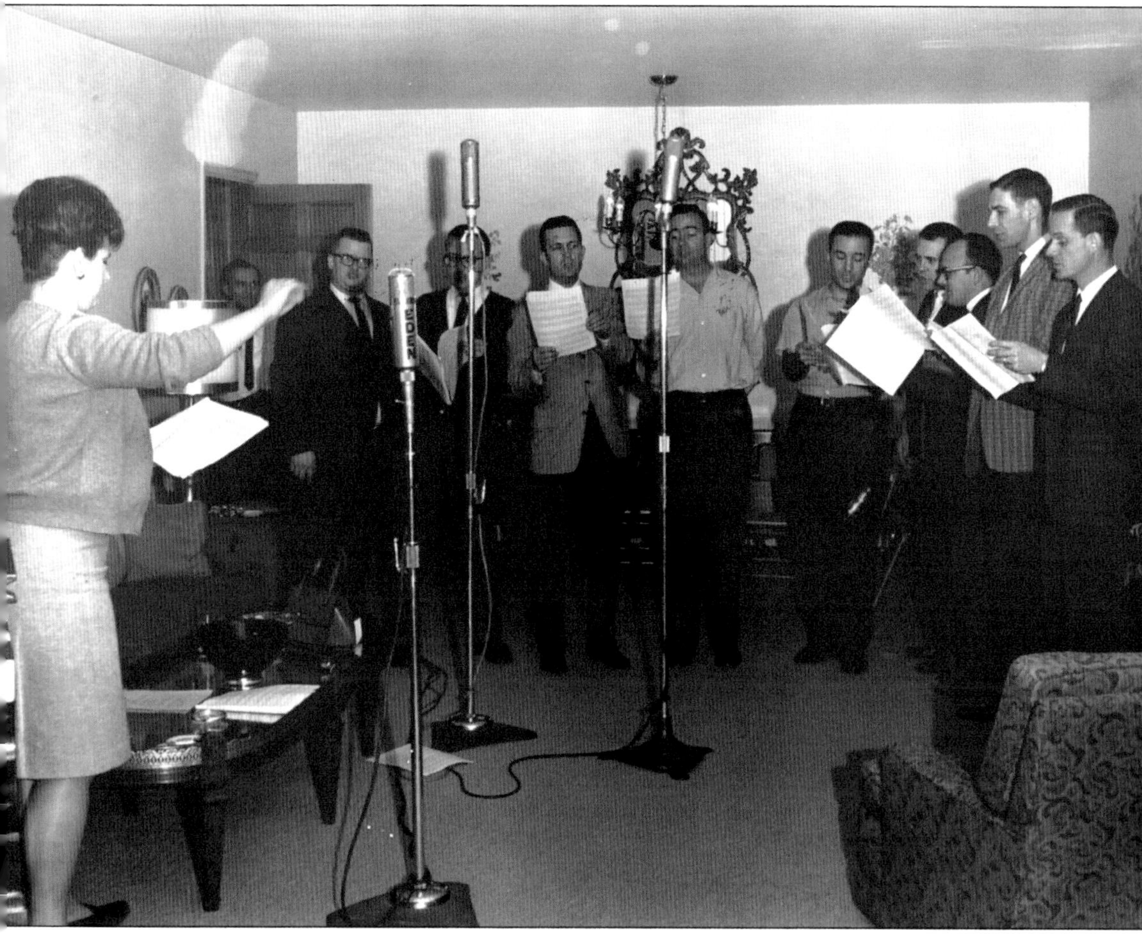

Ivanna Conrad is directing a chorus or choir. This may be a live radio broadcast in the studio on the second floor of the music store. These men may be the Corydon Singers: Rev. William Huckabone, Jerry Bradshaw, Dr. David Dukes, Harry Carpenter, Charles Conrad, Paul Conrad, Arthur Eve, Rev. Nelson Chamberlin, and Frank O'Bannon. The Corydon Singers were featured at the Indiana sesquicentennial celebration in 1966.

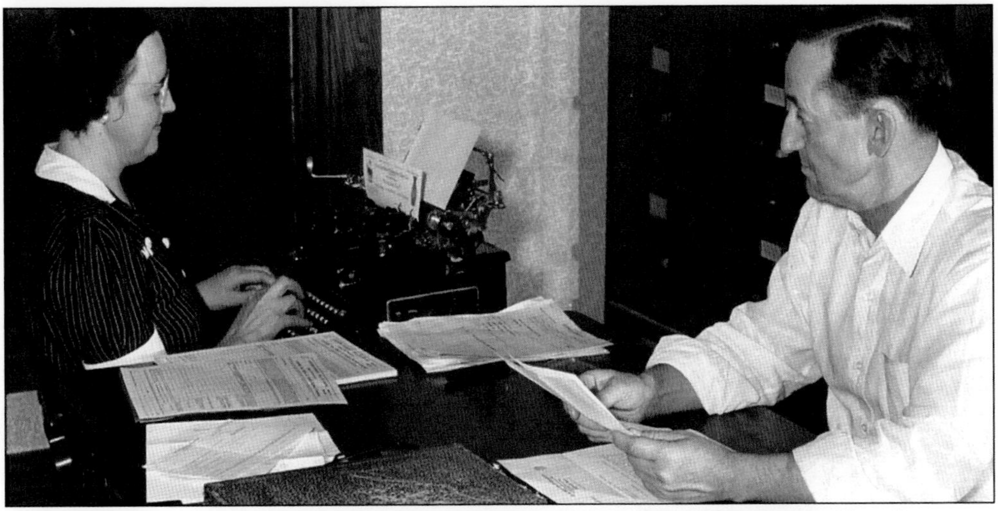

Anna Bacher, secretary, works next to Roscoe Atwood, president of Enterprise Glass Company. Atwood oversaw the move to Corydon. In 1936, the *Corydon Democrat* reported that Cooperative Enterprise Glass Company, dedicated exclusively to making lamp chimneys, had grown for five years, despite the increase in use of electric lights. In the previous year, the furnaces were kept in production for 61 continuous weeks, skipping the usual summer maintenance shutdown to keep up with demand, even though there were 11 other chimney factories across the country.

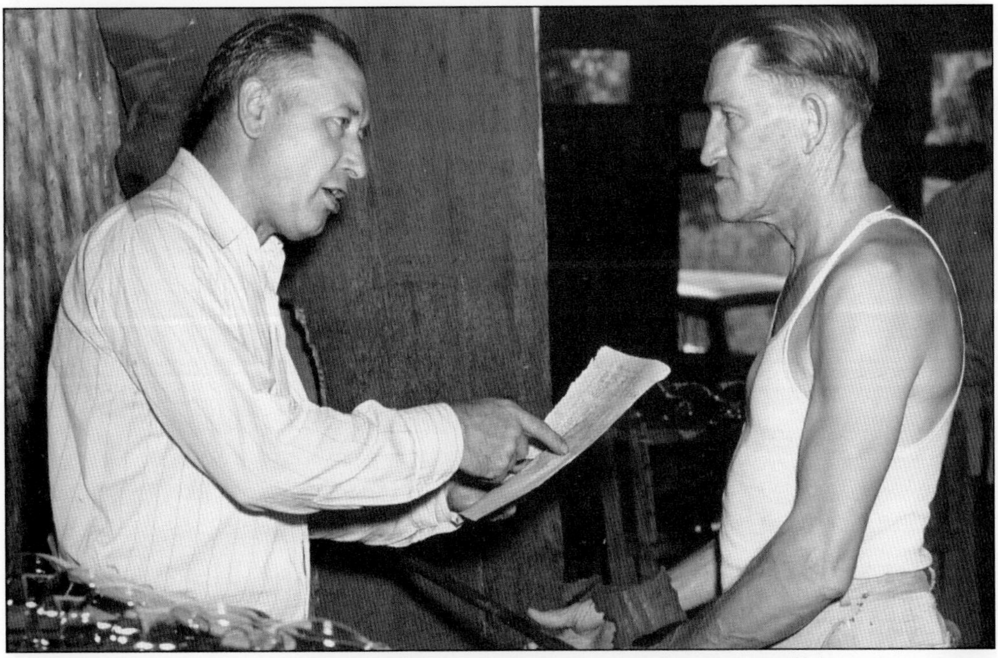

Expert glassblower Vic Zimmerman (left) consults with coworker Ora Griffith at Cooperative Enterprise Glass Company. The blow pipe in Griffith's hands and the wrist guard on his right arm indicate that he is a gatherer, the man who balances a globe of molten glass preparing for the blower. Each chimney was hand-made by a three man crew: the gatherer, the blower, and the finisher. A skilled worker collected a globule of molten glass onto the blowpipe. The artisan called the blower blew his breath through the tube to create the chimney, which was then removed by the finisher, the least skilled of the three.

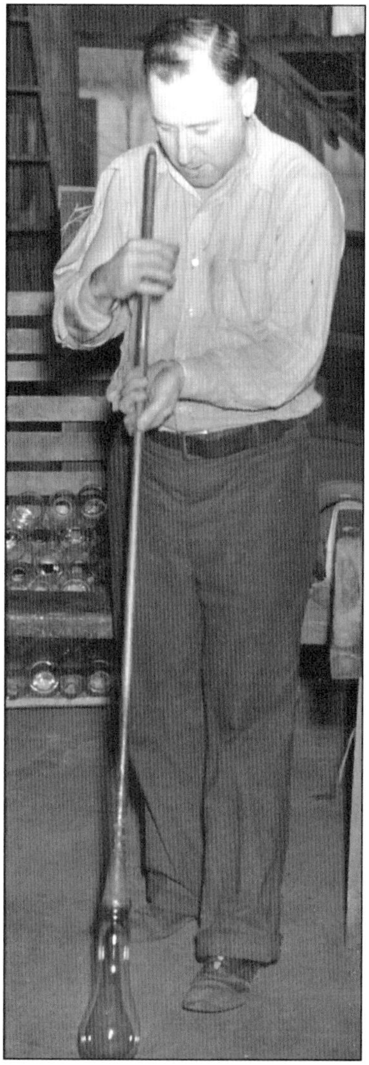

The Cooperative Enterprise Glass Company relocated to Corydon in 1925, after its North Vernon plant was destroyed by a fire on March 17 of that year. Inexpensive natural gas from the new gas fields south of Corydon prompted the move. Victor Zimmerman (seen here) and Mel Van Valican were two of the glass blowers who produced lamp chimneys at the factory. Victor Zimmerman went on to found the Zimmerman Art Glass Factory. Tragically, he was killed by his former business partner, who then turned the gun on himself. His firm, however, continues with his sons and grandsons.

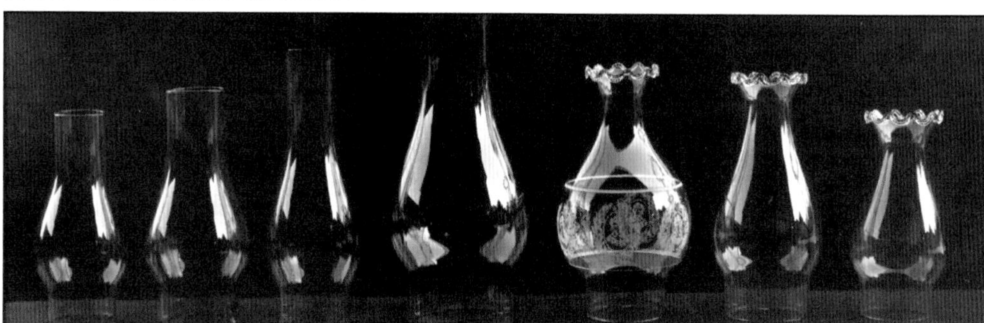

An array of delicate Enterprise Glass products shows the skill of the glassblowers. In 1947, six special lamp chimneys were made by Ross Griffith. They were made to specifications from the organization that maintained Mount Vernon, home of George Washington. Roscoe Atwood, president of Enterprise, repaid the compliment of being entrusted to create the glass pieces by donating them to the historic home.

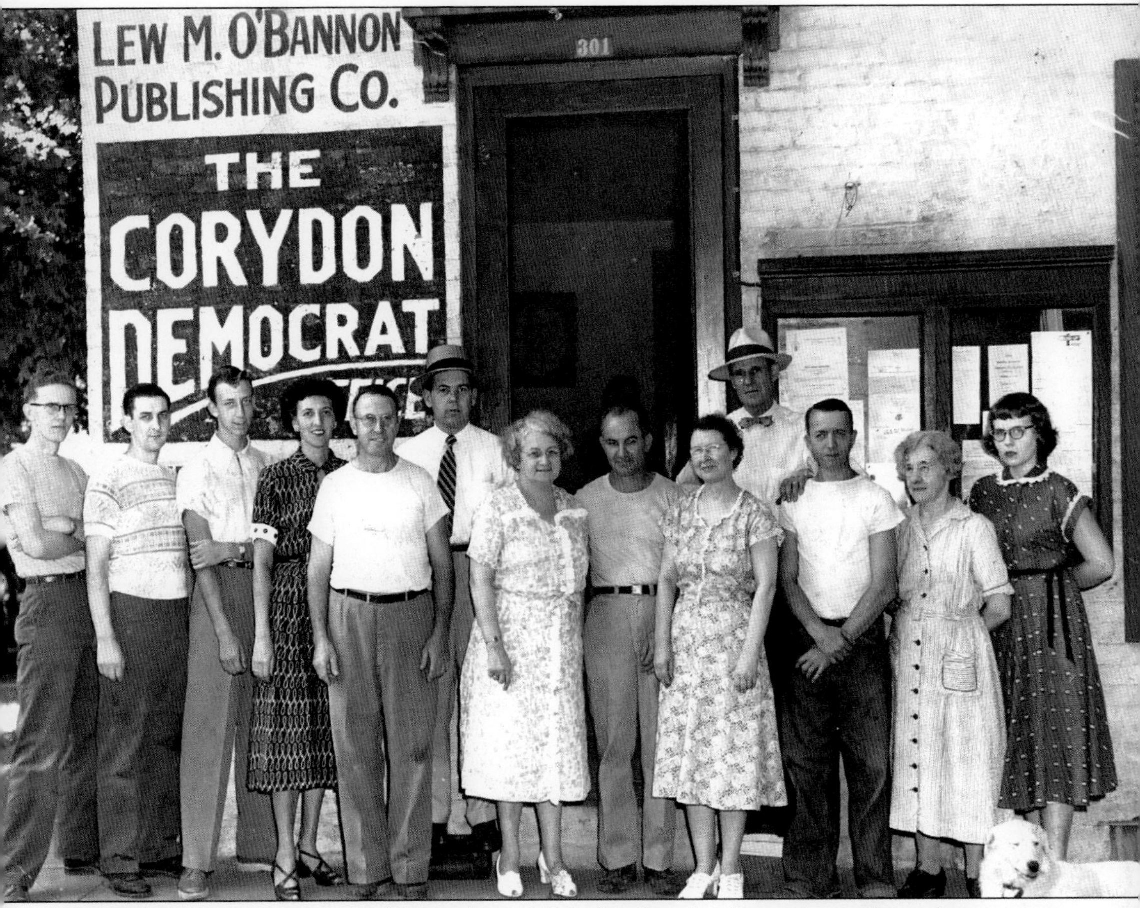

Established by Simeon K. Wolfe, in April 1856, the *Corydon Democrat* is the only surviving newspaper in Harrison County. Lew M. O'Bannon bought it in 1907, and it is presently produced by O'Bannon Publishing Company. The staff poses in 1950. They are, from left to right, Guido Gibson, George Hess, Charlie Burch, Dorothy Splain, Kenneth Flock, J. D. Williams, Lucine K. Gailey, Bob Rainbolt, Hazel Nenor, Robert P. O'Bannon, Ermal Kellem, Sallie Feller, and Margaret Pflanz Jacobi.

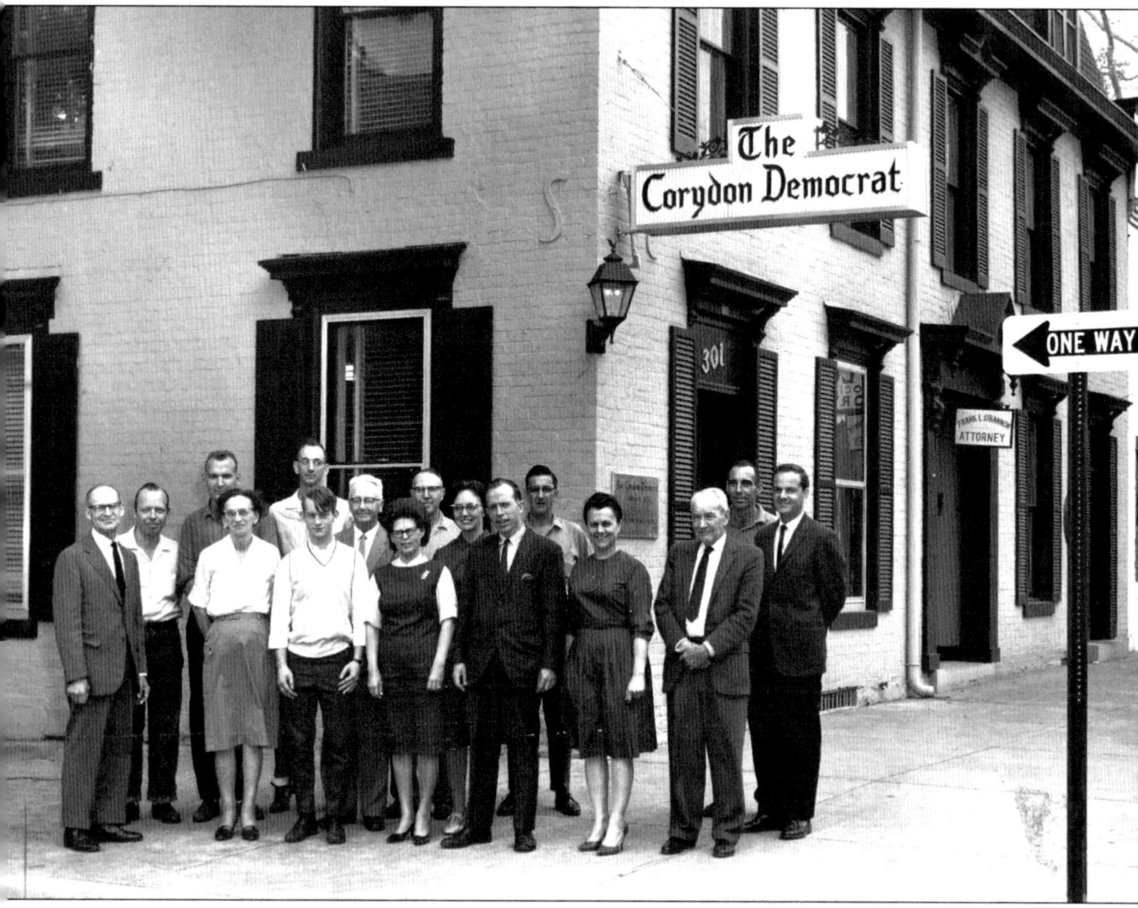

In the 1960s, the *Corydon Democrat* staff assembled on the other side of the corner. They are, from left to right, Bob O'Bannon, Melvin Green, Don McMonigle, Emma Frakes, Vernon Denbo, Eldon Mason, Ed Prewitt, Ruby Rooksby, Kenneth Flock, Daris Miller, Fred Cromwell, George Hess, Phyllis Heishman, Earle Hitch, John Harbaugh, and Frank O'Bannon. Frank O'Bannon would be governor of Indiana from January 13, 1997, to September 13, 2003.

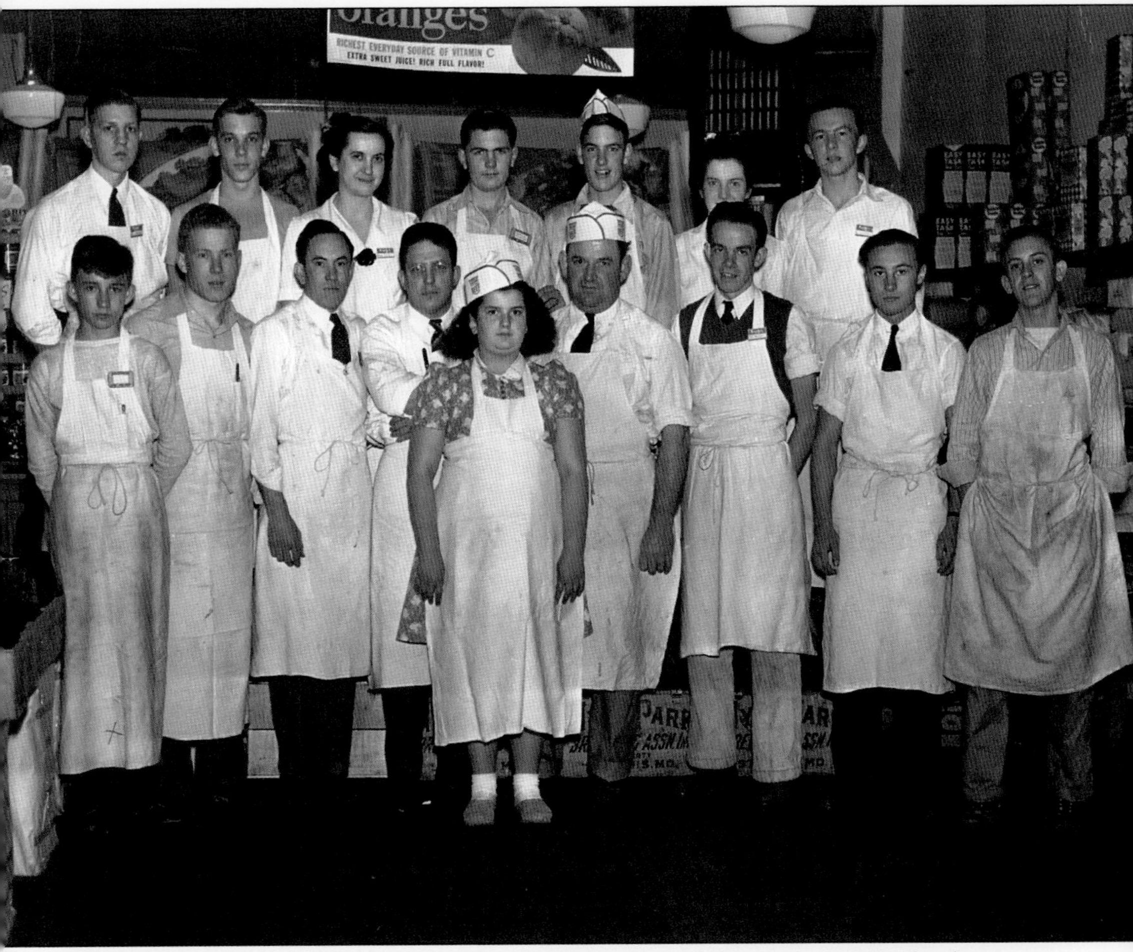

The Corydon Kroger Store was located on North Capitol Avenue in 1940. Employees are identified as follows: (first row) Ray Glenn, unidentified, assistant manager Bob Amy, manager Claude LeMasters, LeMasters's daughter, store butcher, Ted Mossler, ? Chinn, and John Orwick; (second row) Calvin ?, Bill Davidson, unidentified, James Shireman, James Best, unidentified, and George Rosenbarger.

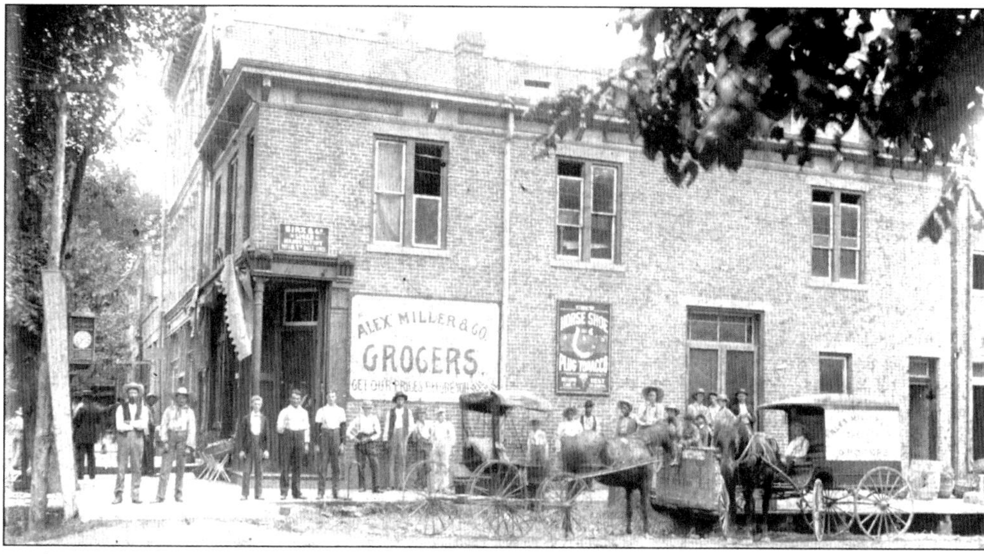

In the early 1900s, Millers operated four of Corydon's grocery stores. Fred Griffin made note of Silas M. Miller (1836–1914) on the northeast corner of Walnut Street and Capitol Avenue; Cortez M. Miller (1843–1918), a Civil War veteran, at 112 North Elm Street; Robert Leffler Miller (1855–1939), brother of Cortez and located just across the square; and Shoudy A. "Sam" Miller (1889–1970), first at East Chestnut Street, then at the corner of Elm and Chestnut Streets. Unfortunately, Alex Miller is not included in the list.

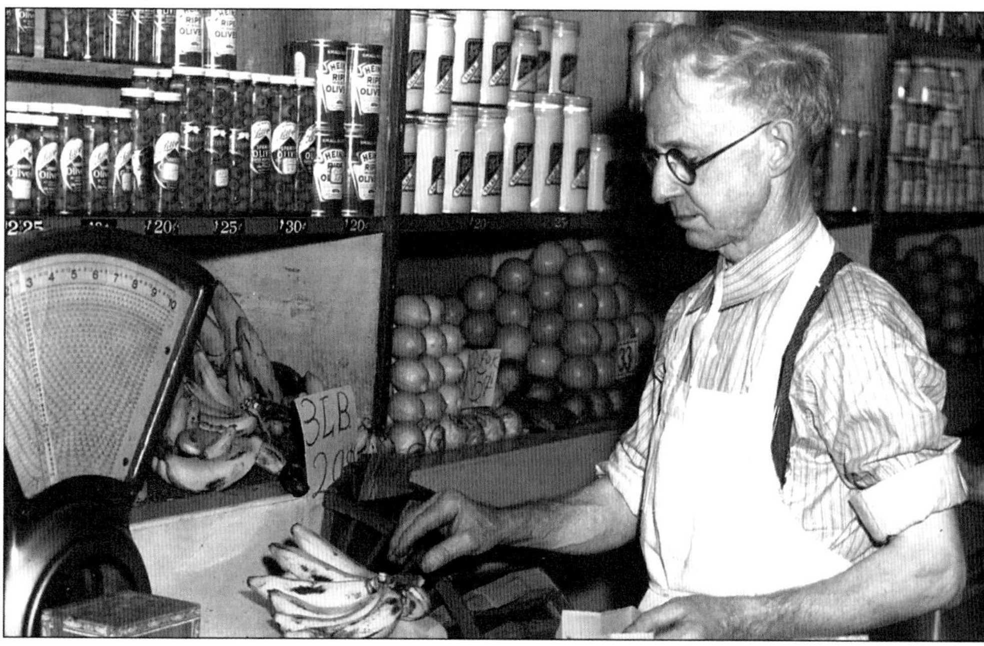

H. T. Hudson is seen in his grocery store on the east side of the square in 1941. In addition to running his business, Hudson was also treasurer of the Corydon Chamber of Commerce, and was a member and president of the Corydon Town Board from 1928 to 1932. Curiously, he was known to many friends as Sam. It seems that his father, Capt. William Henry Harrison Hudson, was considering the name Samuel Tilden should his expected baby be a boy. Yet his first name was Harry. Might the "Tilden" have survived in H. T. Hudson?

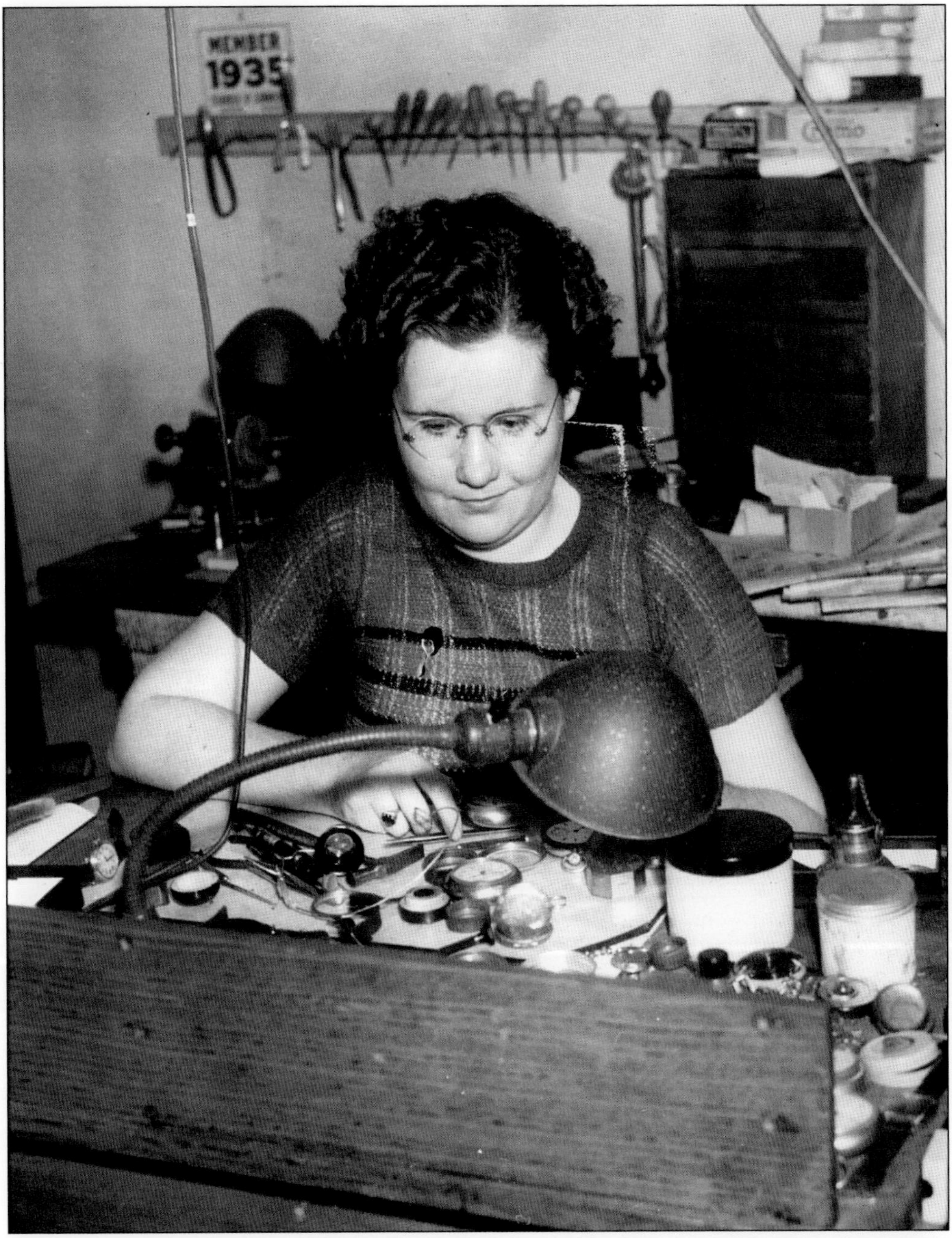

Elva Cunningham was featured in a May 20, 1936, story in the *Corydon Democrat*. Joining her brother in the jewelry business, the 21-year-old apparently became the only female jeweler in the state of Indiana. Like any jeweler, she spent much of her time cleaning and reconditioning watches.

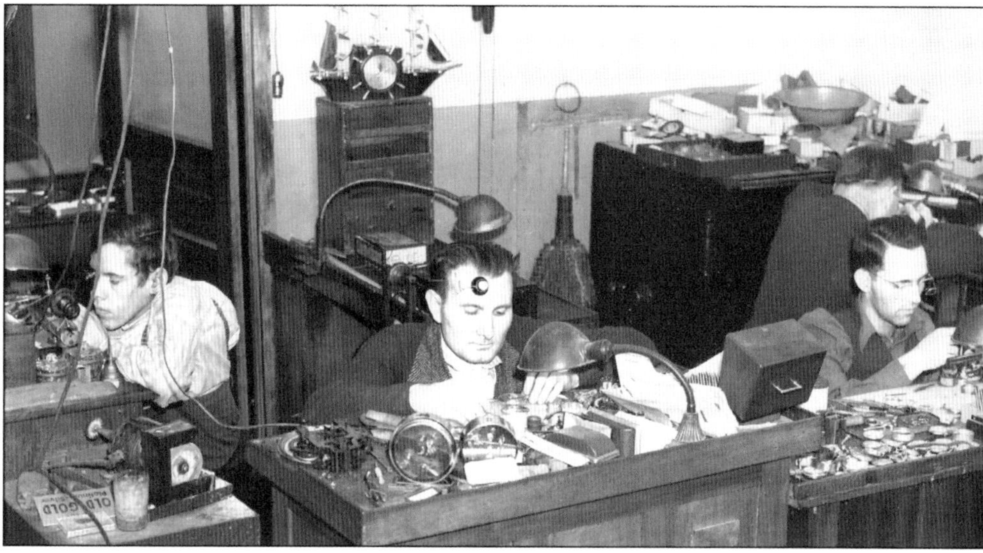

This is the classroom at Cunningham's Horology (watchmaking) School. Floyd Cunningham is second from the left. Founded in 1946 to teach veterans of World War II, the school flourished for a few years. All jewelry stores needed a watchmaker for cleaning and repairing fine, often heirloom, clocks and watches. Students might be single or married, and the school advertised for living quarters for students while they were studying. In 1947, Cunningham bought the Wright Building, the sandstone post office building on Chestnut Street. Huff Furniture Company had occupied the first floor during the war years, with offices upstairs. Cunningham remodeled to open a jewelry store on the first floor, while housing the horology school on the second floor. The school had about 80 students at a time, and those who completed the two-year program were in demand among employers.

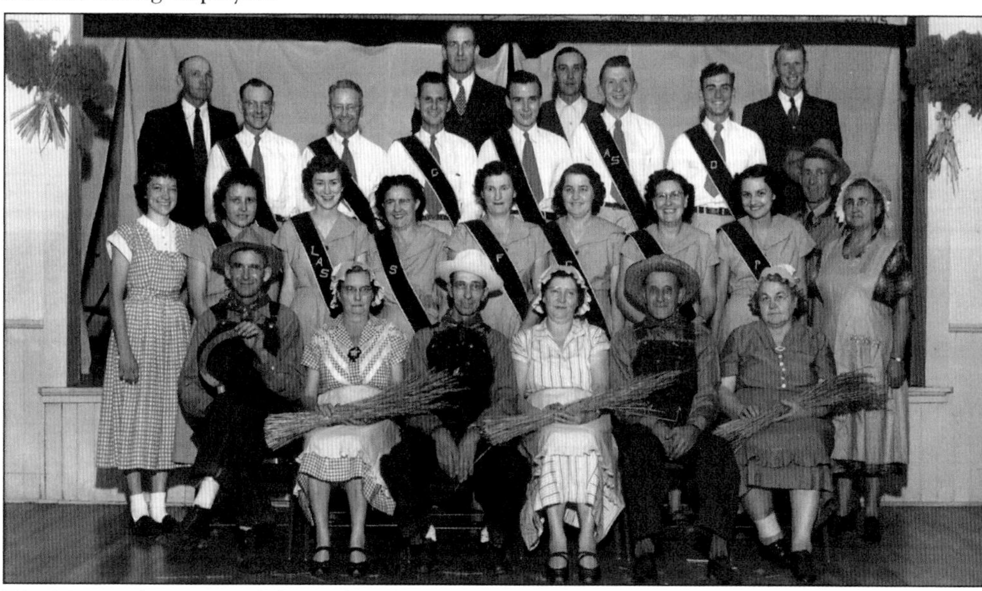

The National Grange of the Order of Patrons of Husbandry was founded in 1867 to promote the interests of farmers. In the great tradition of America, the Grange bettered the business prospects of farmers and provided its members with opportunity for fellowship and nonsense. In 1950, the Harrison County Grange gathered for business and fun.

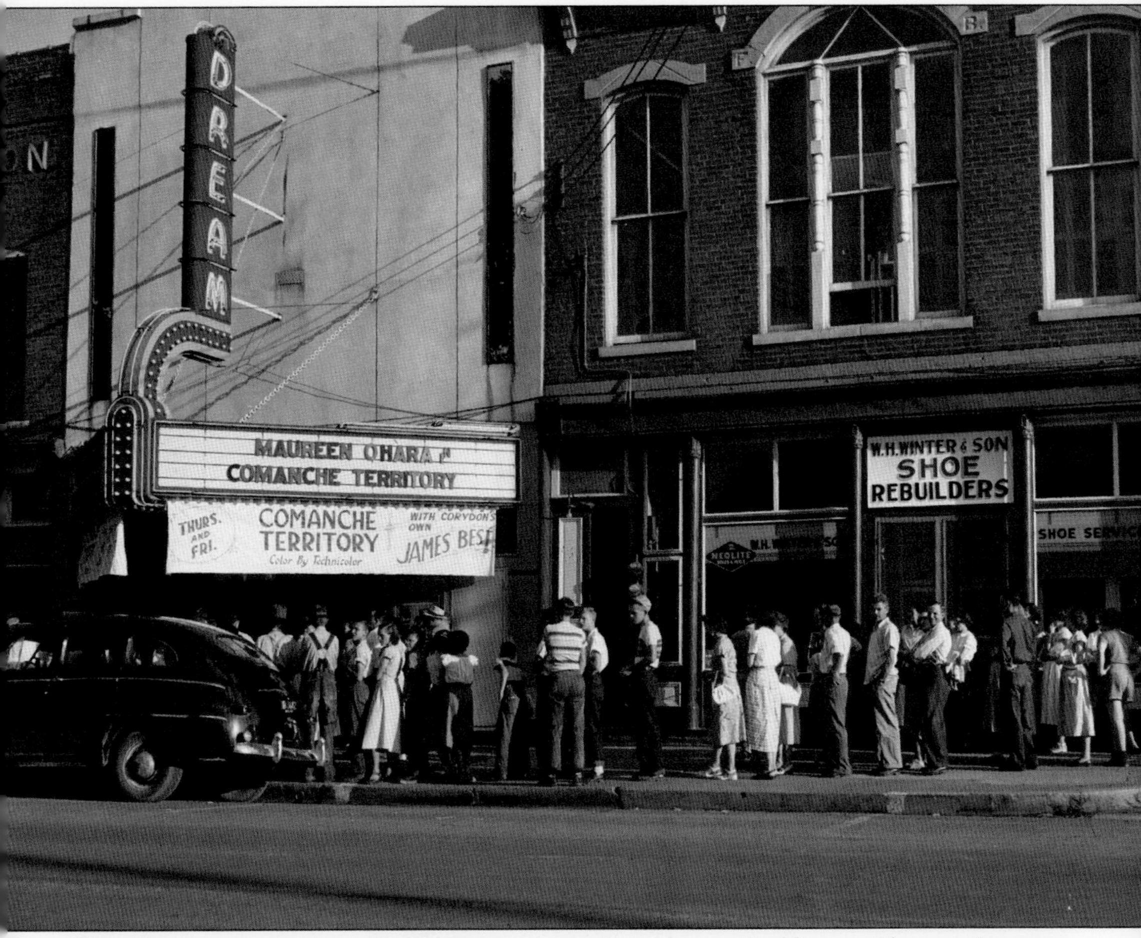

Shaw Grimes originated the Dream Theatre in the Beanblossom Building on Chestnut Street at Elm Street, later moving to Capitol Avenue. Various owners operated the theater until it burned on April 17, 1966. This crowd is lined up for the premiere of the movie *Comanche Territory*, which was the debut movie of actor James Best.

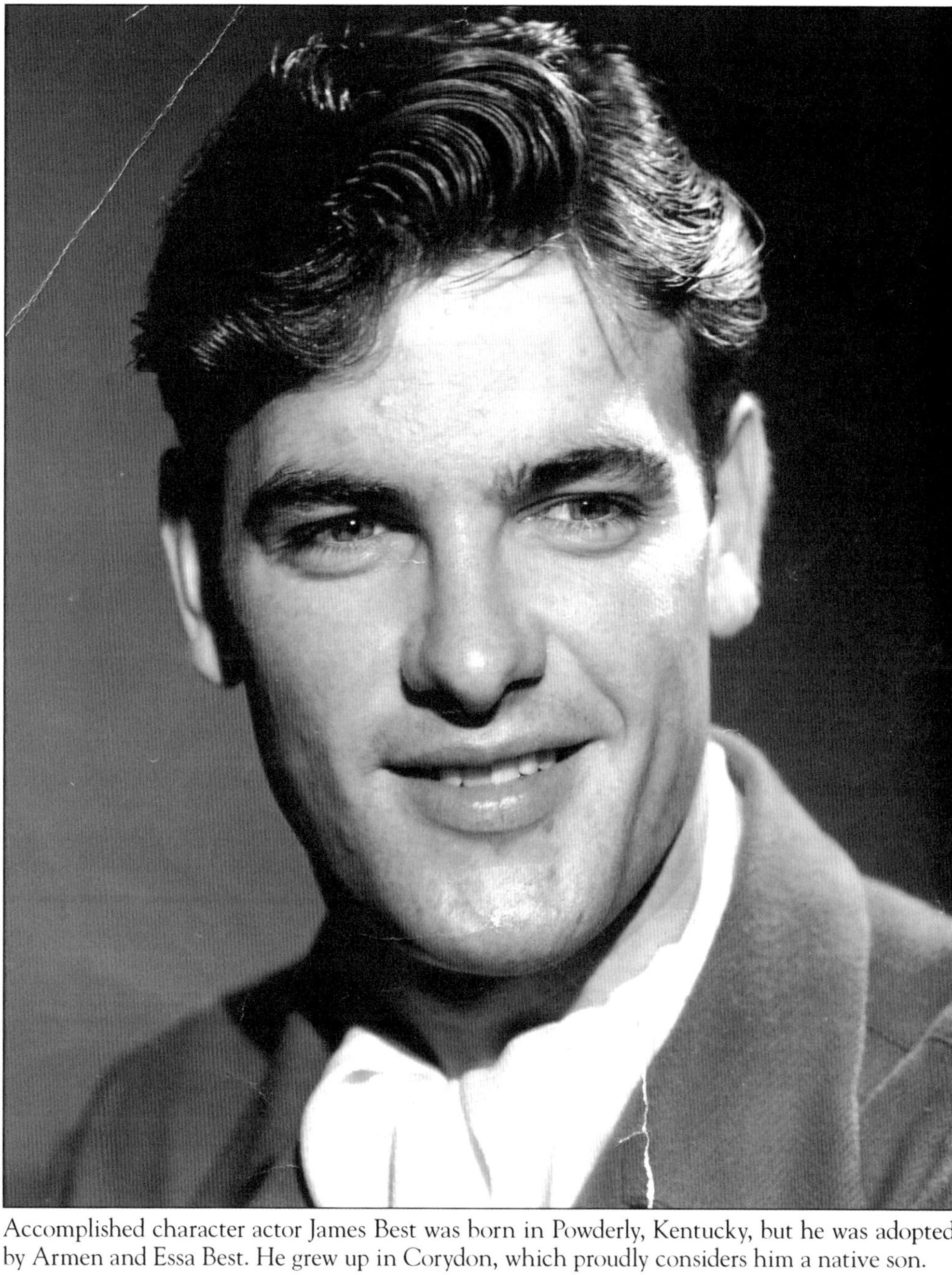

Accomplished character actor James Best was born in Powderly, Kentucky, but he was adopted by Armen and Essa Best. He grew up in Corydon, which proudly considers him a native son.

Five

SCHOOLS

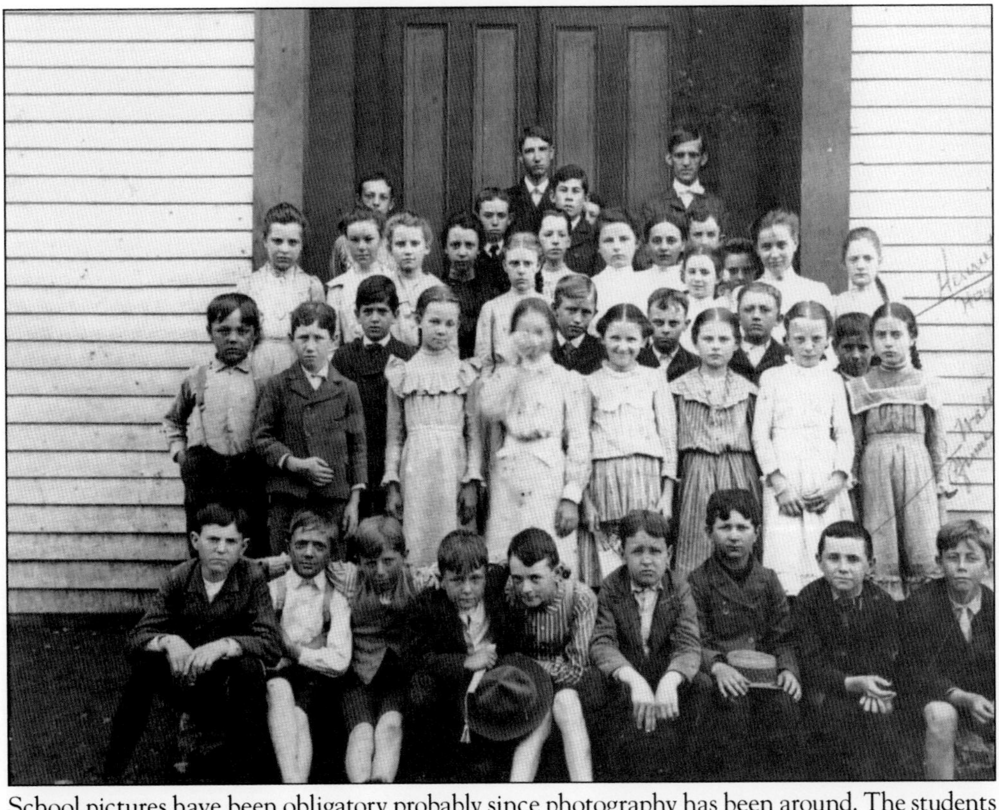

School pictures have been obligatory probably since photography has been around. The students are gathered in front of the old grade school, around 1915. Dennis Pennington kept the first school in Harrison County, teaching his own 14 children and accepting any children in the neighborhood for tuition of a penny or some barter goods. The first known school in Corydon was kept by a Dr. West, who taught in a cabin near the confluence of the creeks. At various times, the state office building, the Corydon Capitol building, and the Governor Hendricks Headquarters all served as school quarters. In 1839, the old Harrison County Seminary building (the state office building) was deemed unsuitable for school use, and in 1845, the Lutheran church building across the street was purchased for a school. It served until it burned, around 1872. At that time, a building specifically intended as a school was constructed.

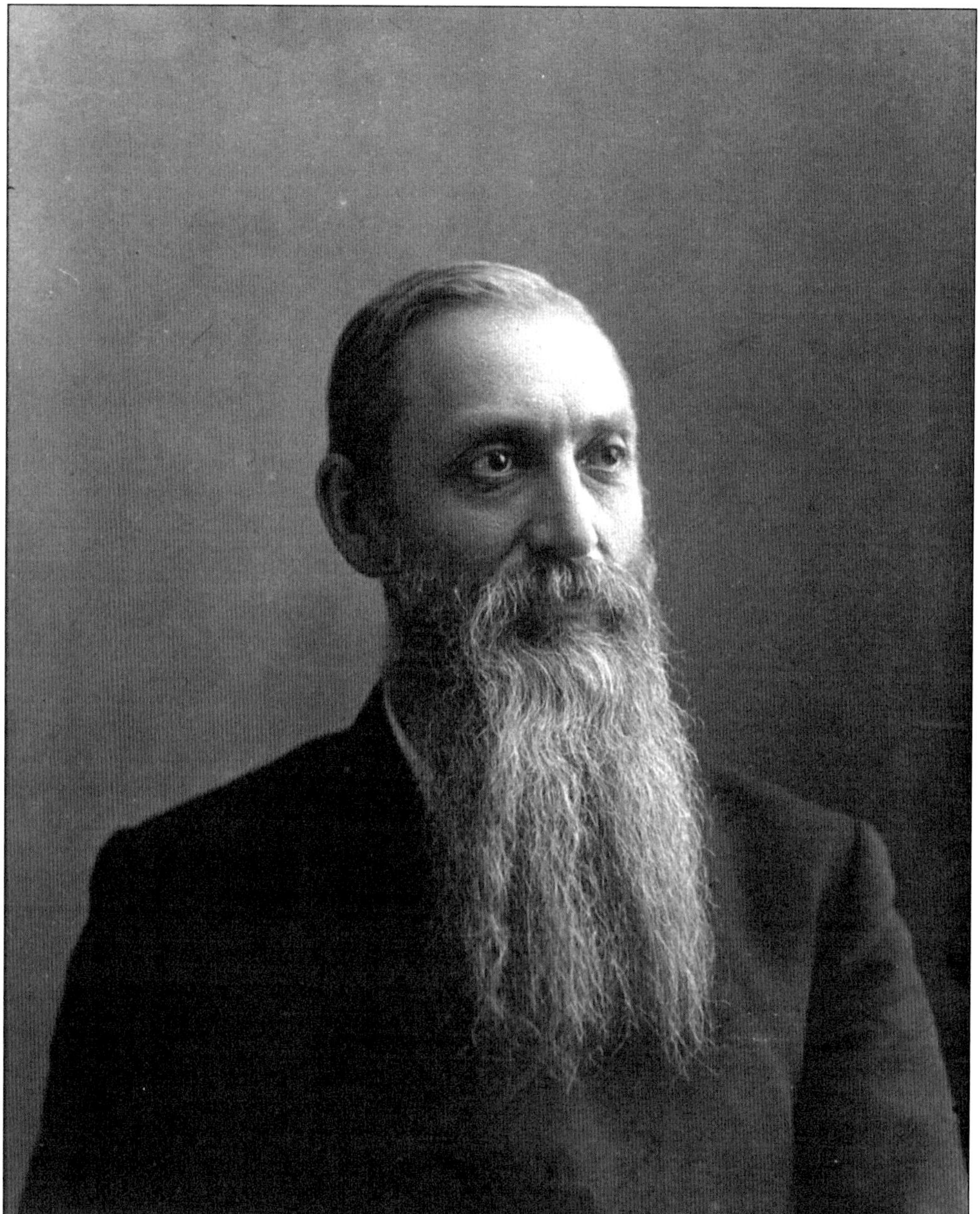

Prof. Joseph Potts Funk, born near Elizabeth in Harrison County, went to the university and became a teacher. In 1876, he came to Corydon, founded the Corydon High School, and served as superintendent of schools until 1887, when he went to New Albany to become principal of the high school, where he remained until his death in 1904. The Corydon High School existed until the August 1, 1950, consolidation of the Corydon and Harrison Township Schools.

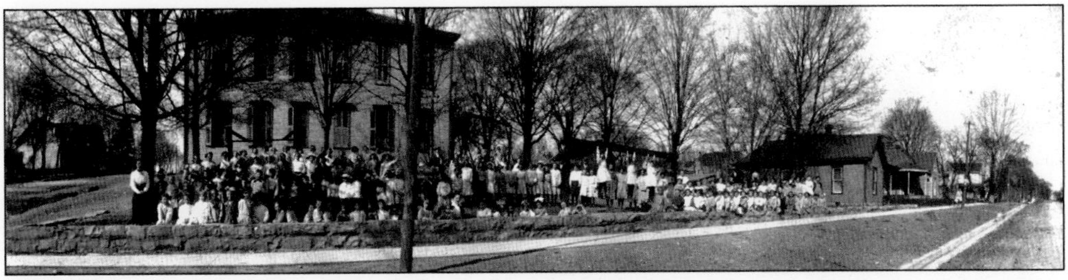

The students and teachers of the Corydon Grade School gathered in the school yard in 1912. The frame school at the corner of Mulberry and Walnut Streets was used until January 1915, when a new grade school building on the corner of High and Mulberry Streets (just north of this building) was completed.

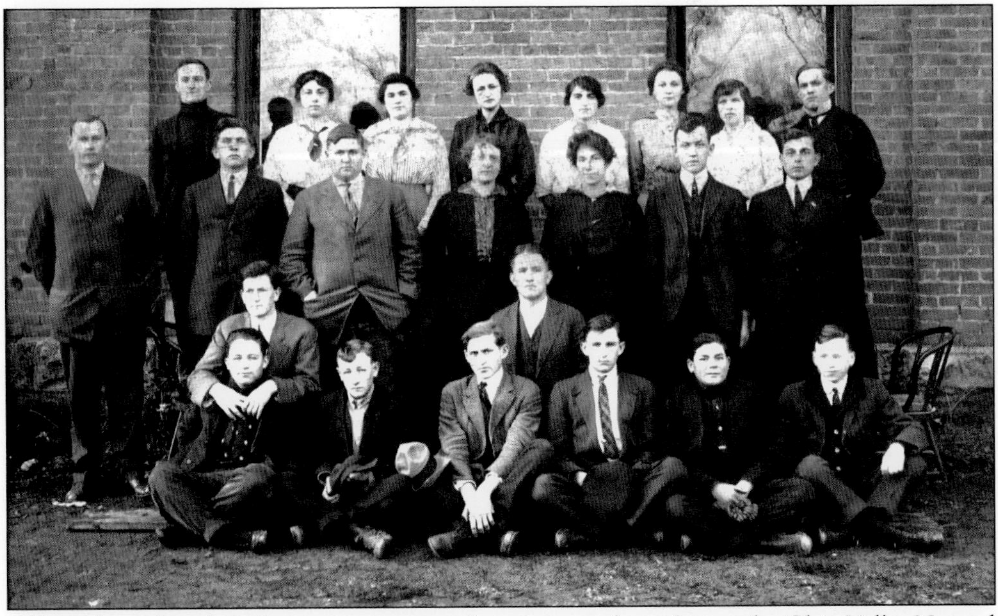

Although unidentified, these young men and women may be a class at the Ohio Valley Normal College, 1896–1908. Possibly around 200 teachers set out from this college to staff the one-room and early rural schools in southern Indiana. The building became Corydon High School.

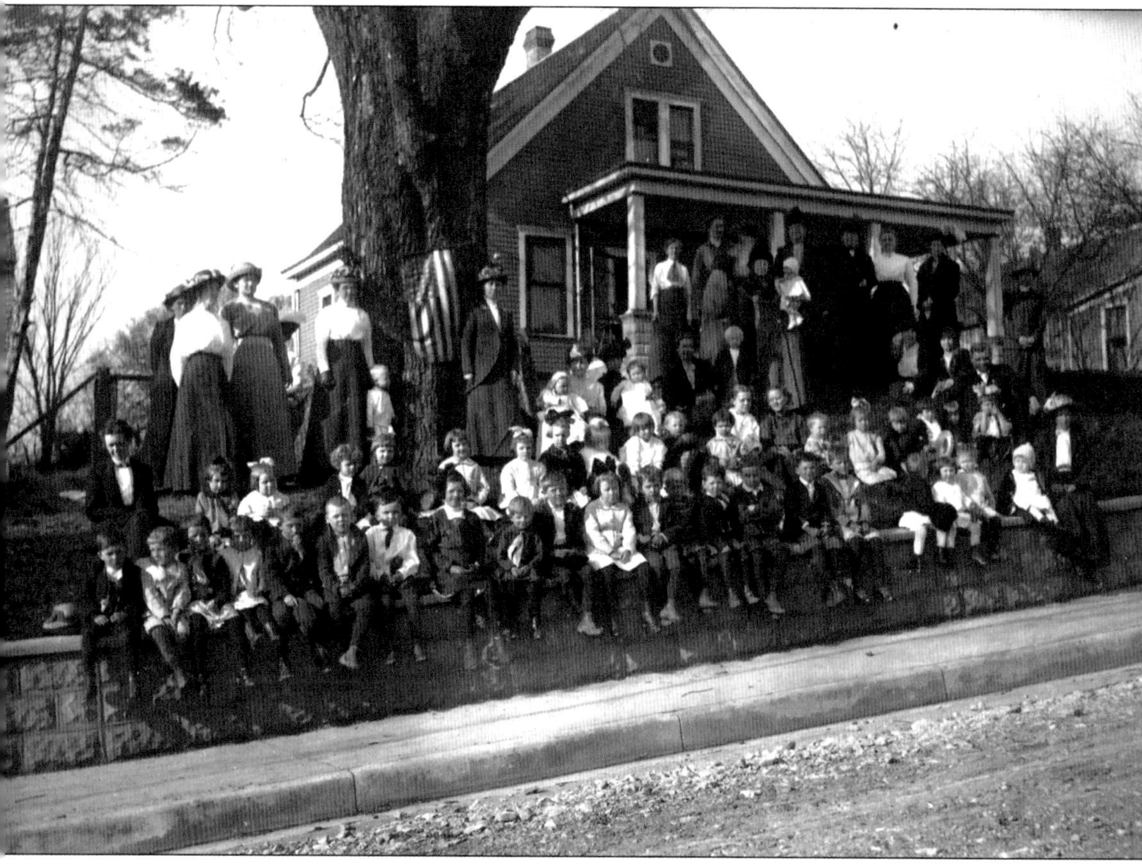

The schoolchildren and their teachers are assembled under the Constitution Elm, around the beginning of the 20th century. The Westfall house, reputedly the oldest house in Corydon, is just visible to the left. Other houses line the street. A coping has been built, which helped to hold the roots of the enormous tree and protect it somewhat from the construction of the sidewalk and paved street. The historic tree was a popular spot for photographs of all occasions in Corydon.

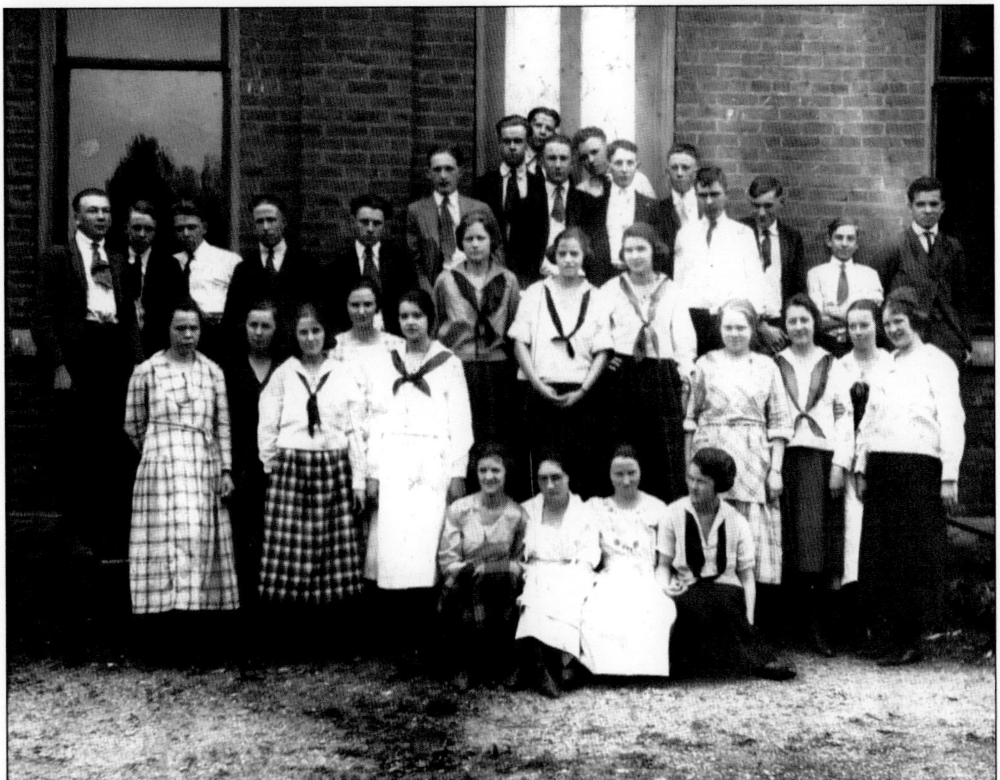

Also unidentified, these students may be at the Corydon High School. The building in back is probably the old Ohio Valley Normal College.

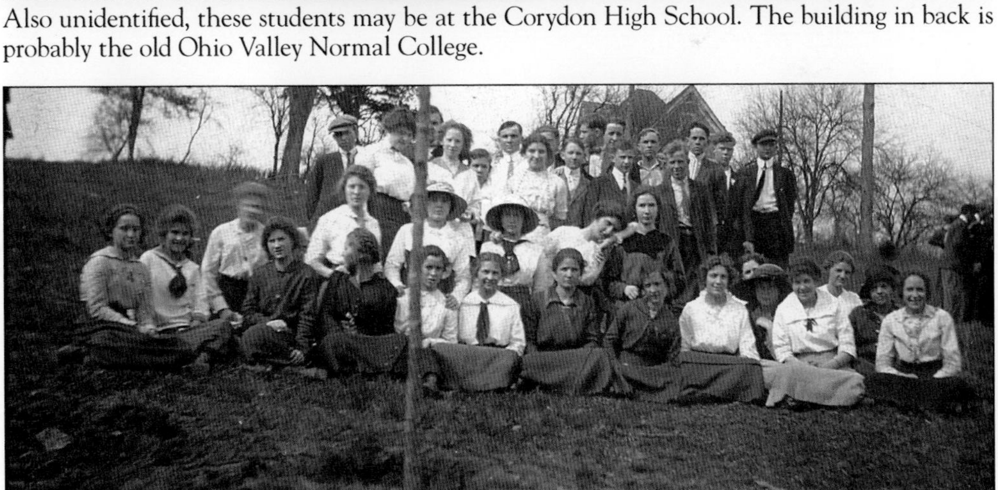

The Corydon High School class of 1916 gathered for a photograph on the hill behind the school. In later years, no one remembered why, but perhaps to plant the tree in the foreground. Included are (first row) Jessie Quebbeman, Frances Birx, Ruth Keller, Christine Reising, Anna Kirkham, Leona Melton, Ruth Shuck, Effie Brown, Catherin Wilson, Edna Sharp, Lin Black, Mollie Keller, and Margaret Denbo; (second row) Edith Saffer, Ozaline Davis, Faith Dropsey, unidentified leaning girl, and Salome Mossler; (third row) unidentified, David Herschel Ward, Benton Windell, Irene Dellinger, Kenneth R. Ward, Bob O'Bannon, Ernest Reas, Russell Rothrock, Reaugh Jordan, and Clarence Brown.

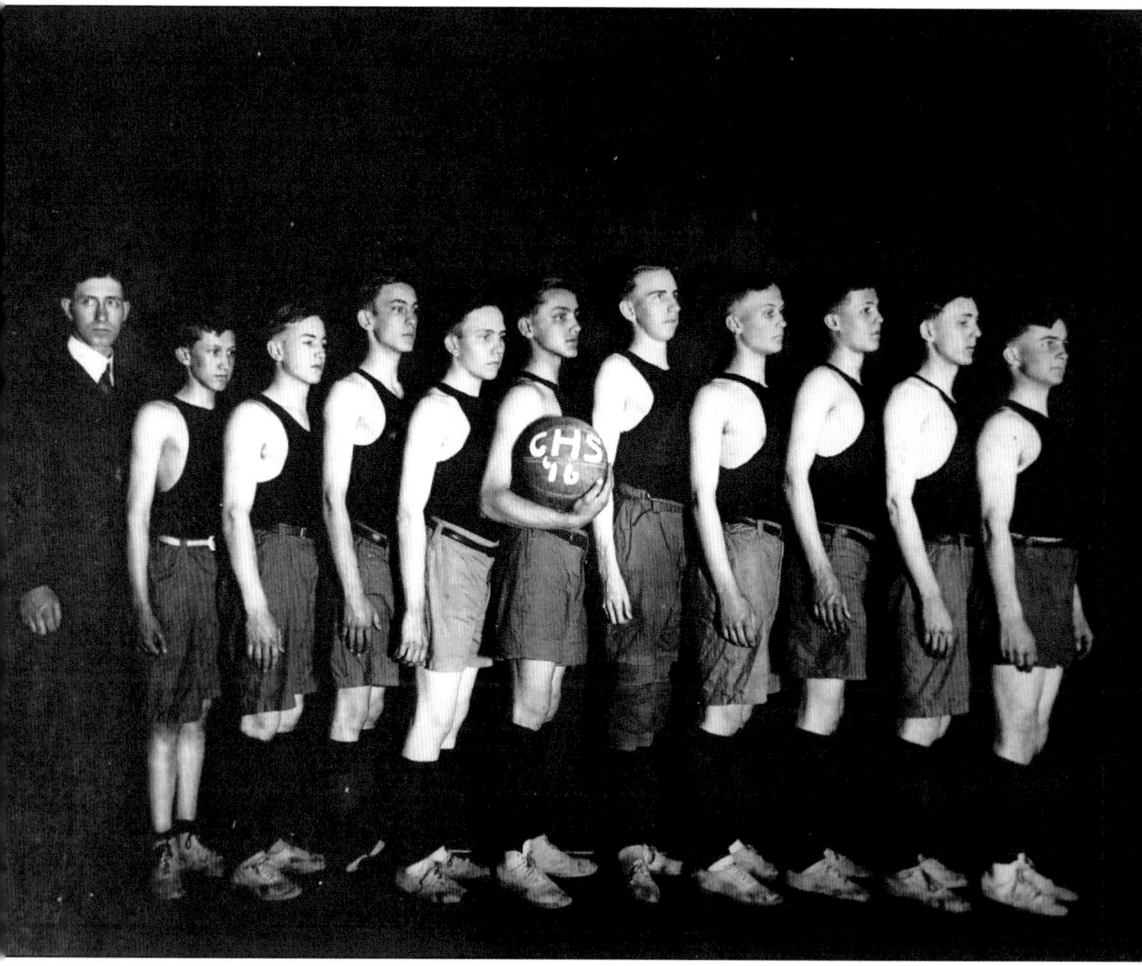

Corydon High School had its first basketball team in 1916. From left to right are coach Walter Bean, Glen Reas, Harry Morris, Harbin Fouts, ? Wolfe, Bill Frederick, Herbert Sonner, Alan Jordan, Dewey Hickman, Roscoe Stevens, and Claude Davis.

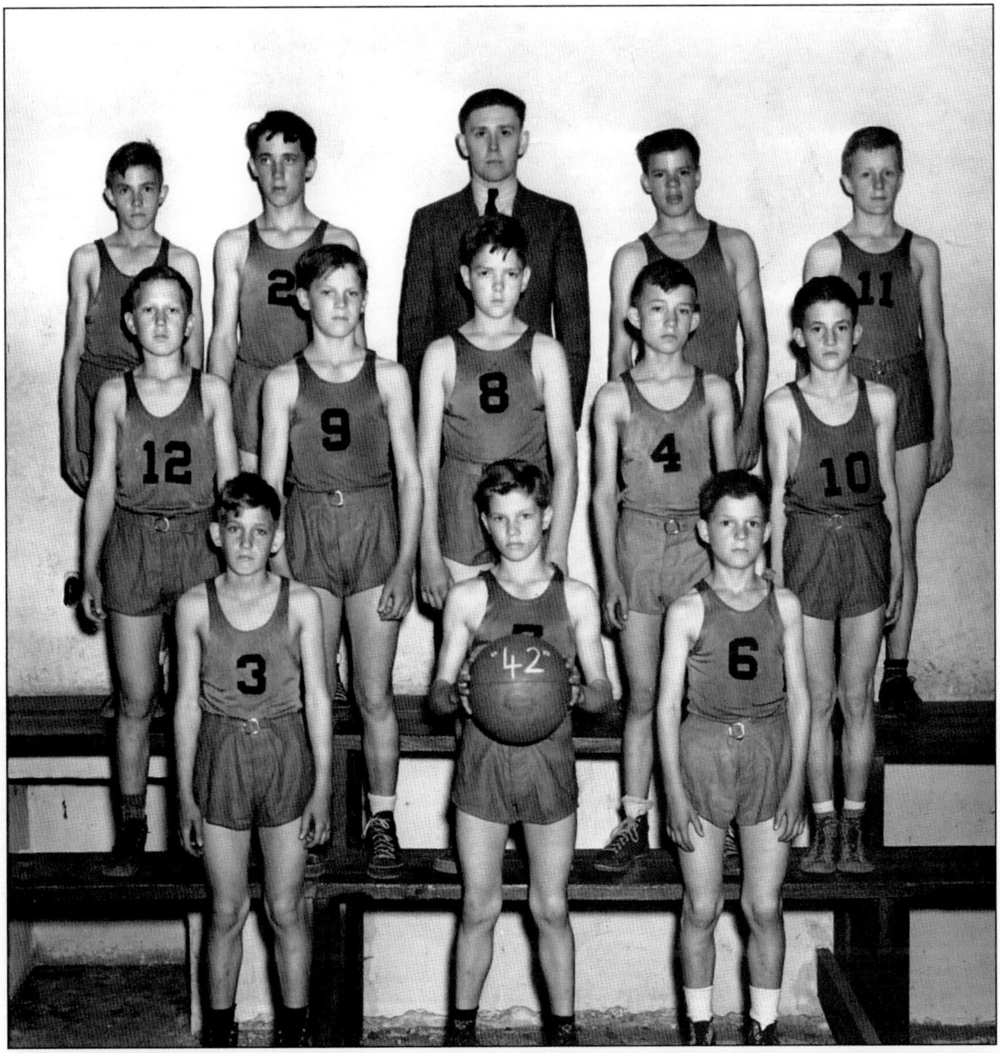

By 1942, Corydon Grade School had a basketball team. From left to right are (first row) John Chinn, Bob Hurst, and Frank O'Bannon; (second row) Moon Ernst, Bill Orwick, Fred Frederick, Ray Glenn, and Casey Boss; (third row) Doug Robson, Jack Kirkham, coach Carlton Franks, Junior Timberlake, and John Saffer.

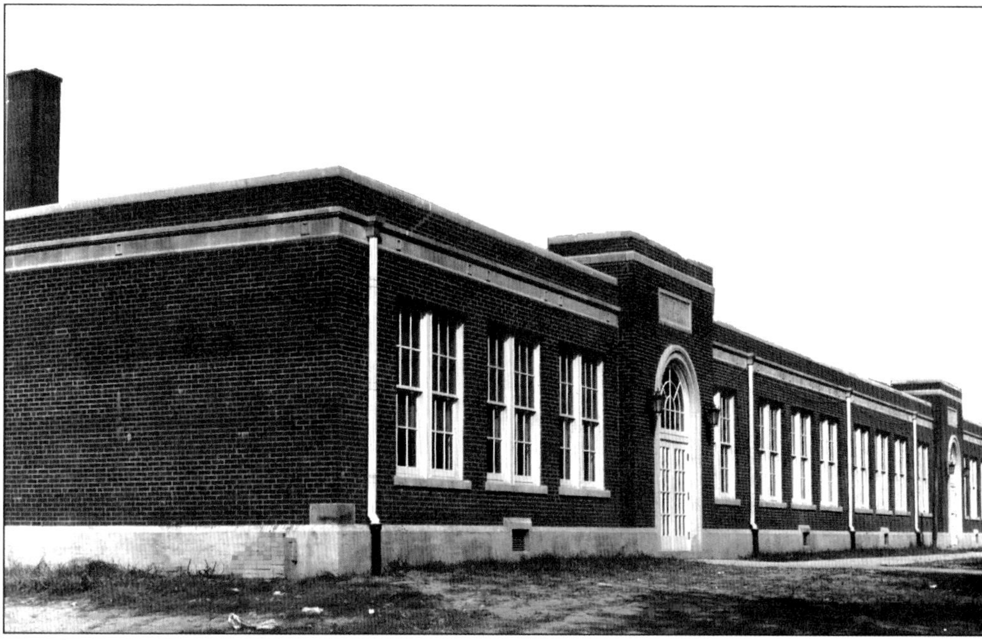

Corydon High School was organized in the building formerly used as the Ohio Normal College, but by the early 1920s, it was deemed unfit for use. The new building was ready for the fall of 1928. Yet many people—taxpayers—were unhappy. Some considered the gymnasium an extravagance. Some railed that the building had no architectural beauty and resembled a factory. Worse, some remarked that, if it had a fence around it, it would look like a prison. The students, of course, picked up on the criticisms and referred to it as the "Soap Factory" or the "Corydon Public Penitentiary No. 2."

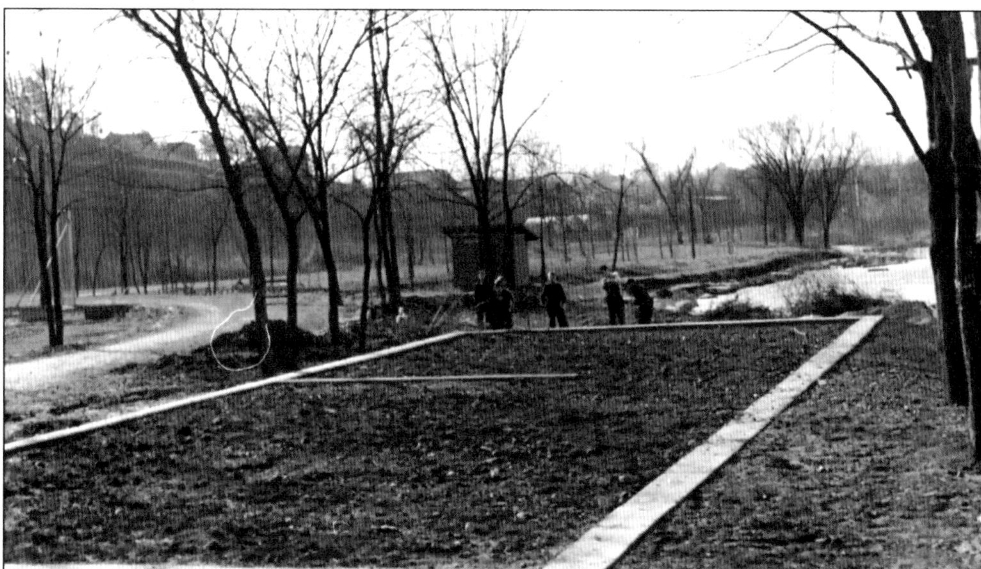

The playground of the high school was separated from it by a public street. Students had to cross back and forth, which was certainly less than ideal. Traffic, however, was minimal and there were no reported accidents. What did derail sports were the frequent inundations from the adjacent creek, which often turned the highest point into an island.

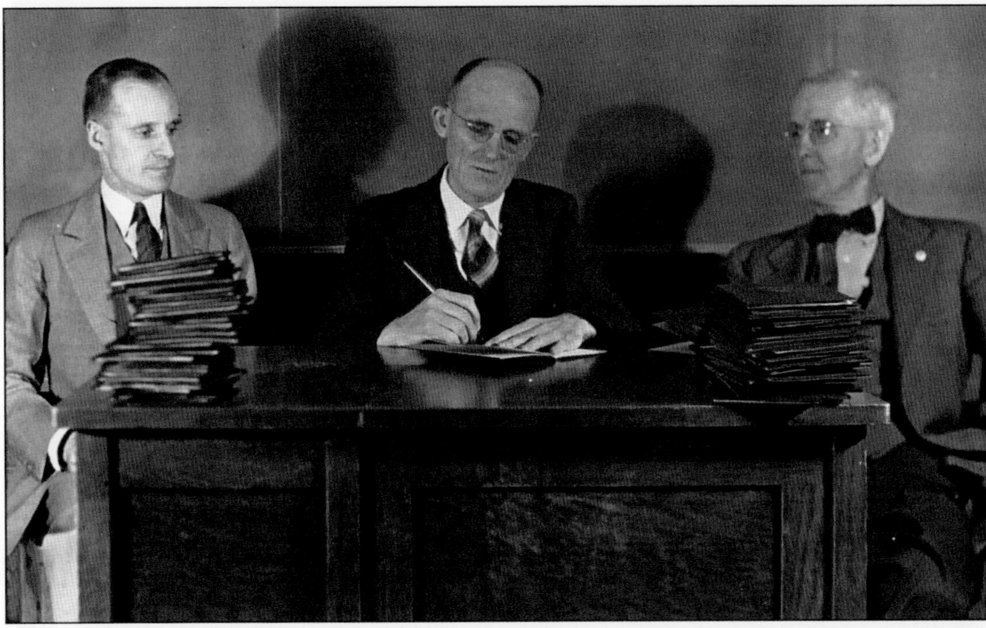

In this photograph, from left to right, Robert P. O'Bannon, Walter Gilham, and Maurice Griffin appear to be signing high school diplomas, or some sort of recognition. School boards were closely in touch with communities and town councils. It was literally possible to know and name everyone in the town. Schools were held closely accountable for both content and viewpoint of what was taught.

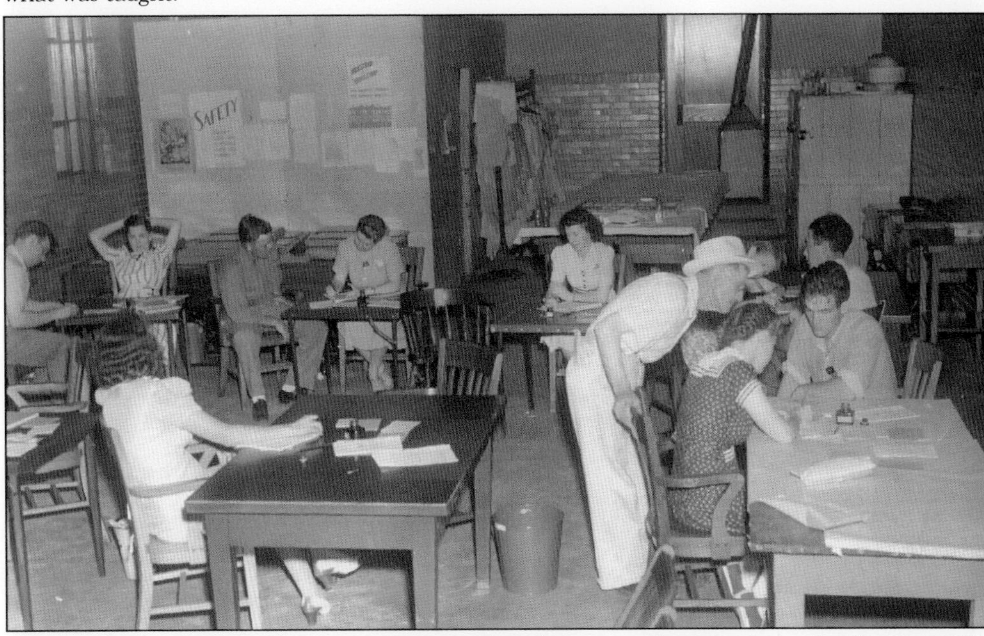

These students, around 1950, are not identified but they are working on some school project. The ink pots suggest perhaps the school newspaper or the yearbook. Students often began their work careers directly after high school graduation, and school experience was important to employers. High school students worked on a portfolio of work to take with them. Prospective bosses would also check school attendance and consistency of effort throughout school.

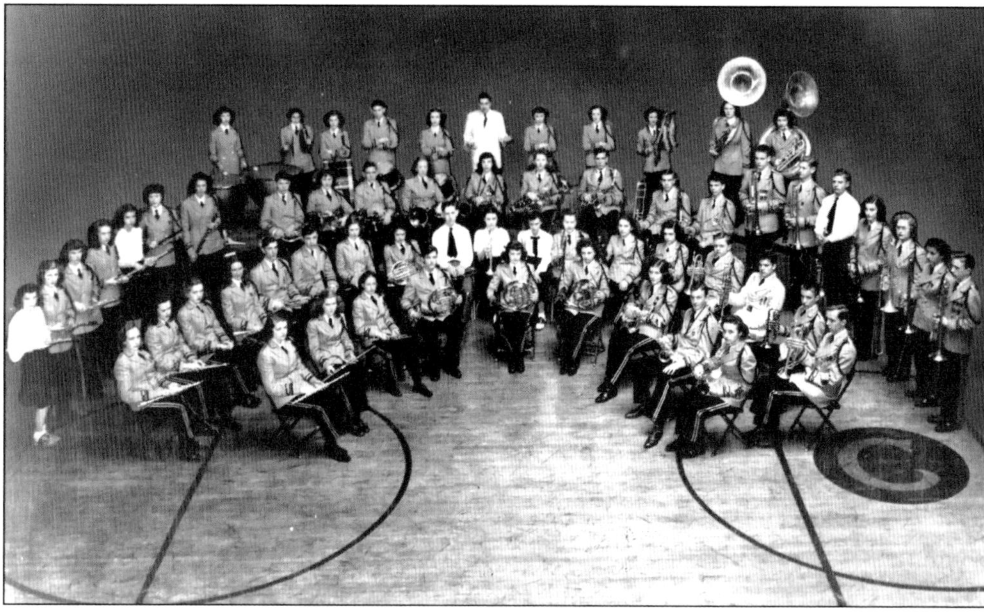

Director Jack Walts poses with the Corydon High School band in the school gymnasium in the 1940s. The large band seems to reflect the importance of music in the community. Named for a character in a song, Corydon has had many bands, orchestras, and choirs throughout its history.

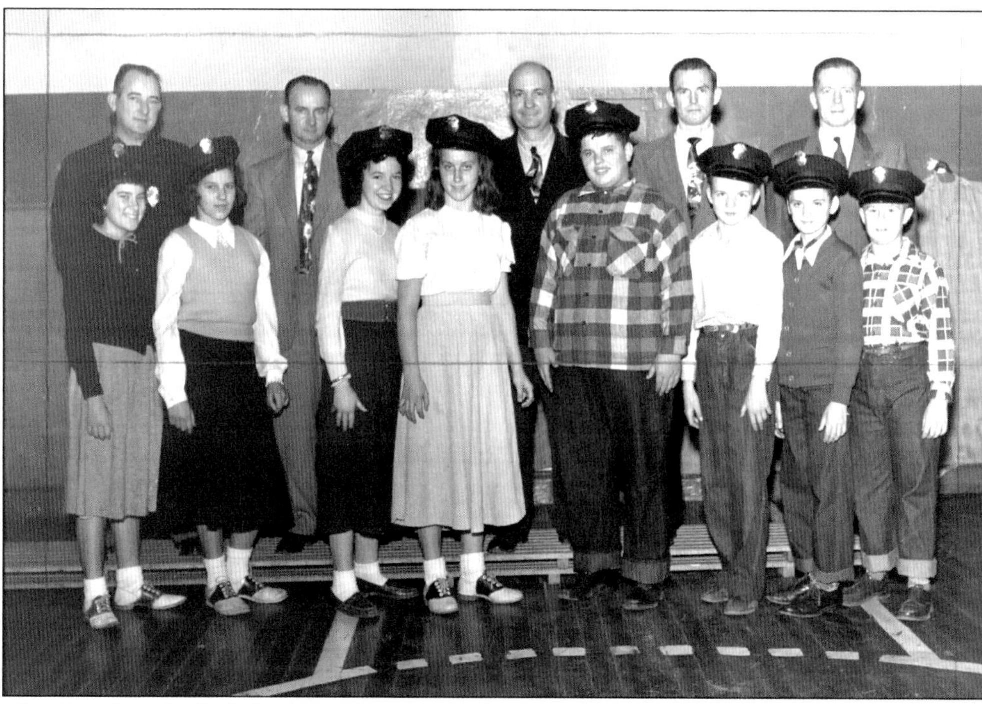

This Corydon Grade School patrol appears to be from the late 1940s or early 1950s. Five adults mentoring eight students attests to the importance of the safety patrol program in schools. Being on the safety patrol was an important responsibility, and students chosen were proud of the recognition. They were role models for their peers and younger students.

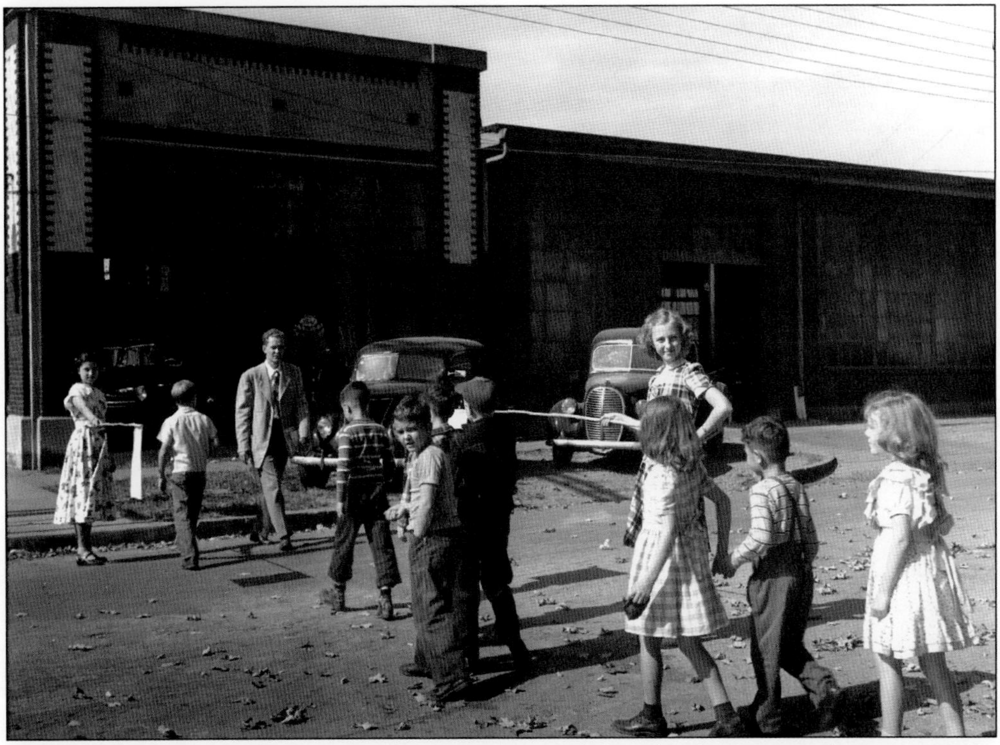

The American Automobile Association (AAA) started the school safety patrol program in the early 1920s. Even as automobile traffic increased, there were no accidents where student crossing guards were on duty. In this photograph, an adult takes advantage of the vigilance of Shirley Johnson (left) and Helen York (right).

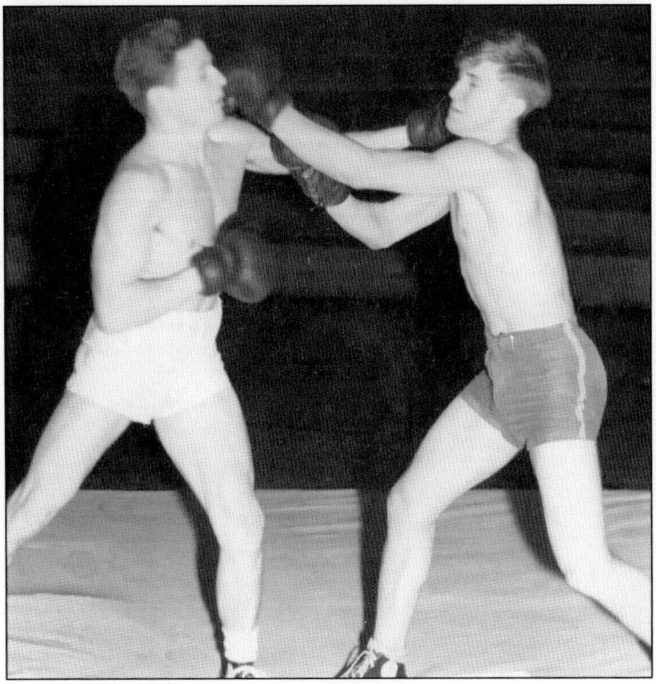

Corydon schools offered all sorts of sports. The students were, and are, enthusiastic participants. Many townsfolk besides players' families enjoy attending games. Friday and Saturday nights are still spent at football and basketball games. Boxing, however, is now seldom part of school programs. August Yockum (left) and Donald Dear are seen sparring in the 1940s.

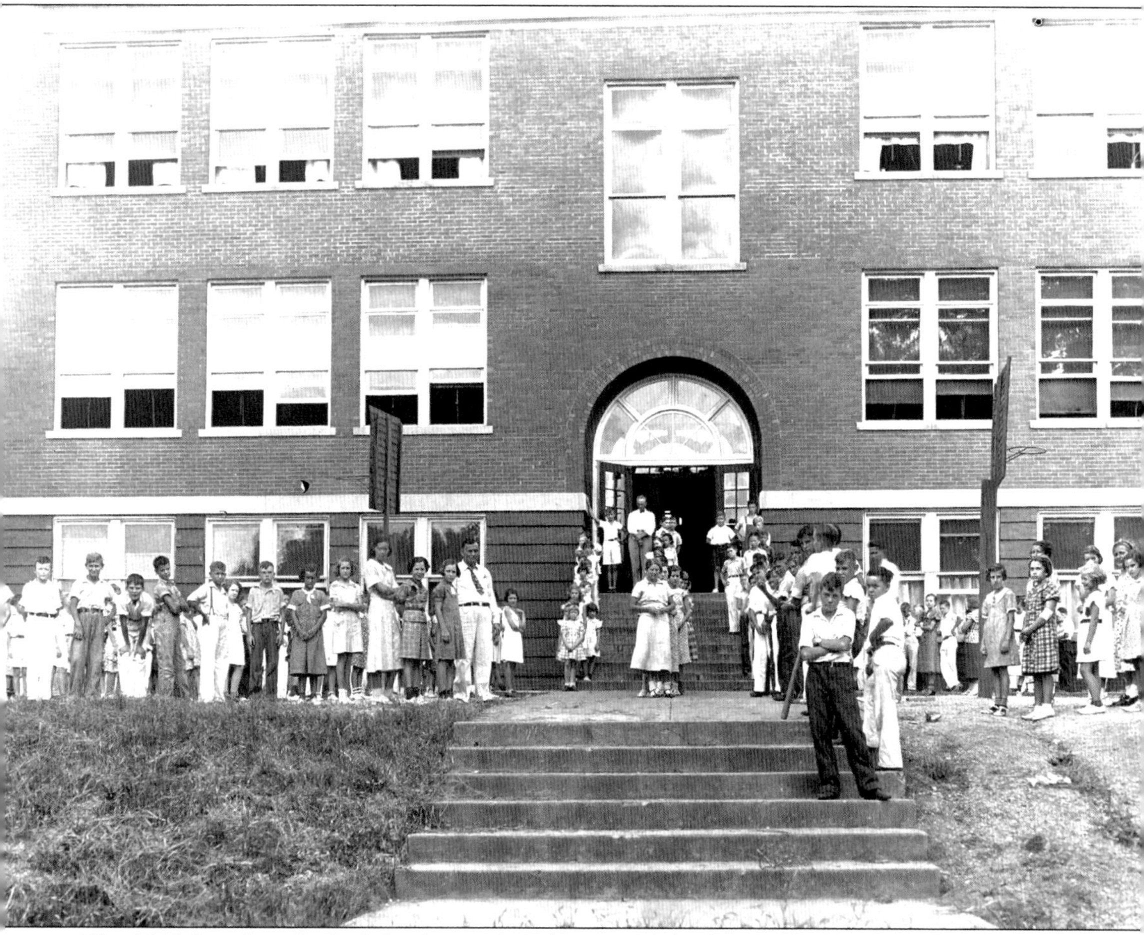

The 1915 Corydon Grade School served students until the late 20th century. Like homes and businesses of the time, opening the large windows was the only "cooling system" available, but school was not started until after Labor Day, and adjourned by Memorial Day. Students were needed for planting and harvesting.

Six

Harrison County Fair

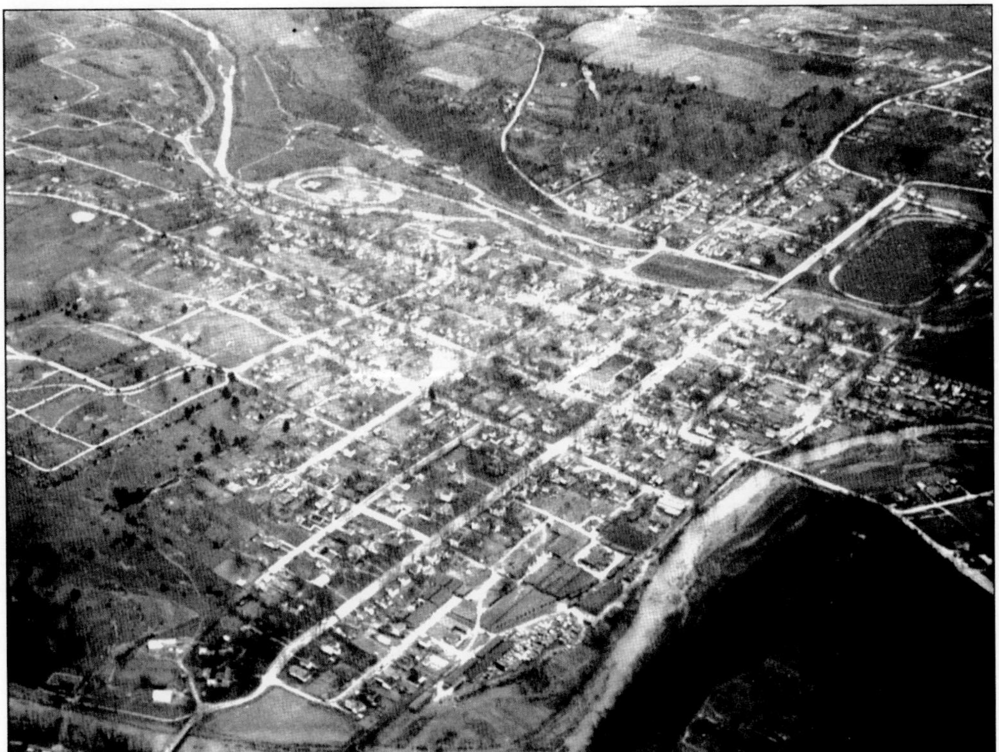

The Harrison County Fairgrounds is a landmark in Corydon, its half-mile racetrack easily identifiable from the air. The Harrison County Agricultural Society held its first fair in 1859. Despite the Civil War, World War I, World War II, the Great Depression, and the transformed economic base of the 21st century, 2009 marks the 150th consecutive Harrison County Fair, the oldest in the state.

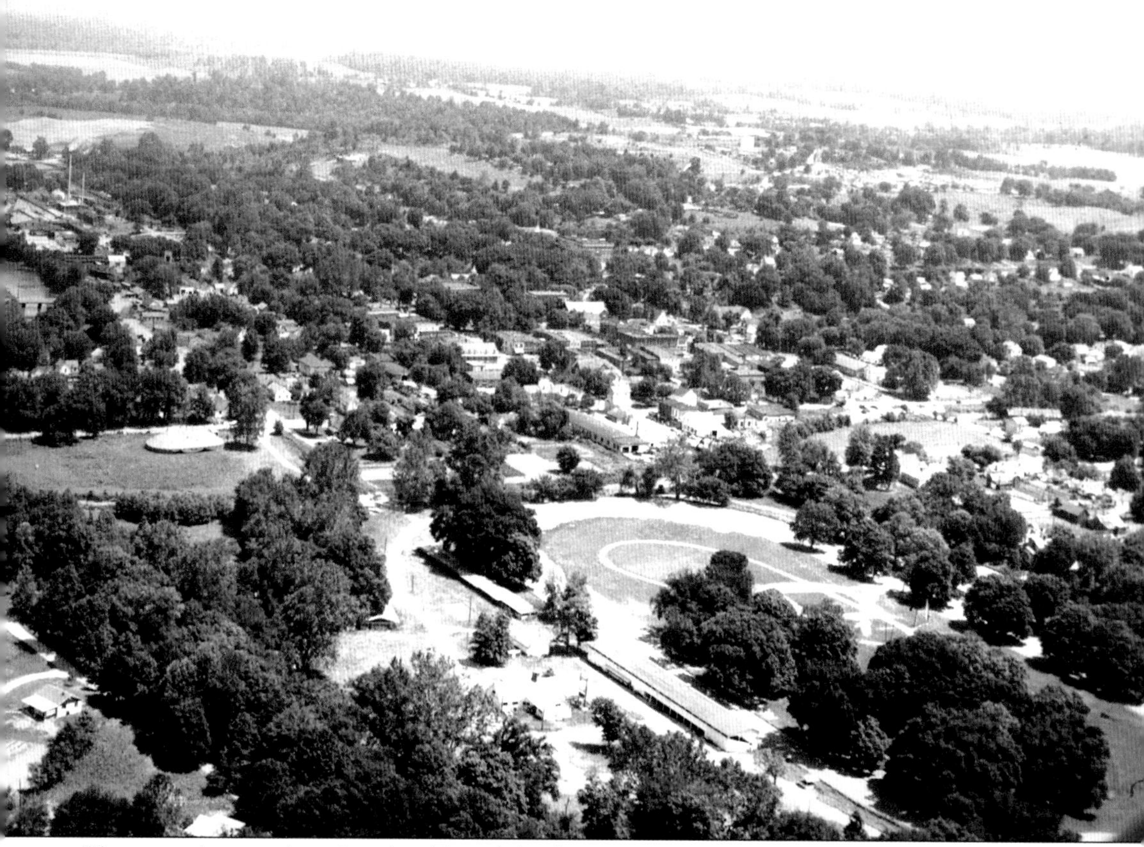

Closer in, the grandstand and stables of the fair are plain. Horses were essential to life in the 19th and early 20th centuries, and in the late 20th century, Corydon was surrounded by ample pastureland. Many farmers indulged a passion for fine horses.

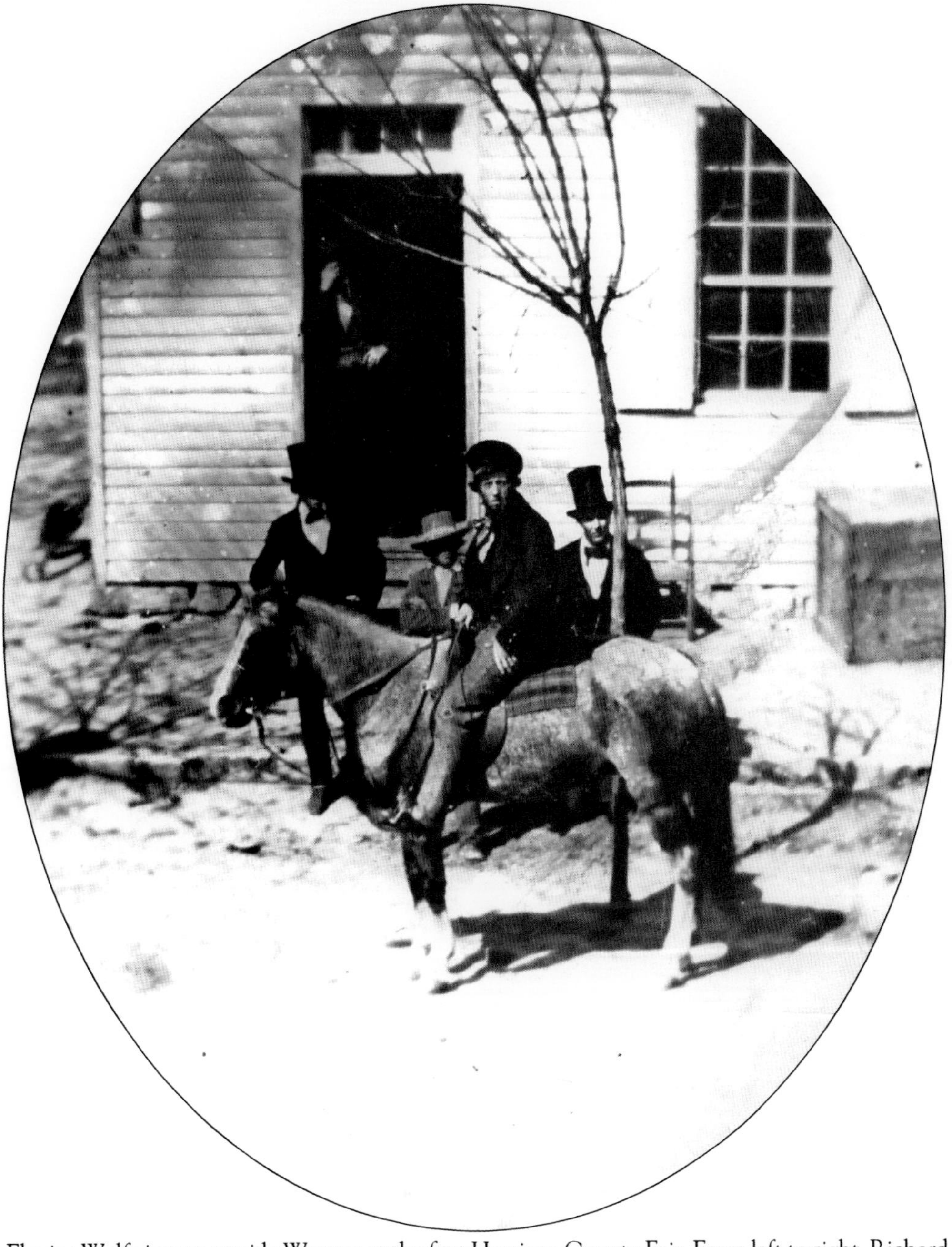

Flavius Wolfe is seen astride Warsaw at the first Harrison County Fair. From left to right, Richard Heth, R. H. Ballard, and John Beard stand behind him.

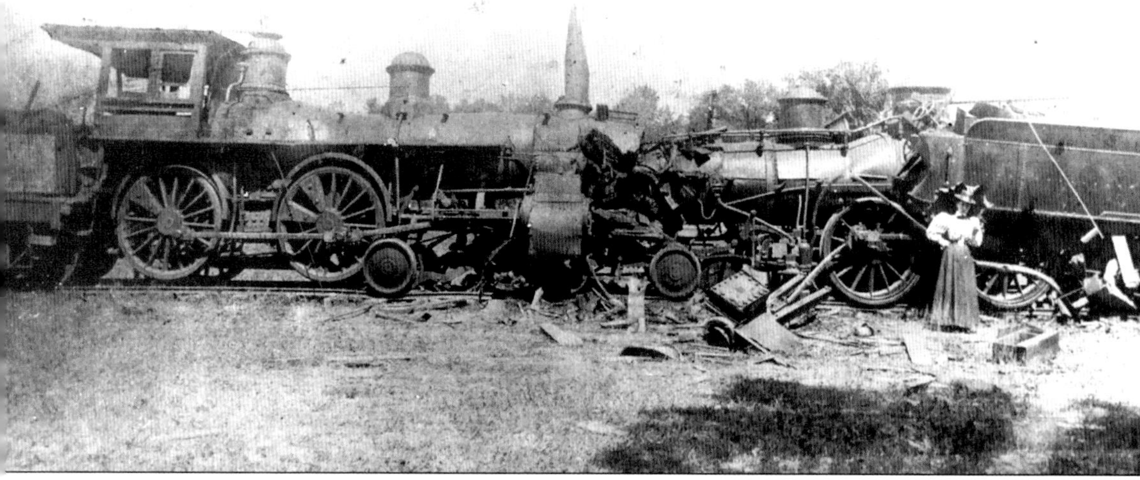

This train wreck was a feature of the fair in 1896. Engines No. 805 and No. 2 crashed head-on on August 26. This collision injured no one, but such spectacles were every bit as dangerous as they would appear. Unexpected power from the locomotives could send the entire mass hurtling into crowds of bystanders. These locomotives were bought for this stunt and were subsequently sold for scrap—at least what was left by souvenir hunters was scraped.

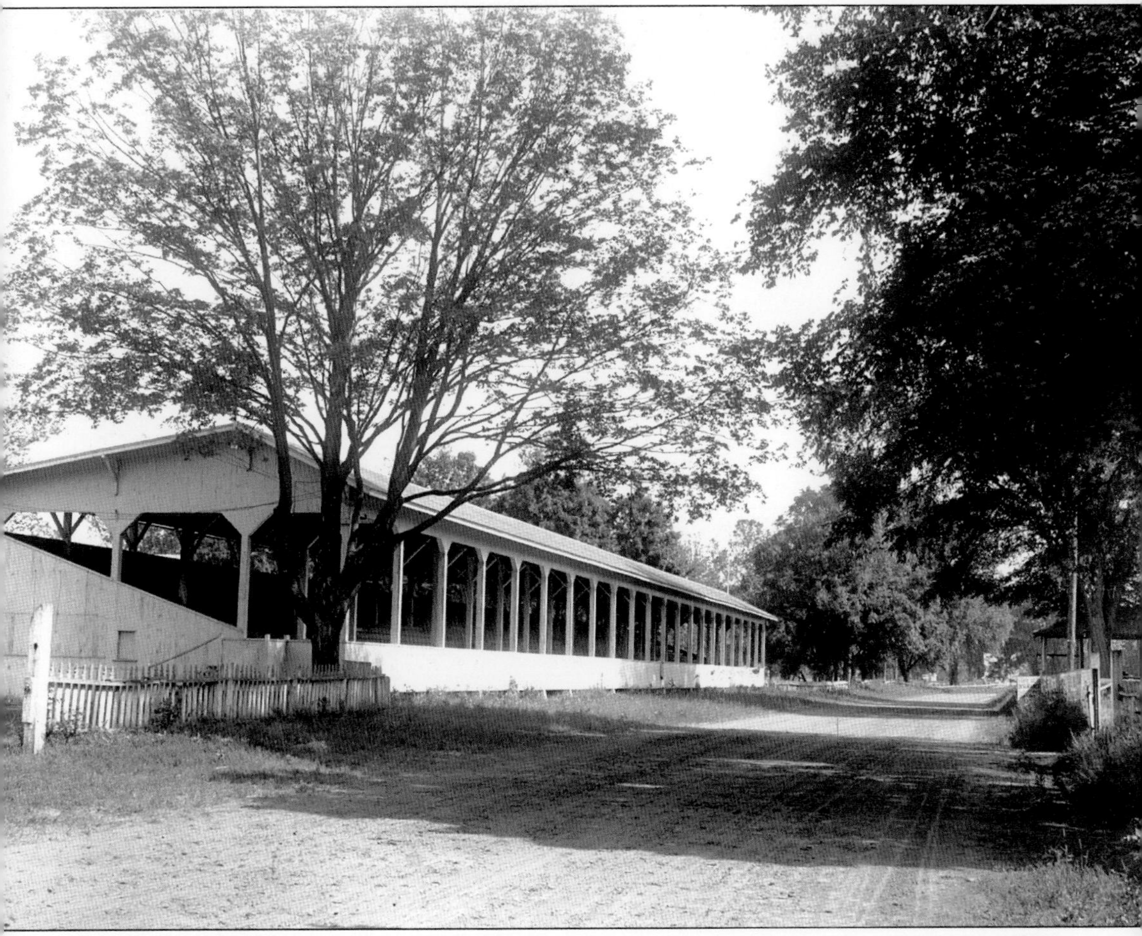

The old grandstand was built in 1927. Display areas were located under the seating area. The building was destroyed by a February 21, 1961, fire. A 16-year-old boy admitted to starting a fire on the wood floor of the north end ticket office. He sometimes left his foster home seeking solitude. He had started the fire to keep warm, and had attempted to put it out twice, before leaving the building. The replacement grandstand came from the former Parkway Field, in Louisville, Kentucky.

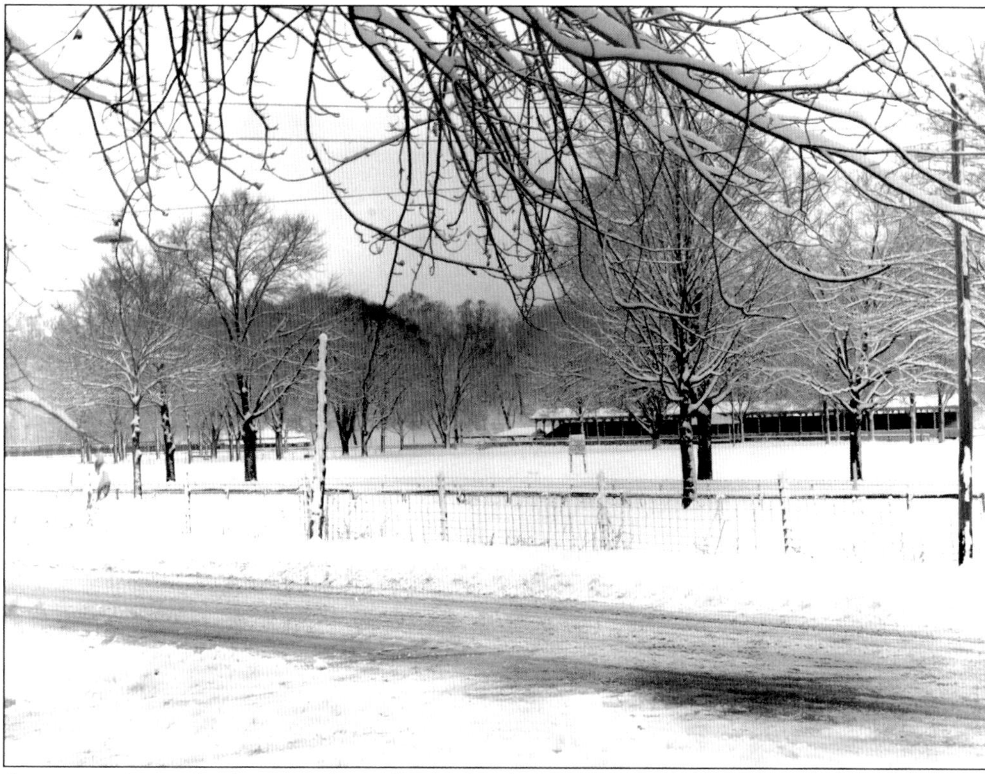

Snow transforms the fairgrounds in this undated photograph. The bandstand is visible in the infield, in front of the grandstand. To the right, out of the photograph, is the grave of Bertha W. Horse racing has always been a grueling sport for the animals. Trotters and pacers are pushed to the limits of their endurance. Pacer Bertha W. had competed on the fairgrounds racetrack for 15 years, and she seldom failed to win. On Wednesday, August 31, 1904, she won the third heat of a half-mile pace in one minute, nine seconds. She showed signs of flagging just before she crossed under the wire, but she continued her effort for about 100 yards more. Then she dropped dead in the traces and on the track. She was buried yards from the scene of her many triumphs.

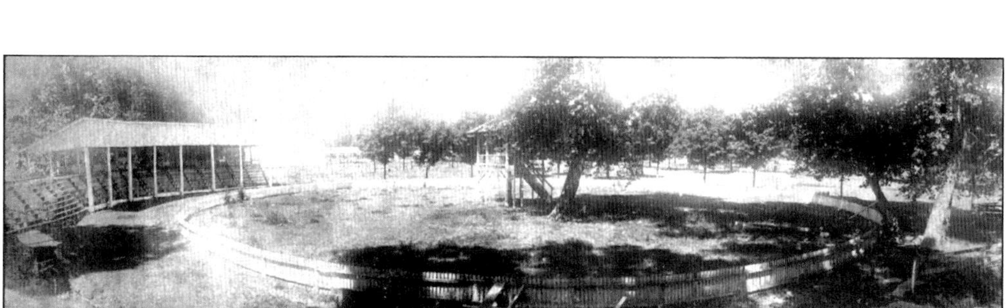

The little ring afforded some shade near the spring. The judges' stand was also shaded by a large tree, at left in the middle.

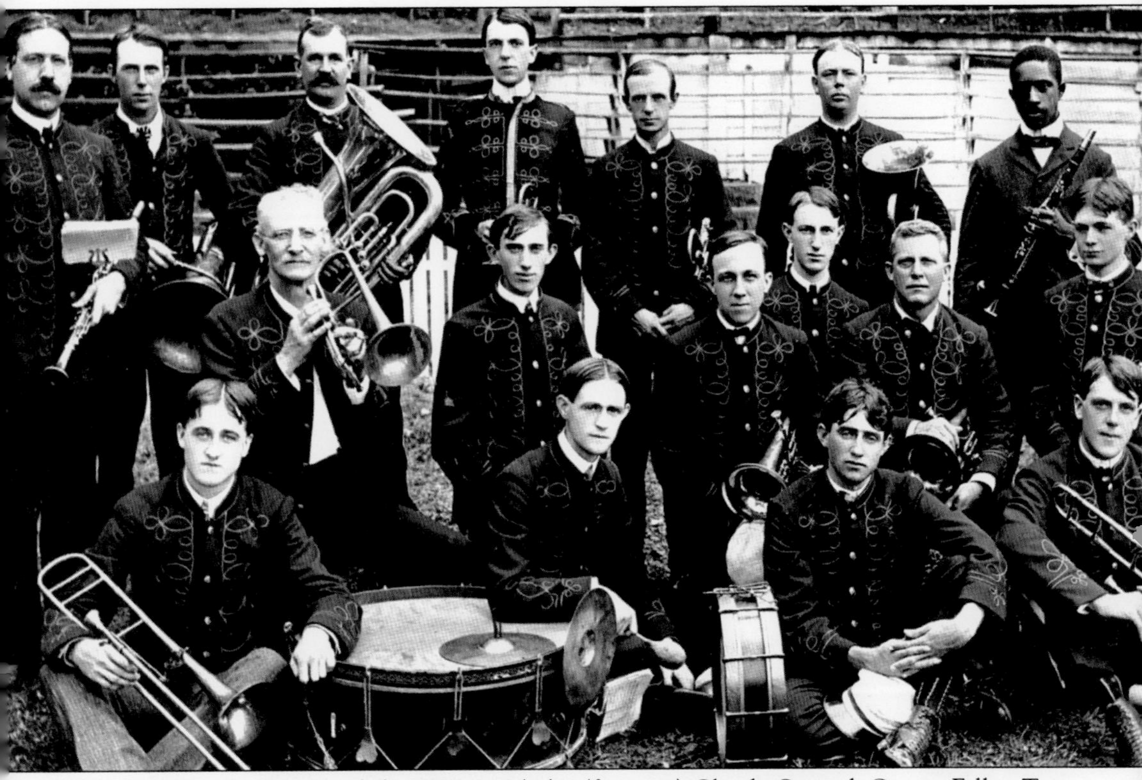

The Corydon Band, around the 1890s, includes (first row) Claude Conrad, George Feller, Toy Brown, and Roscoe Brewster (twin); (second row) Fred Ball, ? Bulleit, Resaugh Miller, Max Stern, John Shuck, and John Trotter; (third row) Giles Mowrer, Benjamin Brewster, Mitchell Rowland, Roger Brewster (twin), James B. Brewster, John Black, and Prof. William H. Fouse. Note that Fouse does not wear a uniform. However, in 1891, he organized the Corydon Colored School. It closed in the 1920s when the students began to attend the Corydon school. It is the oldest African American school still standing in southern Indiana. In the late 20th century, Maxine Brown spearheaded the restoration effort that turned the building into a community center for lectures, musical performances, and other educational programs. It is named in honor of Maxine Brown's aunt Leora Brown, who had taught at the school.

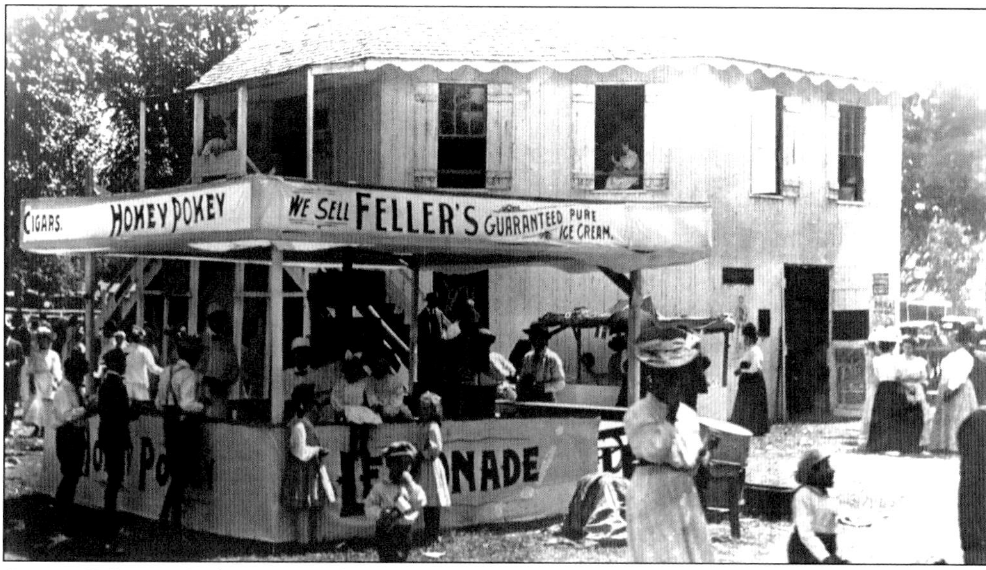

George Feller's refreshment stand is seen here around 1900. Lemonade and ice cream were rare treats before mechanical refrigeration, as was the Hokey Pokey, an early ice pop with no wooden stick, when the Round Hall, in the background, stood in the center field. It was razed in the early 1920s. Many of its exhibits were moved to the Homecomers' Hall, behind the grandstand.

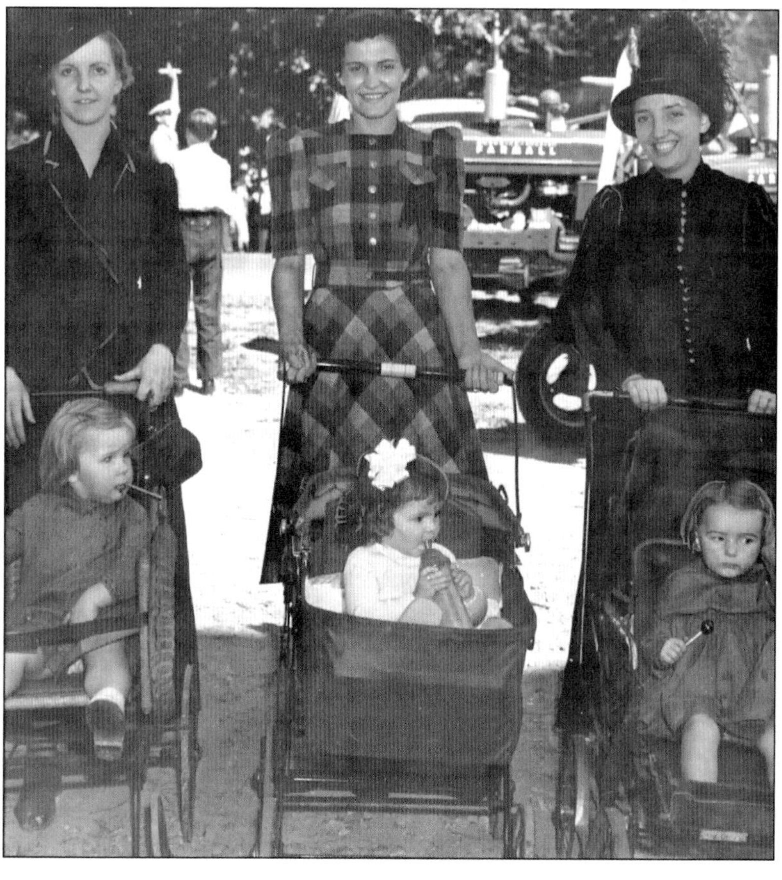

Although not identified, these proud moms may well have brought their daughters to a day at the fair. Perhaps they were veterans of the prettiest baby contest.

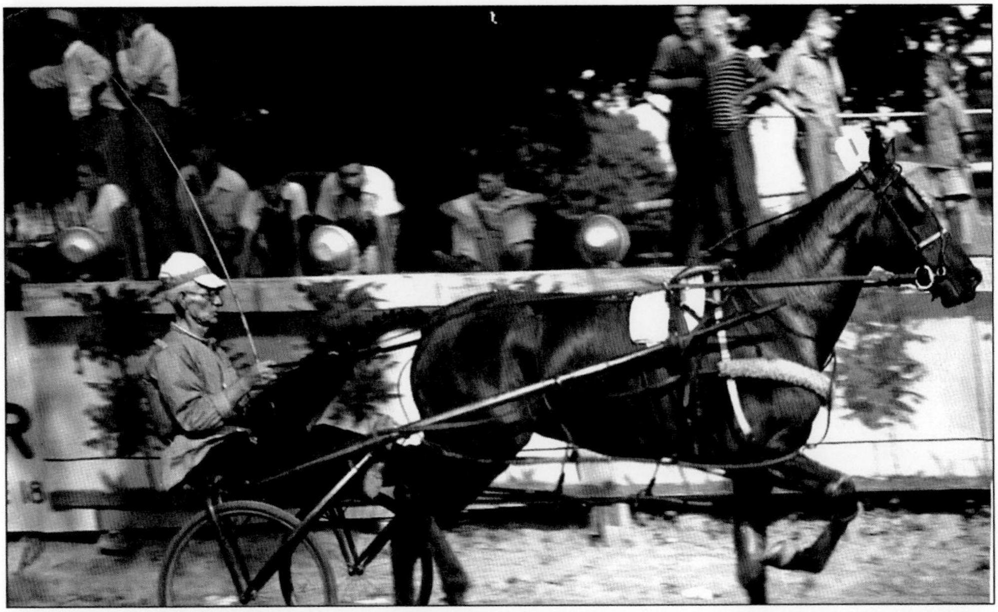

Steve Stepro demonstrates that racing trotting horses is not limited to the young. Corydon native Elmer Conrad was still racing when he was past 80 years old.

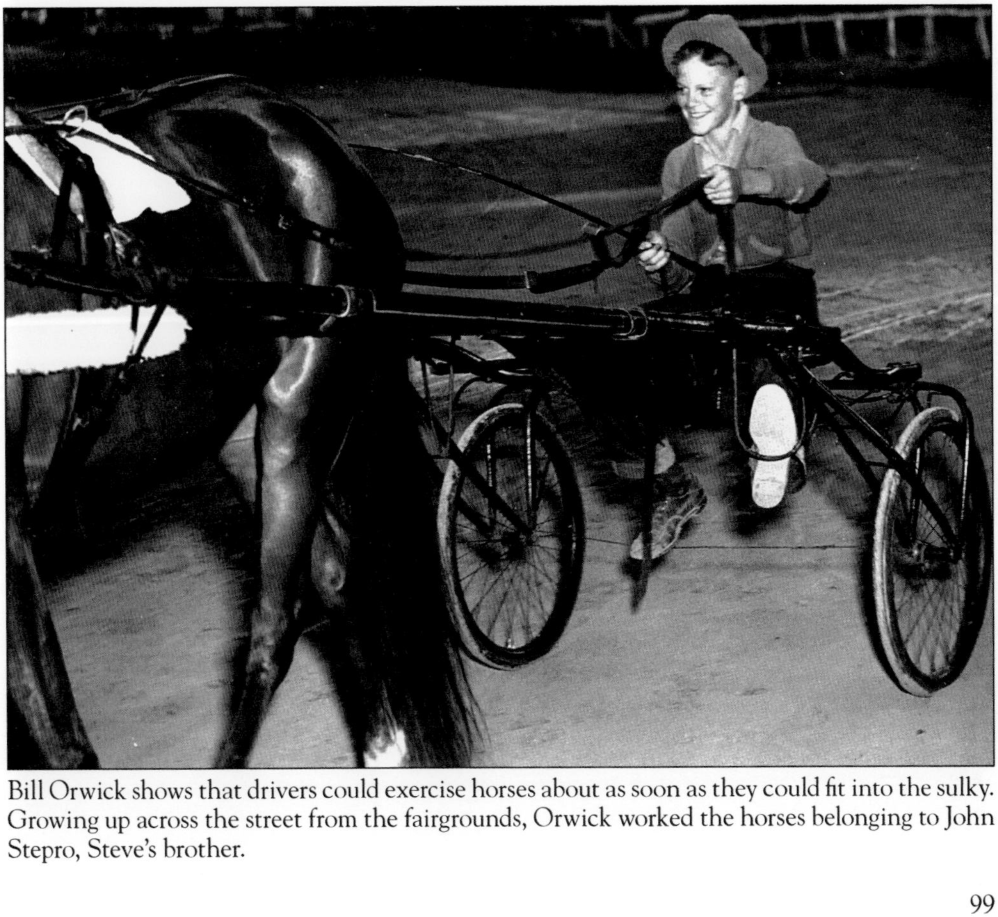

Bill Orwick shows that drivers could exercise horses about as soon as they could fit into the sulky. Growing up across the street from the fairgrounds, Orwick worked the horses belonging to John Stepro, Steve's brother.

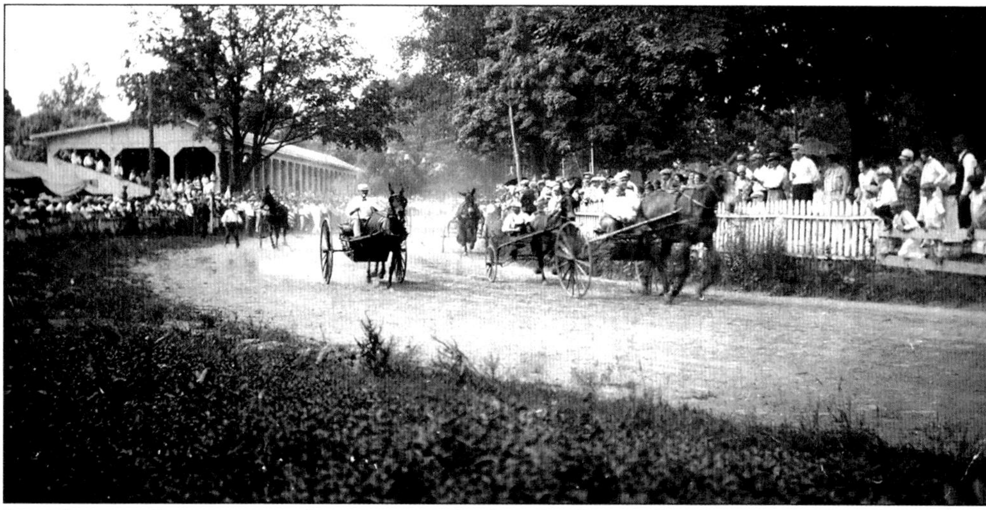

In addition to horse races and pony races, the fair also featured mule races. Definitely not built for speed, mules do more work with less food than horses. They were valued as draft animals in town and on farms.

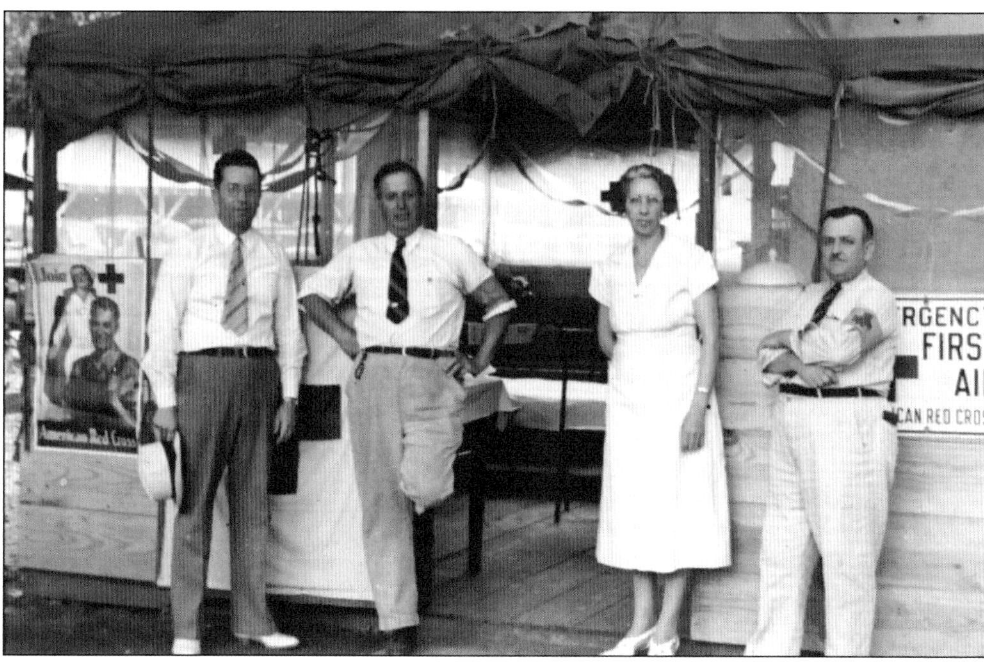

The first aid station at the fair was prepared for cuts and scrapes, upset stomachs from too many treats, as well as heat stroke. These people are not identified, but doctors and nurses were usually close by.

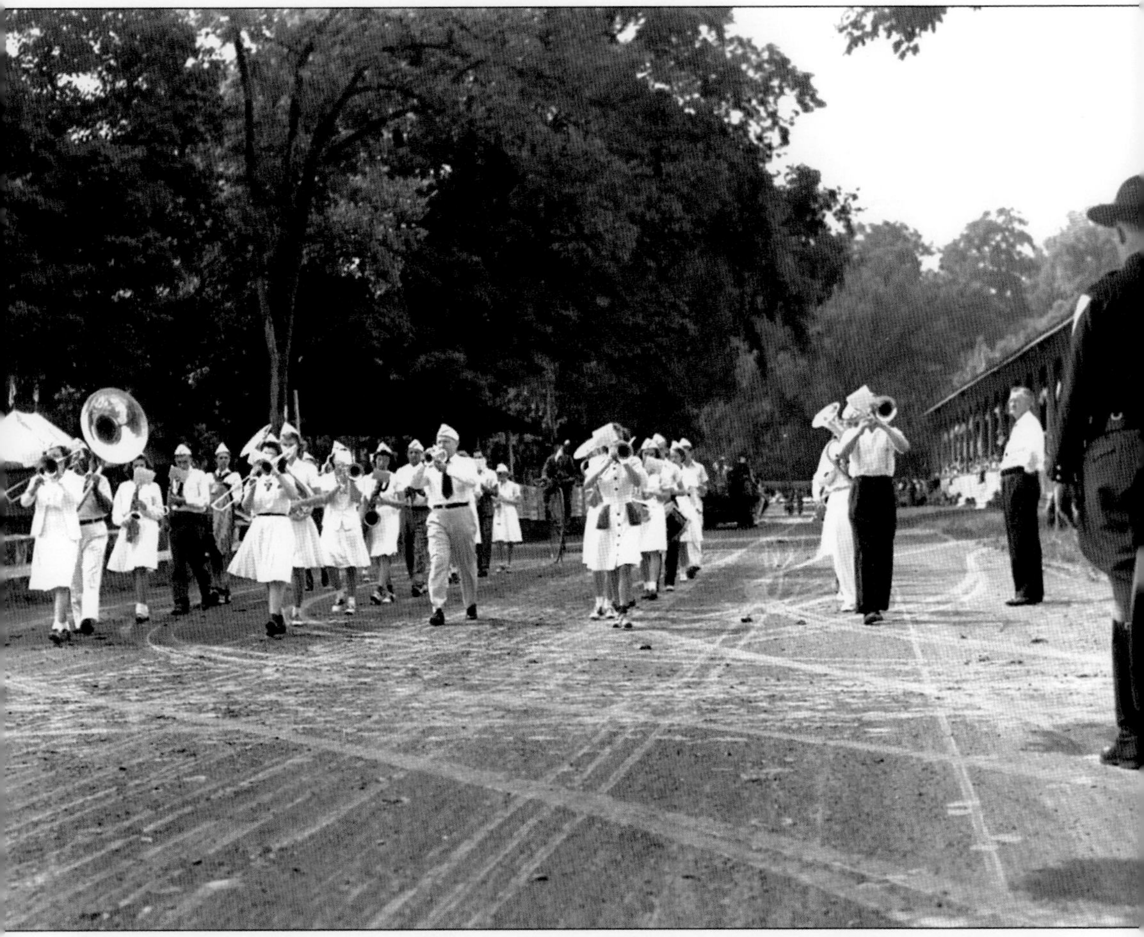

The unidentified band may have been part of fair festivities, or some other event held at the fairgrounds. They are marching on the track. At one-half mile, the smooth, flat oval is a perfect practice place for many types of performers. Also, being dirt, it is gentle on bone and muscle, minimizing the impact of pounding. This brass band may be welcoming a celebrity. Is the Indiana State Police officer at the right part of a security force?

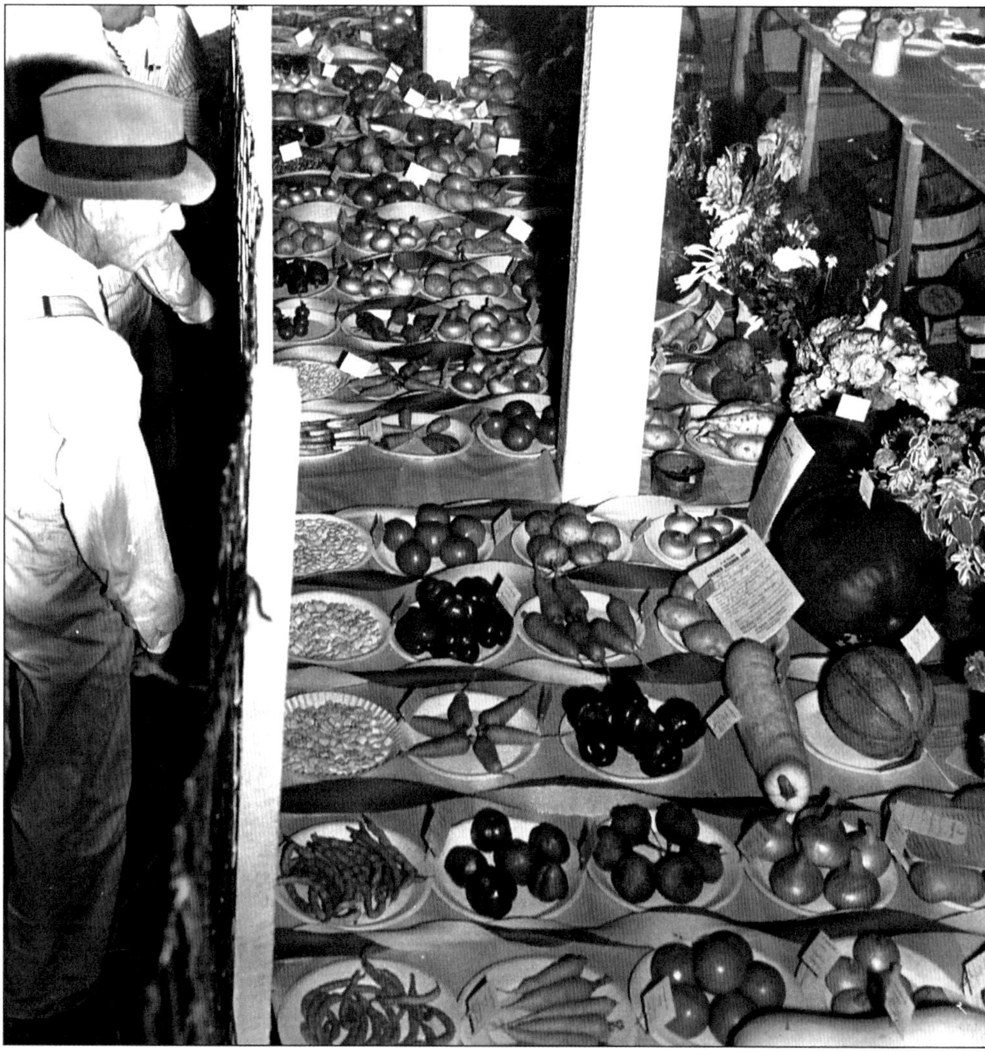

The best fruits, vegetables, and grains came to the fair. The Harrison County Agricultural Society was interested in improving seeds and new varieties were carefully monitored to judge whether they represented an improvement. Southern Indiana soil was not so rich as the Kentucky farmland just across the Ohio River, and early American subsistence-farming practices wore it out in only a few seasons. As the hardwood forests were cut down, the land deteriorated further. As the county seat, Corydon was the center of research and education programs to learn and promote soil conservation and renewable farming techniques.

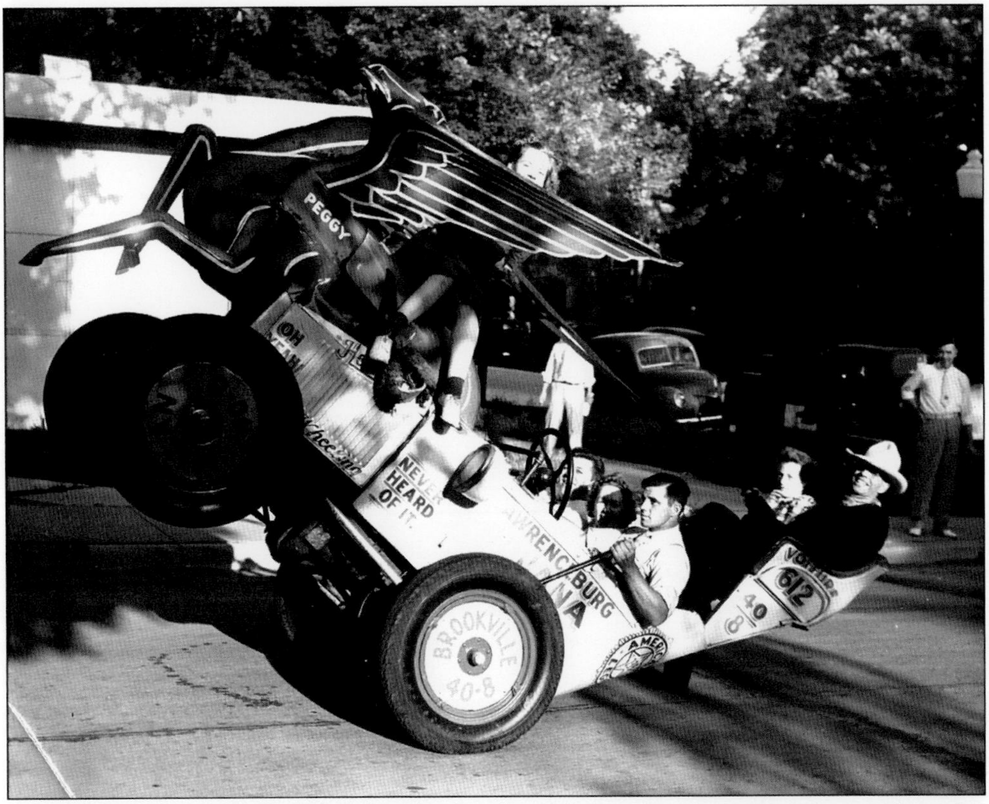

This photograph is not identified, but the fair always featured visiting attractions, such as this funny car. The occupants are not named, but the driver may have toured the country with his bucking bronc.

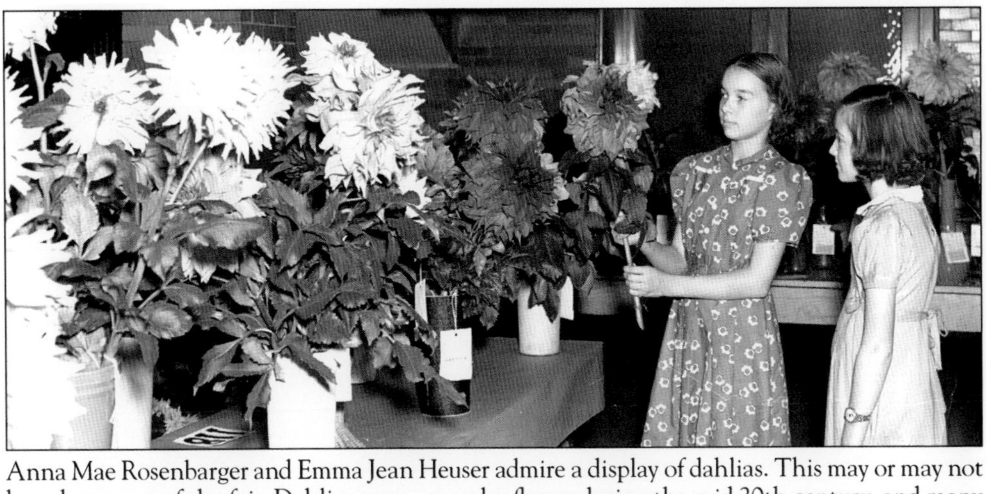

Anna Mae Rosenbarger and Emma Jean Heuser admire a display of dahlias. This may or may not have been part of the fair. Dahlias were a popular flower during the mid-20th century, and many varieties were touted to produce blossoms as big as dinner plates.

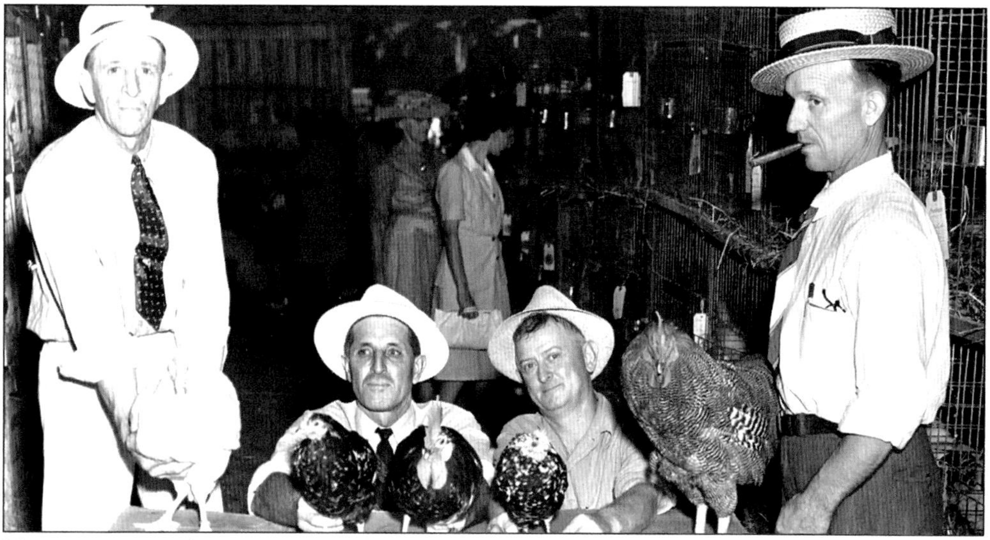

Harrison County began exporting baby chicks around 1900, shipping by railway express. Every chick arrived alive and healthy. By the 1930s, the hatcheries were bringing in more than half a million dollars a year. The first incubators were heated by kerosene lamps and held no more than 150 eggs. The next generation burned coal and was appropriately called the Mammoth Incubator, as its capacity might reach 3,000 eggs. Some 2,000 local farms furnished about 15.2 million eggs per year. Mrs. Charles H. Kintner, of Corydon's Sunshine Hatchery, had Indiana's first 300-egg hen. Kintner's English leghorn high hen laid 329 eggs in the 1926 Alabama contest, only one egg short of tying the United States contest winner that year. When egg size became important, Harrison County farmers had prime breeding stock to develop whatever traits were wanted.

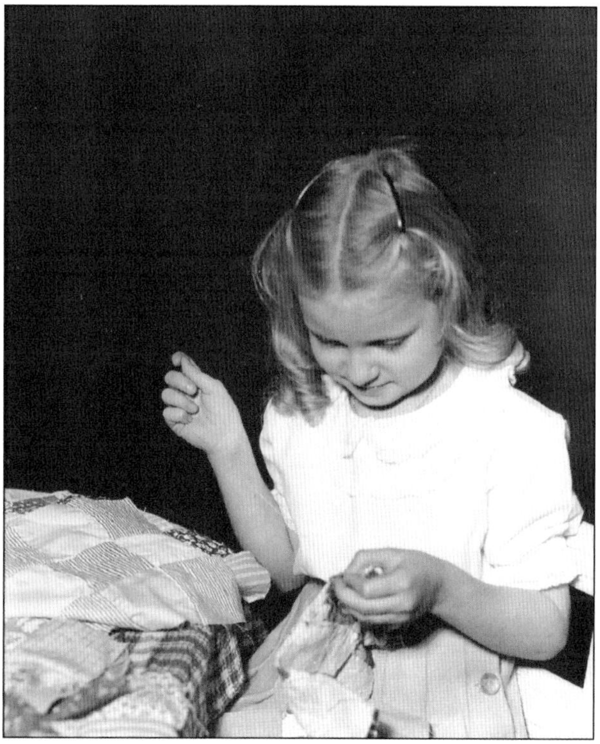

Six-year-old Nancy Mathes works on her quilting in 1949. Quilting was viewed as rest and recreation: it could be done sitting down and it could be done while visiting with friends and family. No scrap of material was ever thrown away. Baskets held large and small pieces of cloth in every color and pattern that the quilter could find. Scraps were traded and the quilts told the story of the family, the community, a special event, and a lifetime of work and giving. The county fair competition might lead to the state fair. Some quilters made quilts from their prize ribbons.

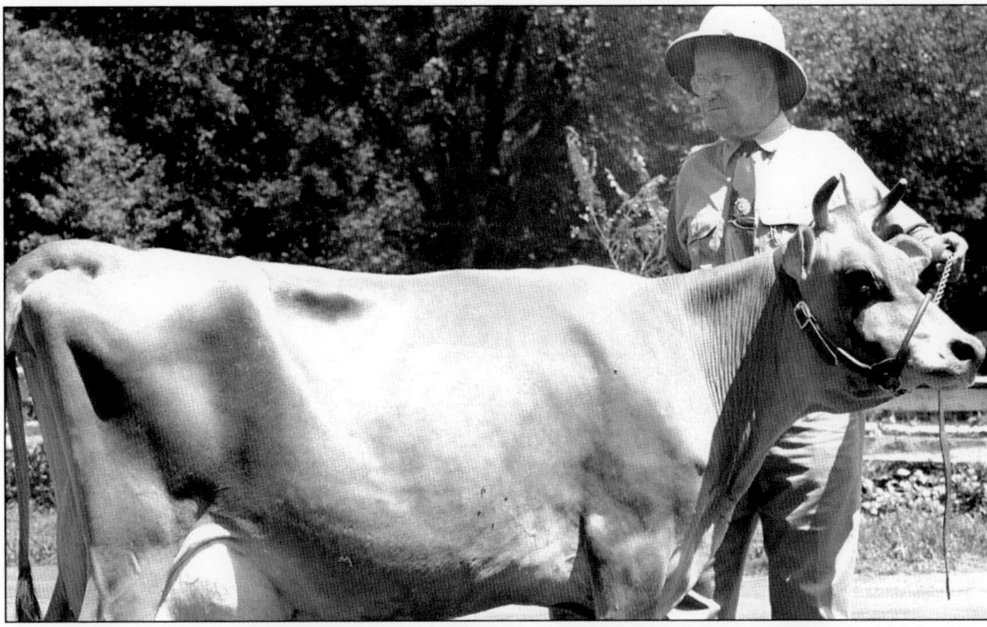

Dr. William E. Amy shows off a prize cow. Dairy cattle were another important industry of the 20th century. Corydon had creameries, a cheese plant, and dairy routes. A goal was set to have each farm in the county have four cows.

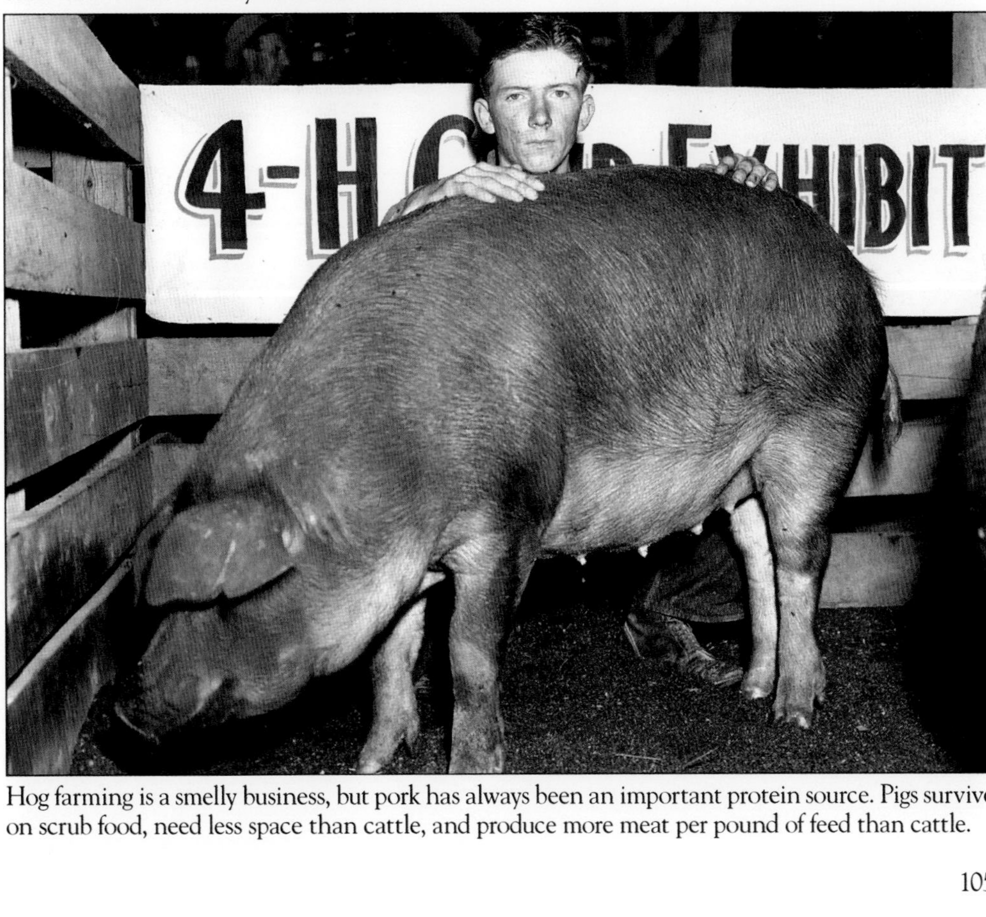

Hog farming is a smelly business, but pork has always been an important protein source. Pigs survive on scrub food, need less space than cattle, and produce more meat per pound of feed than cattle.

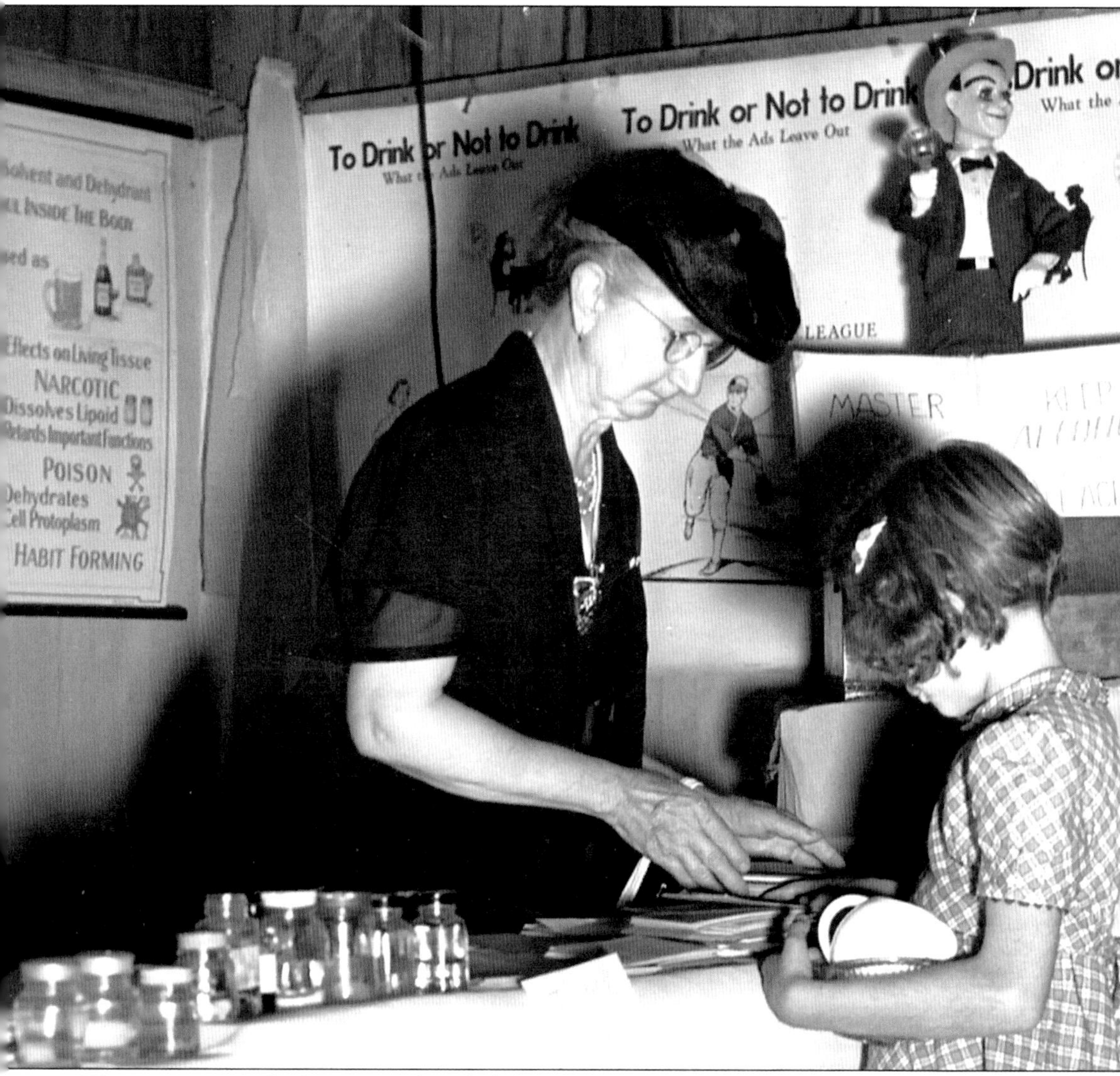

This temperance display is not identified, but it may have been part of the fair. Corydon was a capsule of America as a whole in the struggle over alcohol. Neighbors knew of alcoholism and the suffering of the family; yet abstinence was not a popular idea.

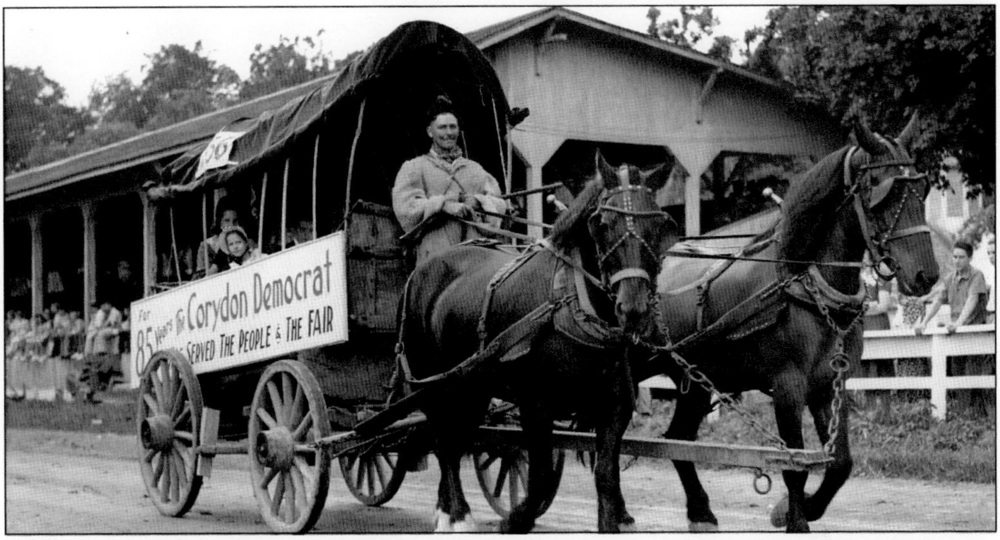

Both established in 1859, the Harrison County Fair and the *Corydon Democrat* celebrate joint anniversaries, here the 85th. This was probably doubly sweet, as it also marked the beginning of the end of World War II. Horse-powered wagons, harrows, ploughs, threshers, and pleasure vehicles were still used until well after the war. Even as diesel and gasoline engines began to take over the work, the wood implements were kept under tarpaulins and harnesses were oiled and kept supple. A man can talk to a horse or mule all day long and get a mighty decent conversation, but a fellow talking to a tractor is just plain crazy!

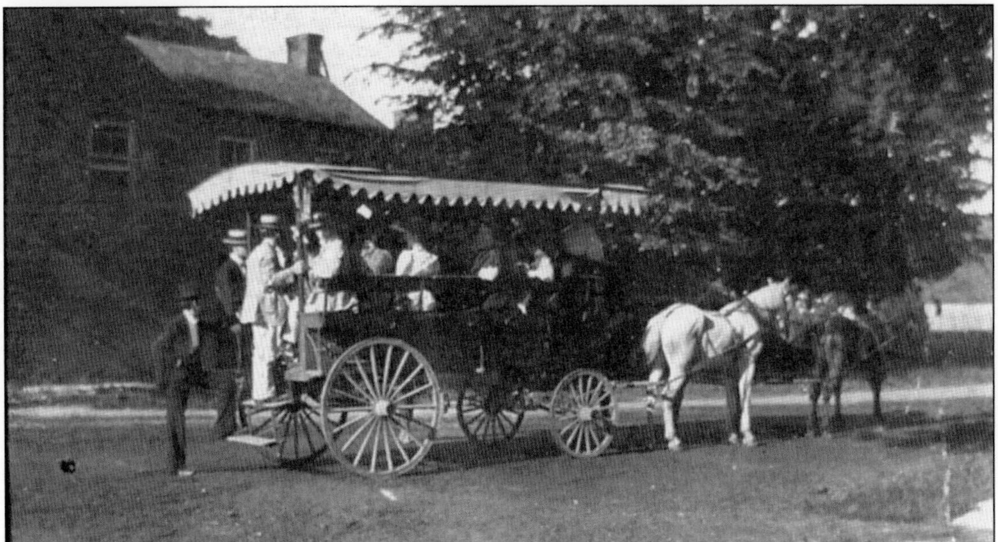

This elegant omnibus-sized surrey is the shuttle from the Kintner House to the Harrison County Fair. People came from all over the area to attend the fair. Exhibitors, judges, vendors, shoppers, and folks who wanted to be present at the spectacle all came. People stayed with relatives and friends if they could. Many participating in the fair camped right at the fairgrounds beside their animals or near their exhibit of produce of crafts. Farmers drove in for the day, as soon as morning chores were done and had to be back home for evening milking and other tasks. But for the wealthy, the hotels provided luxury; soft beds, good food, and door-to-door transportation to the excitement.

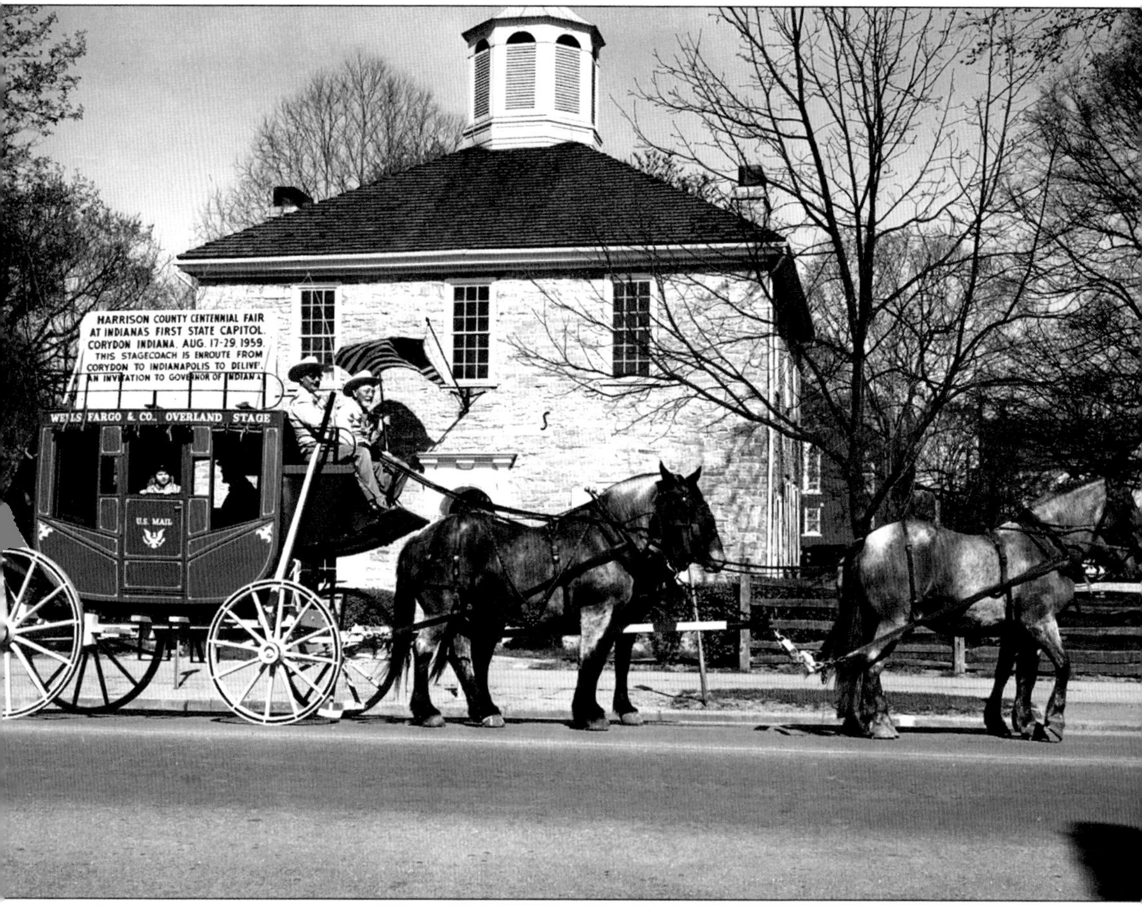

This stagecoach is beginning the trip from Corydon to Indianapolis, retracing the move of the capital city more than 125 years previous. The coach carries an invitation to the governor of Indiana to attend the centennial Harrison County Fair, August 17–29, 1959.

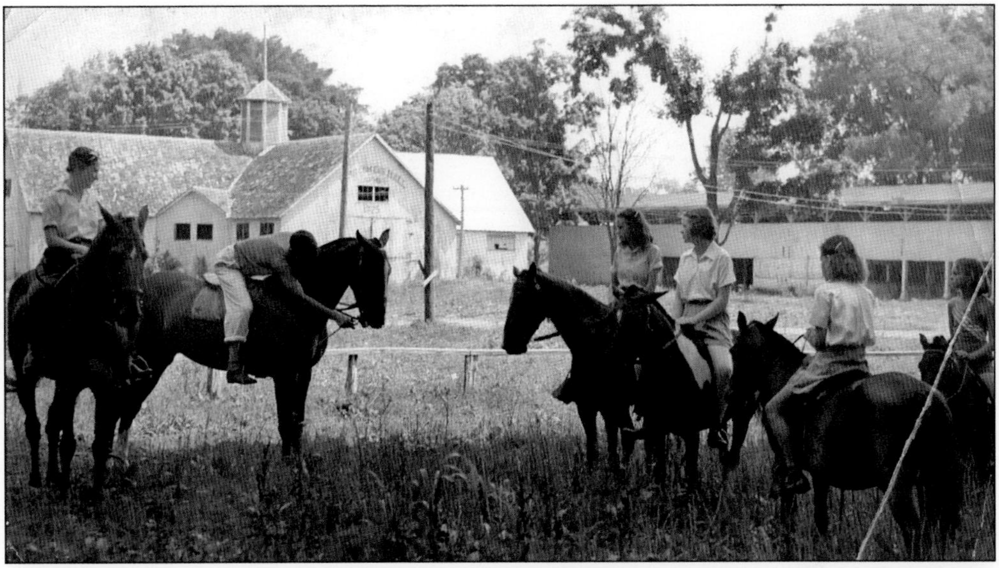

Townspeople kept horses at the stables in the fairgrounds. These young people are identified as Marilyn Miles, Patsy Mason, ? O'Bannon, and ? Hurst. Horses were numerous in Corydon up through the late 20th century. The common childhood passion for a horse of one's own was quite possible to gratify. Town houses still might have a stable, as well as a garage, and a leisurely amble down a block or two of town streets took riders into the country where horses and riders could follow trails at a walk, gallop cross country, or accept the challenge to jump logs and streams.

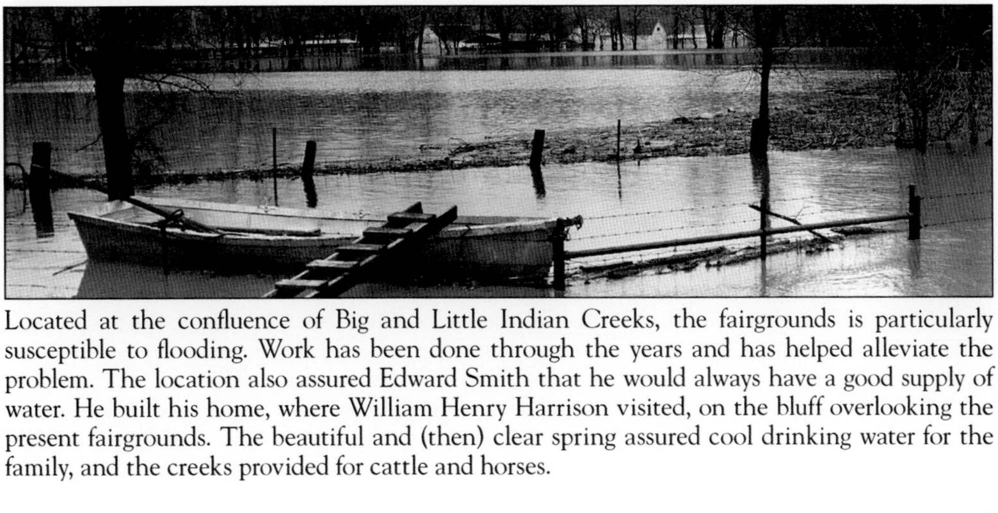

Located at the confluence of Big and Little Indian Creeks, the fairgrounds is particularly susceptible to flooding. Work has been done through the years and has helped alleviate the problem. The location also assured Edward Smith that he would always have a good supply of water. He built his home, where William Henry Harrison visited, on the bluff overlooking the present fairgrounds. The beautiful and (then) clear spring assured cool drinking water for the family, and the creeks provided for cattle and horses.

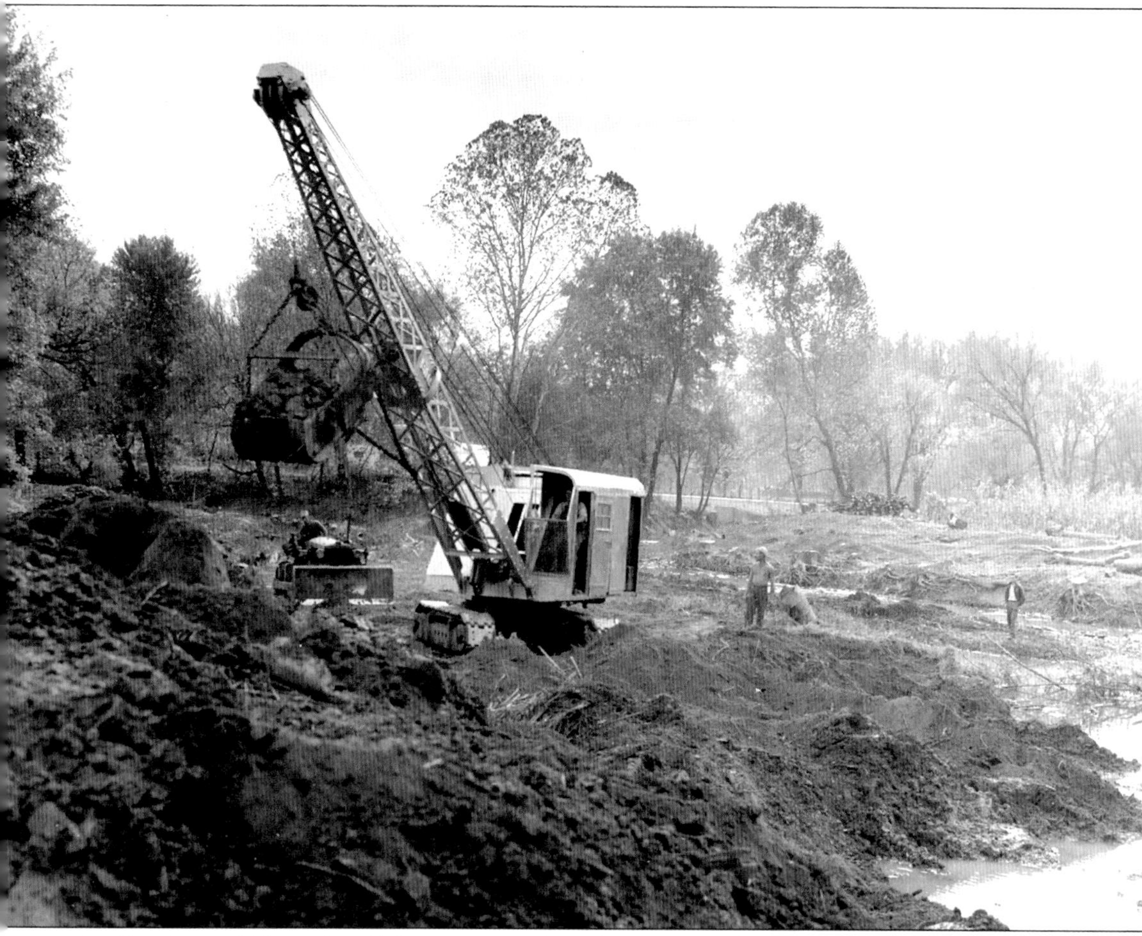

In October and November 1943, this steam shovel, power drag line, and bulldozer were brought from Lingo and Company of Seymour to clear the creek channels. From 100 yards below the confluence of the two creeks, east and north almost to the West Bridge, the channel was dredged and brush along the banks was cleared to improve water flow even in heavy downpours and so lessen flood danger. Little Indian Creek was also straightened shortly afterward, and the land for the fairgrounds extended.

Seven

State Centennial and Sesquicentennial

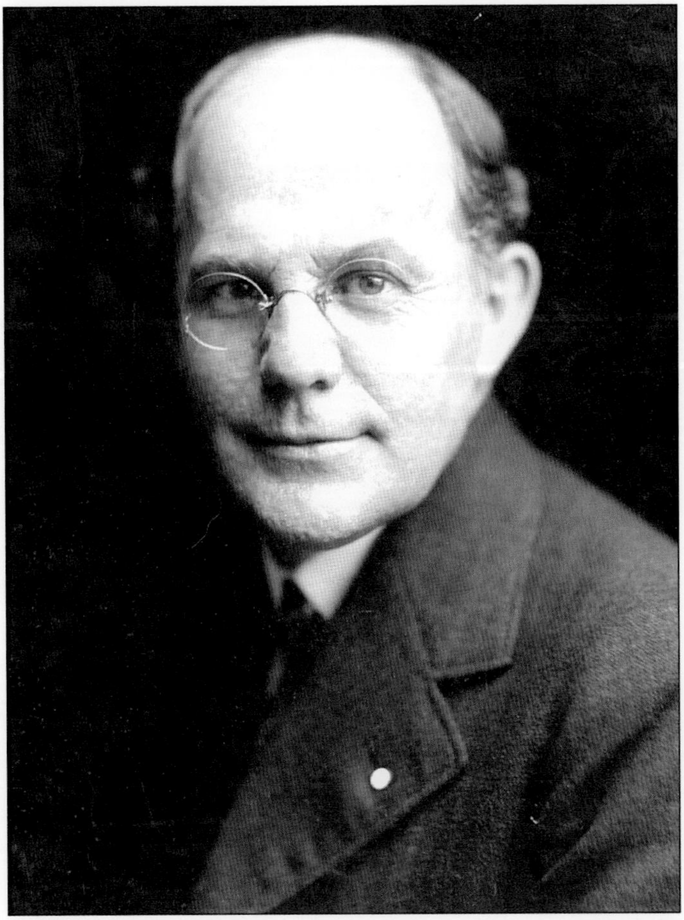

Centennial pageant master William Chauncy Langdon smiles from this portrait, but there is no information about him. He had a large responsibility. Many of the people in Corydon knew the first-hand stories of the time when the state was born in their town.

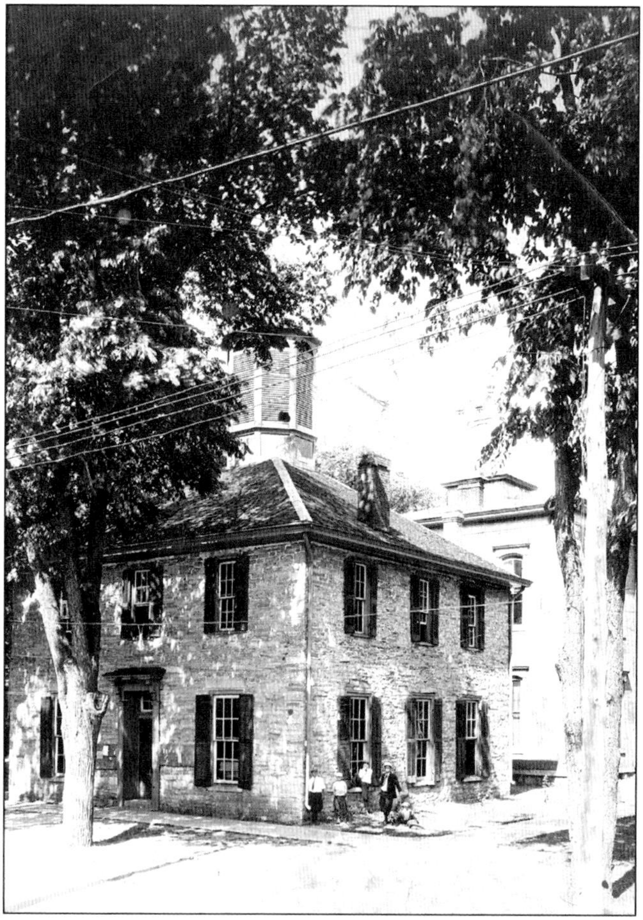

A series of photographs of the historic buildings still standing was made in 1916. This is the Corydon Capitol building, then the Harrison County Courthouse. The brick building in back is the county office building.

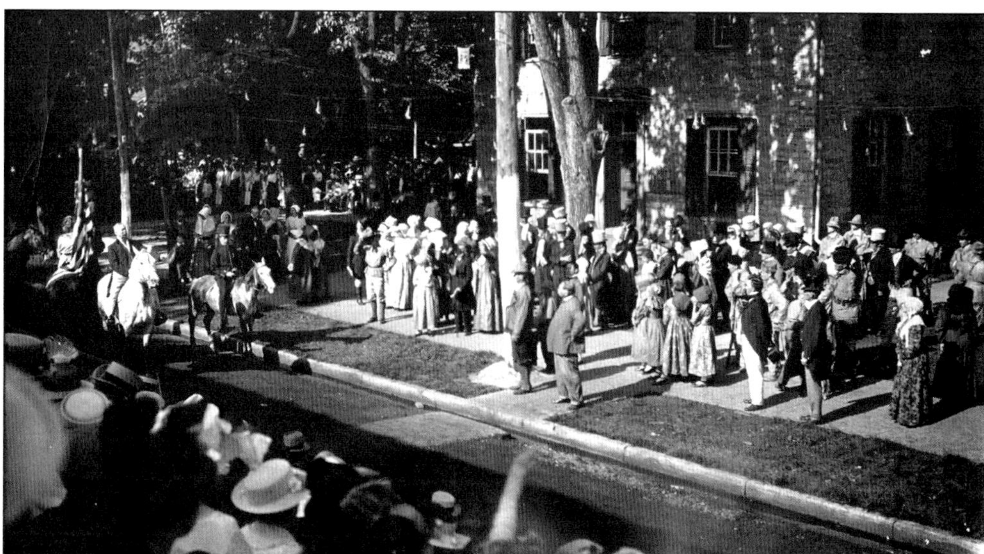

All the people attending the centennial celebrations were encouraged to dress as pioneers. Here the centennial parade passes the Corydon Capitol.

Attorney Lew M. O'Bannon had bought the *Corydon Democrat* newspaper in 1907. Apparently he thoroughly relished the state centennial celebration.

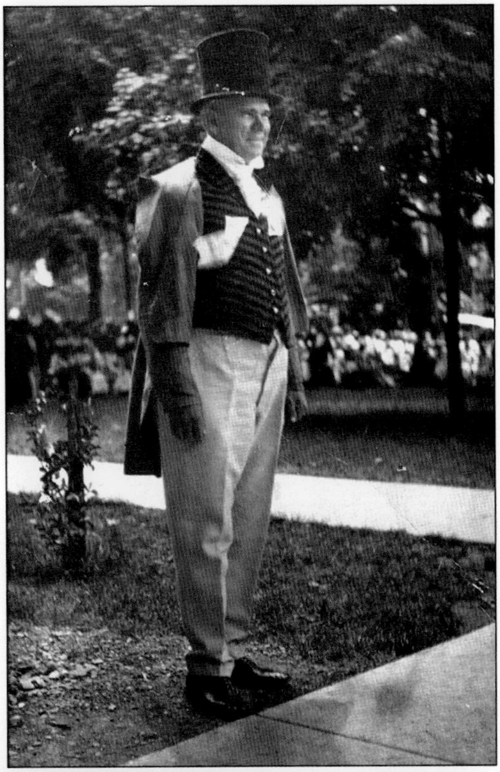

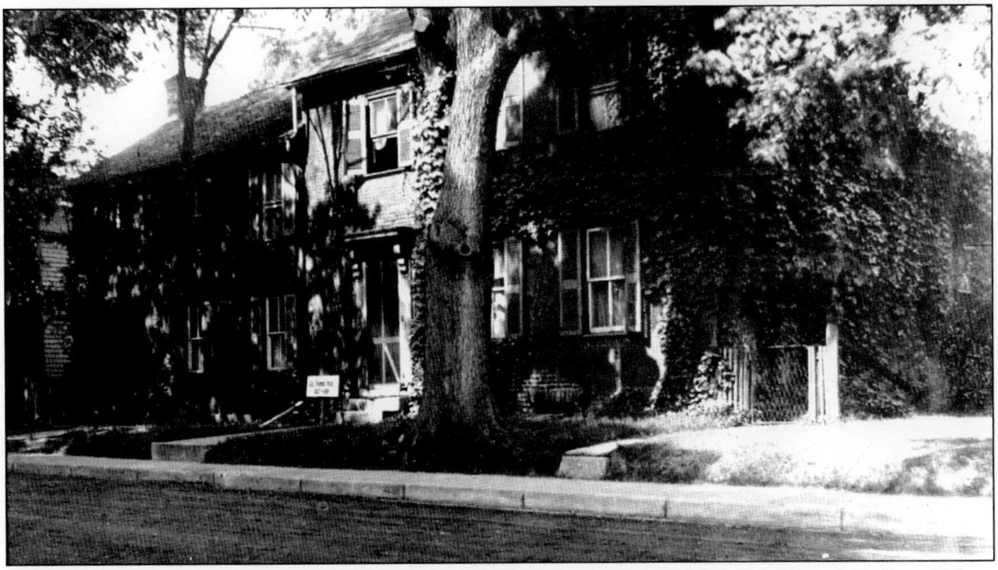

Thomas Posey was the last governor of the Indiana territory, and did not like Corydon. When the capital moved from Vincennes, Posey pleaded ill health and the necessity to be close to his Louisville, Kentucky, physician. He moved to his Jeffersonville, Indiana, property and refused to come to Corydon. His son, Thomas L. Posey, had this Federal-style home built in Corydon in 1817. Although he never married, he reared 14 orphans in this house. The remaining section was owned by the Hoosier Elm Chapter of the Daughters of the American Revolution. It still stands, but is in need of stabilization and renovation.

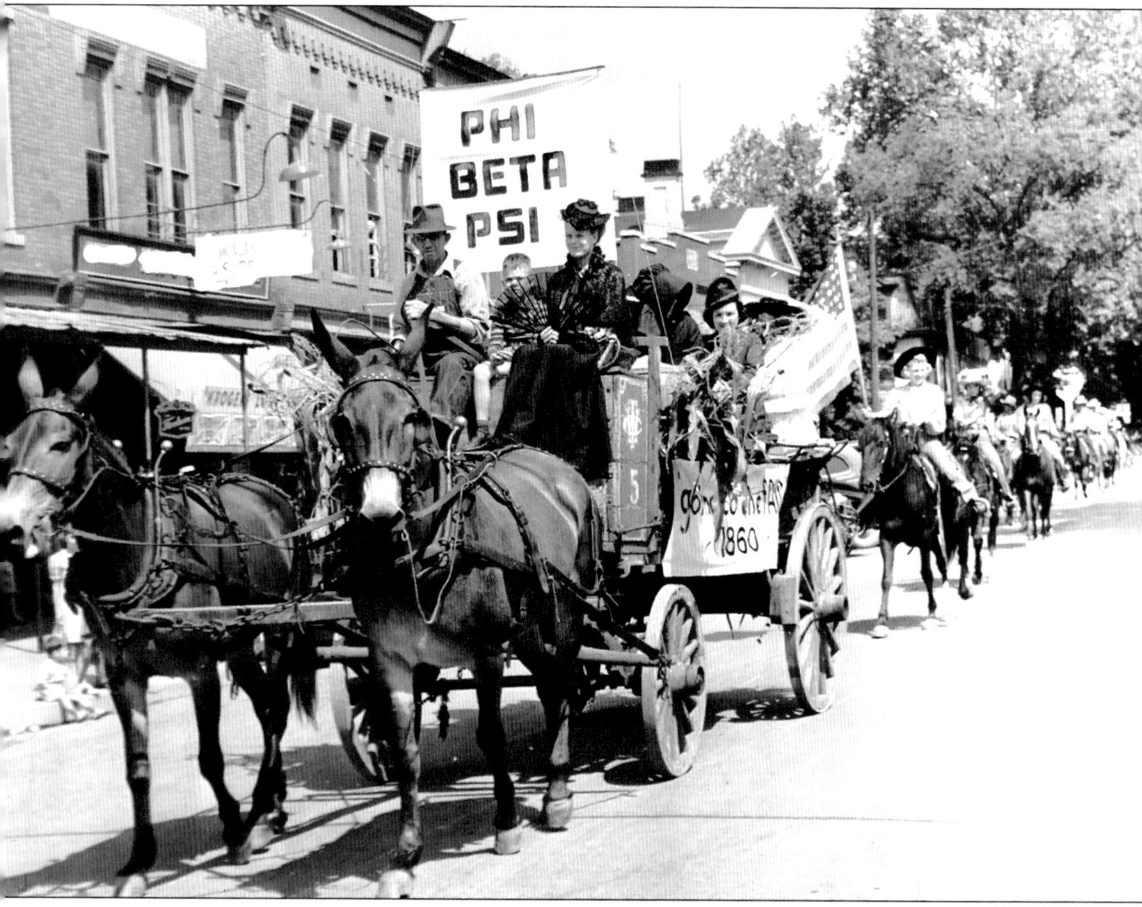

This parade photograph is undated, but seems to be a history celebration. Note the beautiful mules pulling the wagon and the long line of horses and ponies in the procession. A display like this requires more than is at first apparent. The animals must be cared for year round: pasturage, grain, water, and shelter. Hooves must be trimmed and shod. Harnesses are made of leather, which must be regularly oiled and lubricated, and the wooden wagons need maintenance to roll smoothly and not come apart at an inopportune moment. Hitching a team or saddling a horse is more detailed than simply turning a key in an ignition. Finally, but perhaps most importantly, the people handling the animals must know them well. The horses and mules need to trust the driver or rider and not panic in the midst of crowds and noise. Corydon never lacked for draft animals through the late 20th century, but now many parades rely on trucks and automobiles.

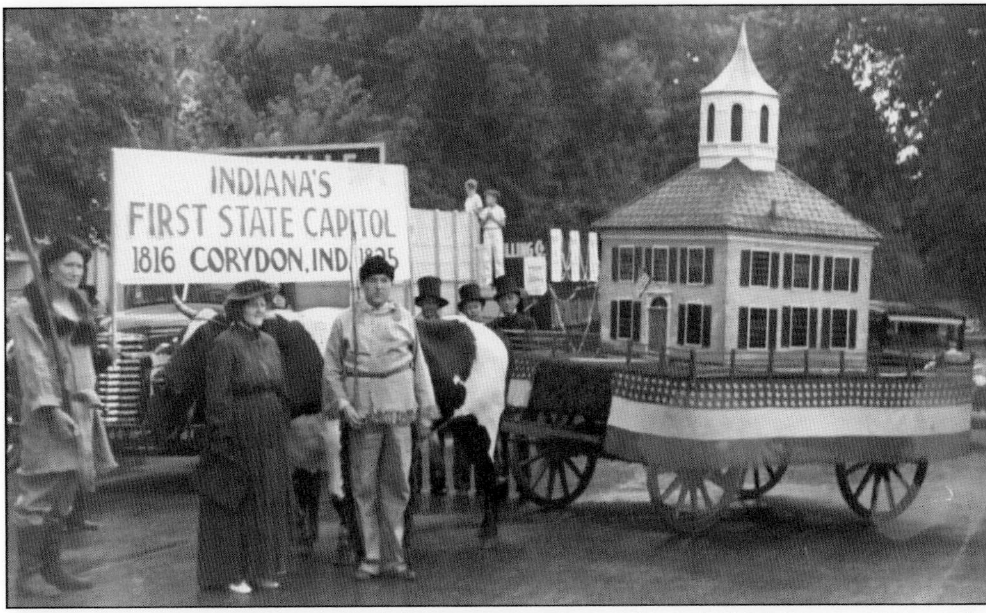

This model of the Corydon Capitol dates to sometime in the early 20th century. Its wooden frame is stuccoed in concrete. It was refurbished at least once, and stood for many years on the lawn of the American Legion post near the South Bridge.

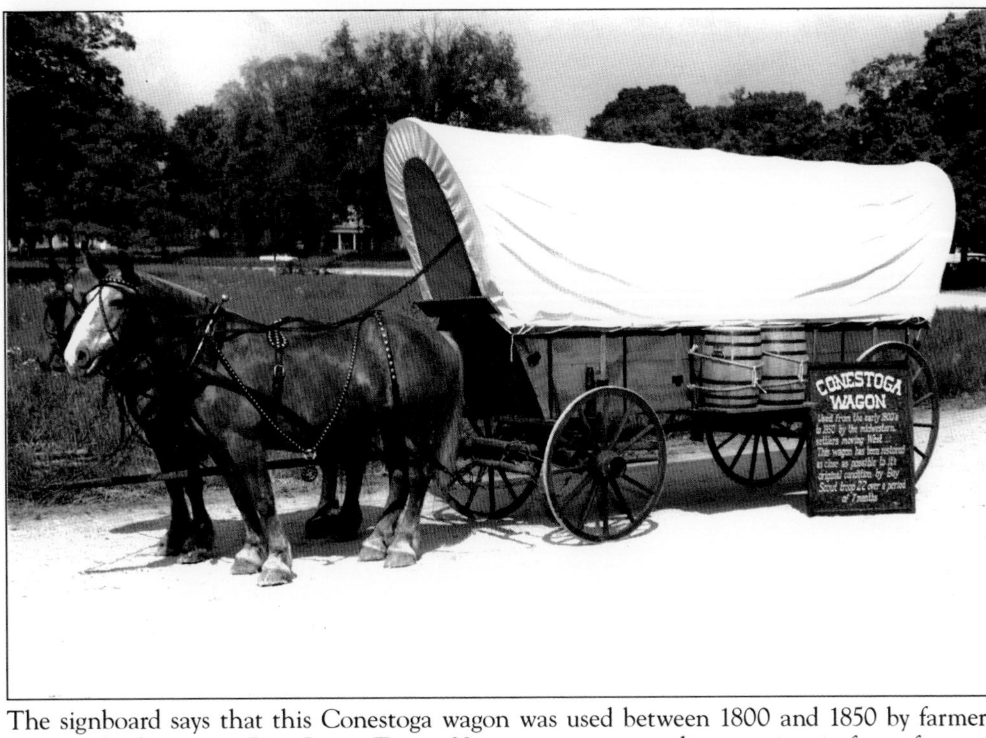

The signboard says that this Conestoga wagon was used between 1800 and 1850 by farmers moving further west. Boy Scout Troop 22 spent seven months restoring it for a featured appearance in the sesquicentennial parade.

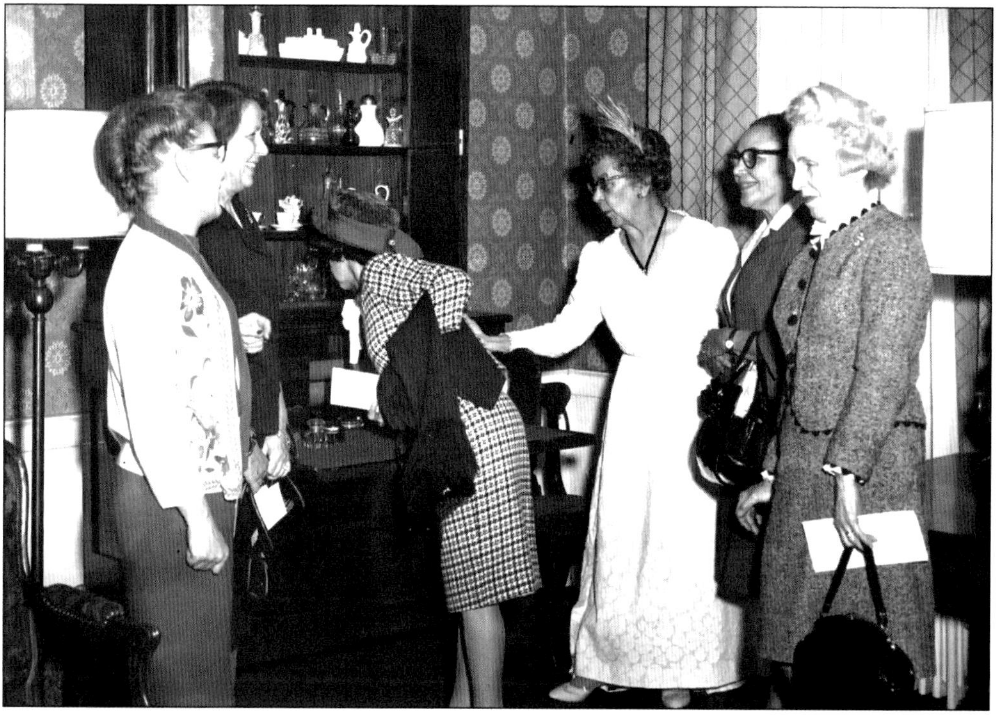

Annis McGrain, third from right, is seen at her home, Cedar Glade. She was in charge of the historic homes portion of the sesquicentennial celebration. She often entertained at Cedar Glade.

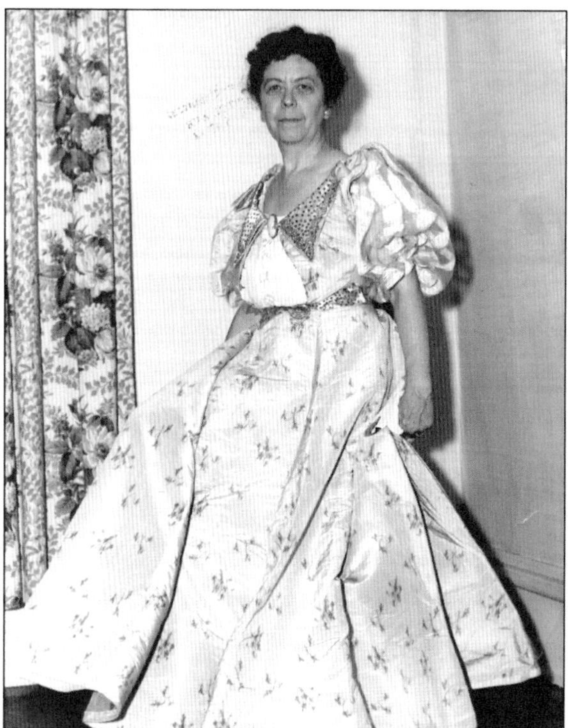

Annis was a community leader in Corydon for most of her life. She was a schoolteacher, then became a real estate agent. Living at Cedar Glade, she was often asked to host various functions. In the post–World War II years, many events were formal, as people relished the postwar prosperity and exuberance. Here she is ready for yet another grand event.

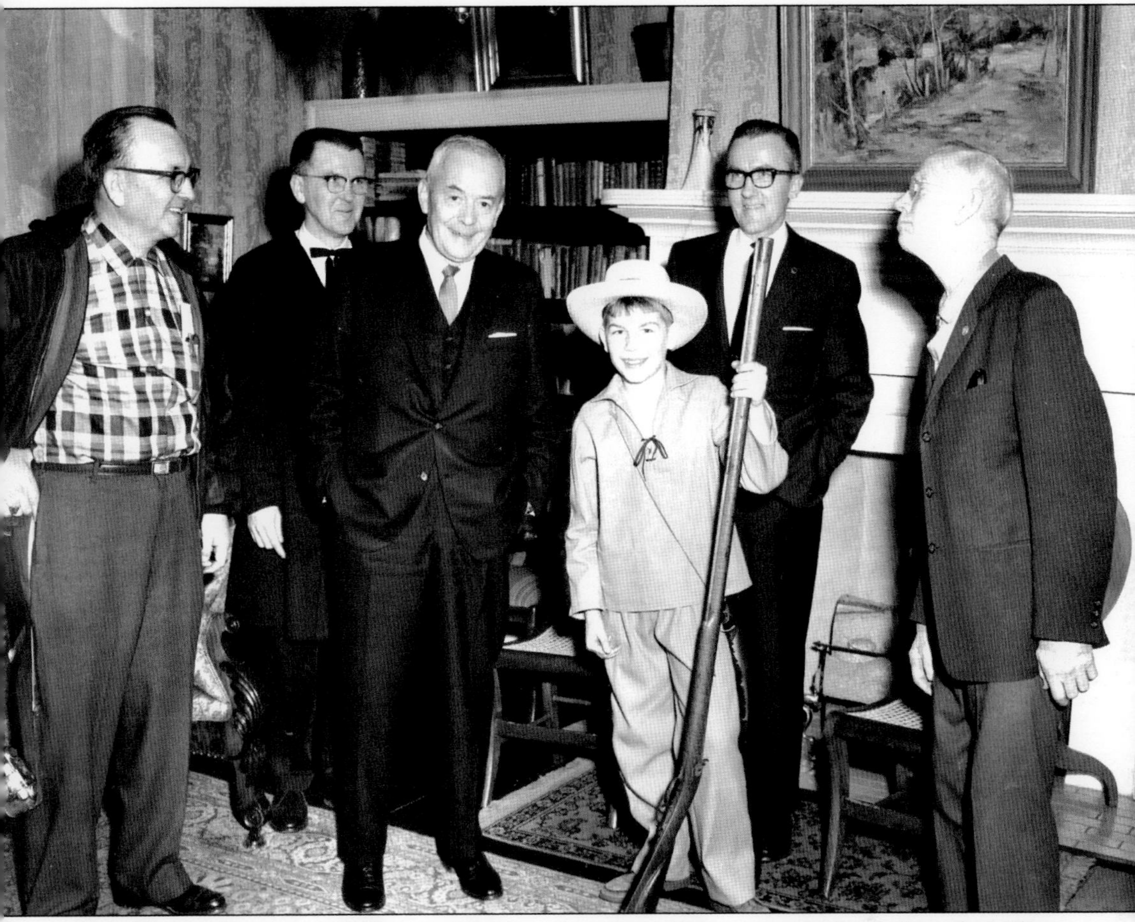

From left to right, Henry Griffin, Fred Griffin, Gov. Roger Brannigan, Fred's son Patrick Griffin, William "Tim" Griffin, and Daniel P. Griffin are in the Porter-Griffin home (Governor Hendricks Headquarters) during the sesquicentennial.

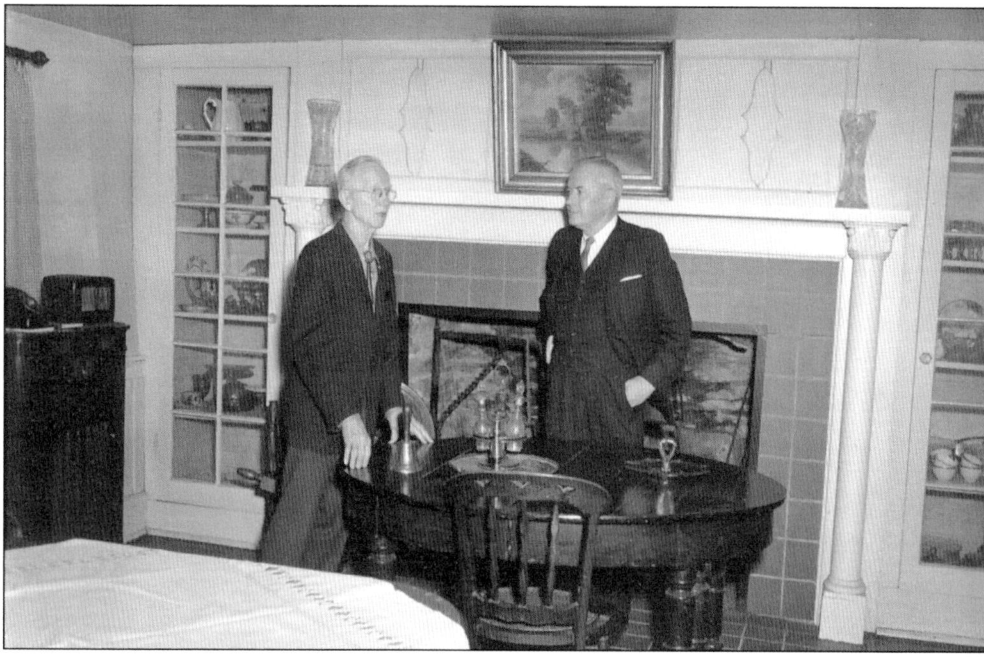

Gov. Roger Brannigan enjoyed his tour of the Porter-Griffin house and the stories of Daniel P. Griffin and the rest of the family.

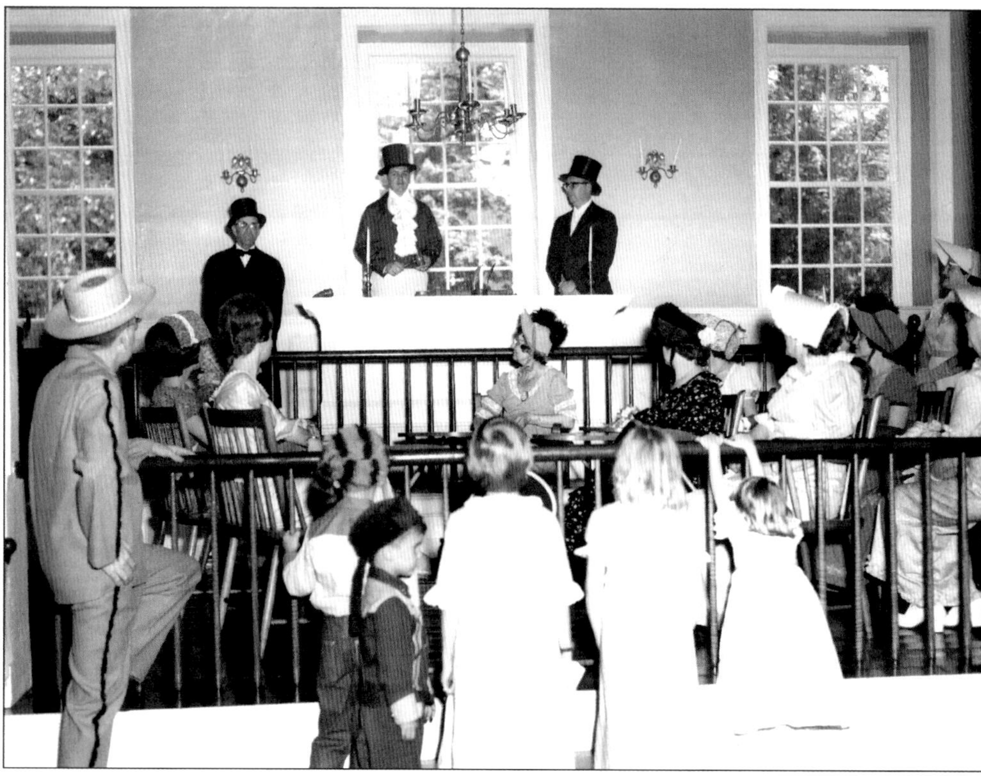

A sesquicentennial pageant was staged in the house of representatives of the Corydon Capitol in 1966.

Eight

Corydon Goes to War

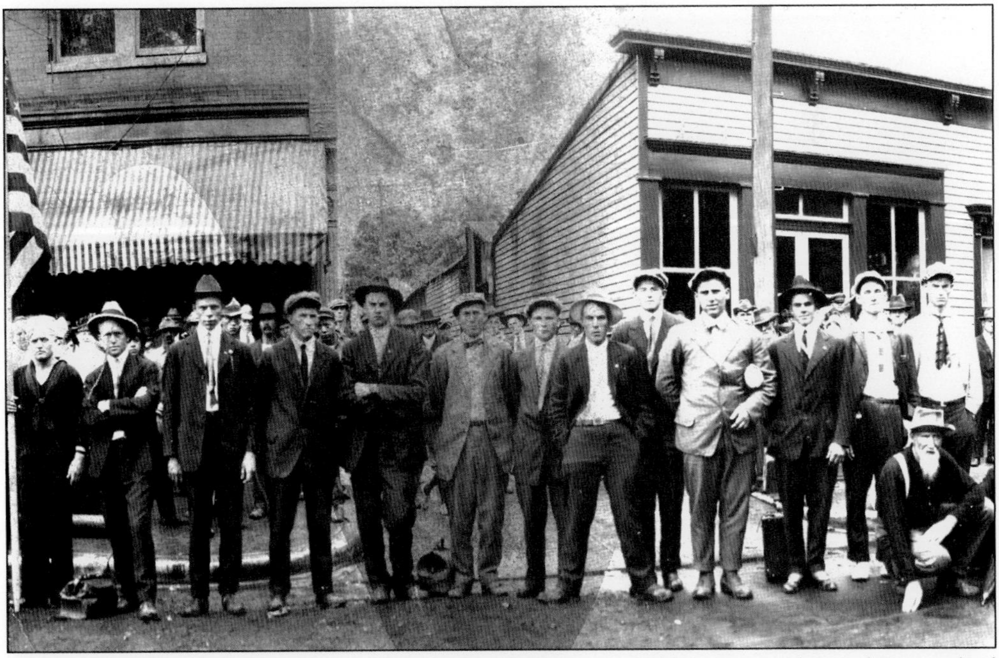

The young men are leaving for service in World War I. Corydon seems to have photographed each group of draftees in World War I and World War II. The United States did not engage in the war until 1917. It was "the war to end all wars," and Americans were determined to finish war for all time.

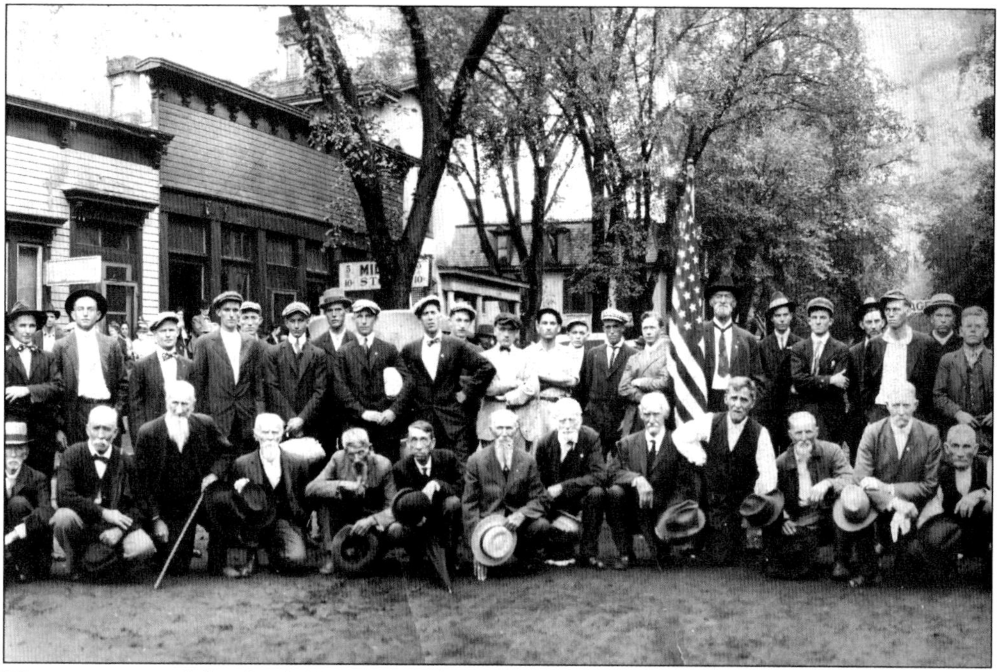

These veterans of the Civil War pose with recruits heading for World War I. The building in back with the mansard roof is the Corydon Democrat building. Corydon has sent its sons to every war back to the War of 1812.

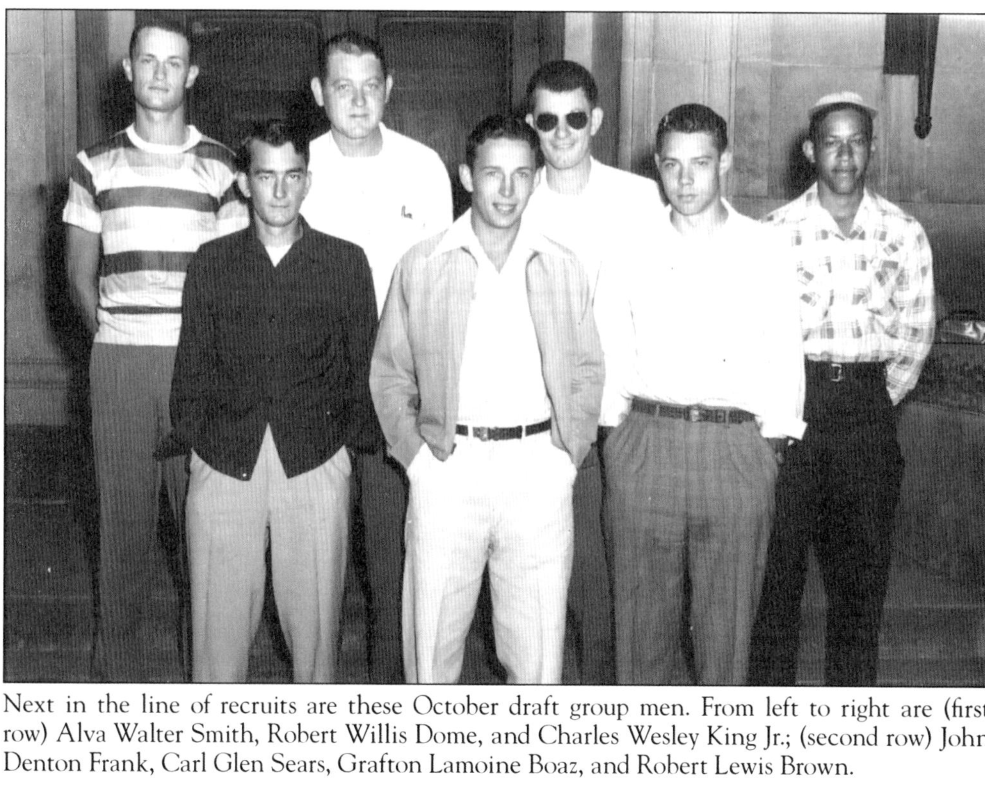

Next in the line of recruits are these October draft group men. From left to right are (first row) Alva Walter Smith, Robert Willis Dome, and Charles Wesley King Jr.; (second row) John Denton Frank, Carl Glen Sears, Grafton Lamoine Boaz, and Robert Lewis Brown.

The lady, the equine, and the occasion are unidentified, but this photograph beautifully illustrates the lifelong determination of Corydon people to live and rejoice in life to the fullest. Perhaps this lady is celebrating the soldier sons, fathers, husbands, and brothers who have won and kept her freedom.

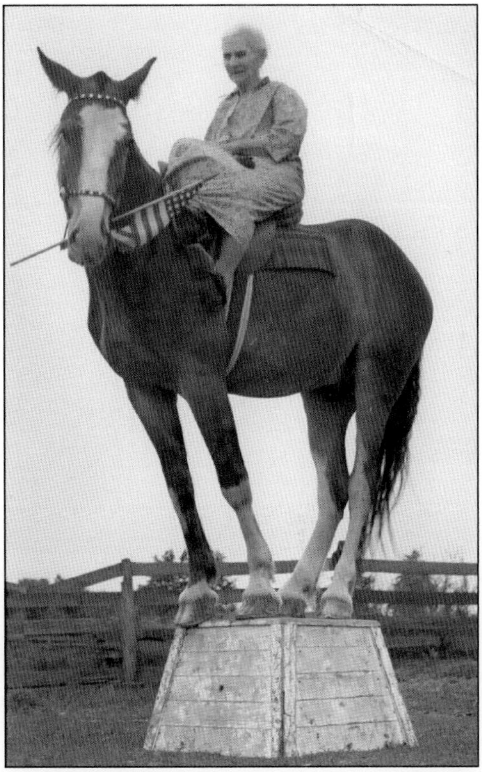

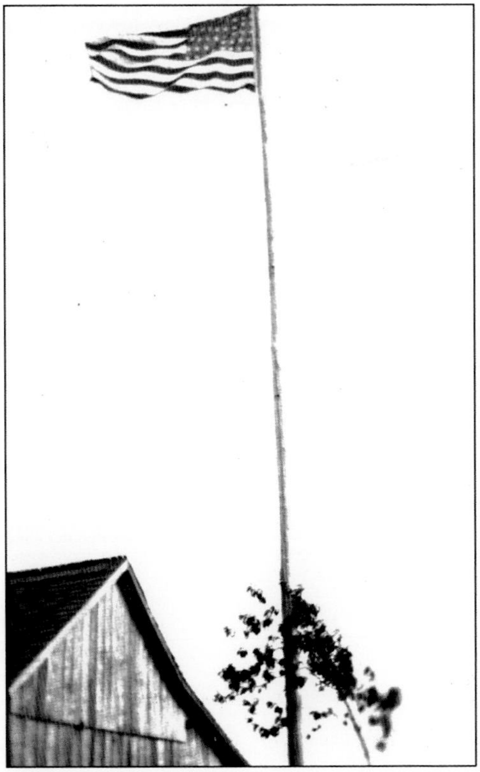

Freedom poles were erected as symbols of patriotism during World War I. Communities vied with one another to put up the tallest pole. This one soared 114 feet over the town square.

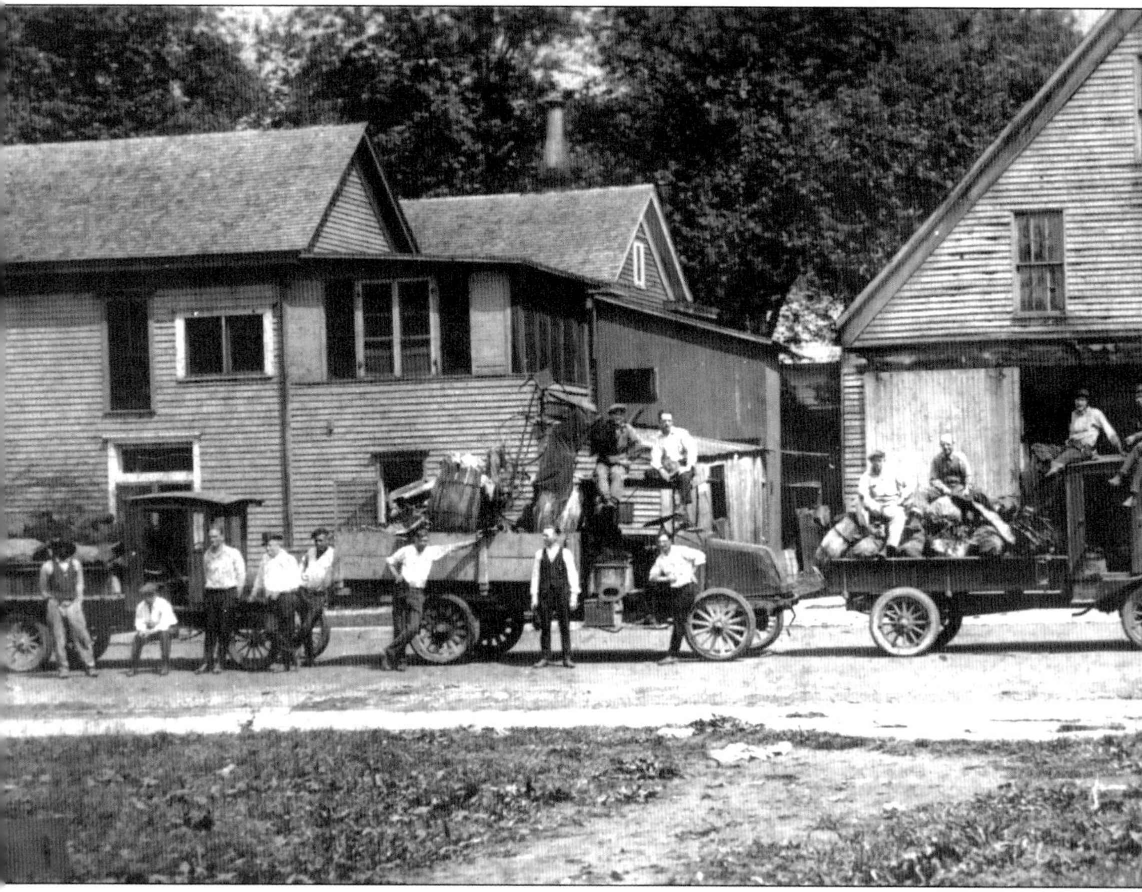

In the spring of 1922, World War I veterans from the Harrison Post of the American Legion hauled away trash in a townwide clean up. The town truck was used, along with four trucks furnished free of charge by the Hurst Hardware Company, J. J. Bulleit and Company, J. L. Rowe and Sons, and Turley and Bocard. The men shoveled and loaded rubbish brought curbside by residents. The women's auxiliary of the post served a noon dinner at the legion headquarters.

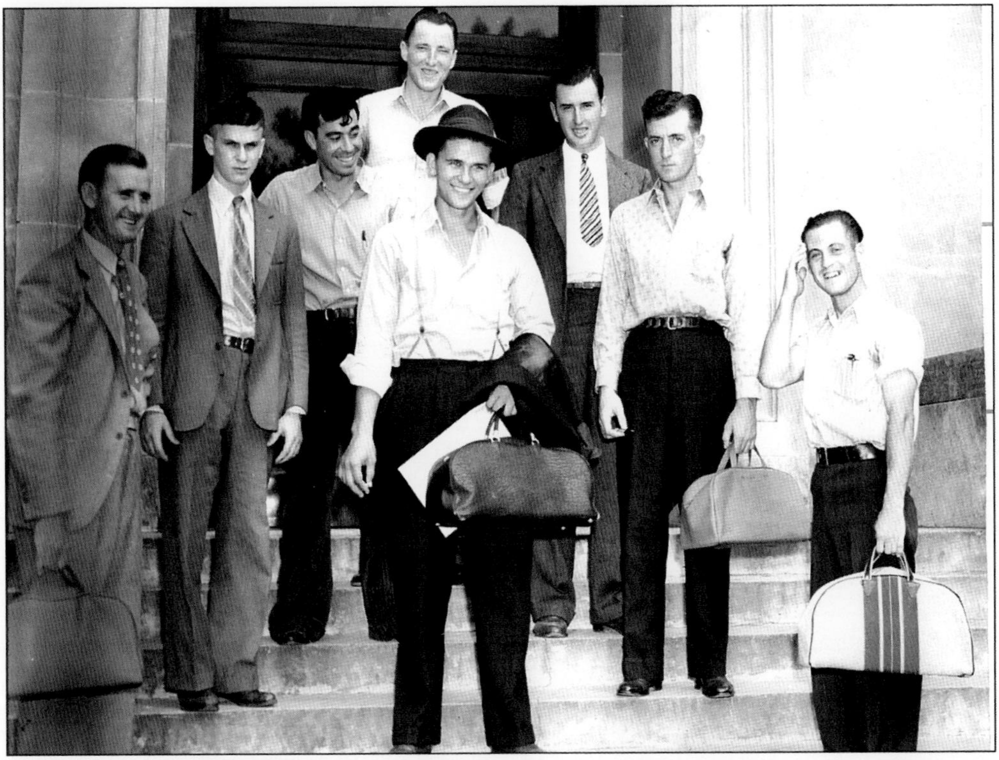

From left to right, Earl William Hays, Lloyd John Biel, Loran Grover Hisey, Lawrence Frederick Baker, Earl Richard Conlee, George William Denbo, Earl Robert Cunningham, and William Kermit Rothrock left Corydon for Louisville's selective service physicals in September 1941. Cunningham did not pass the physical and returned home; all others entered the military.

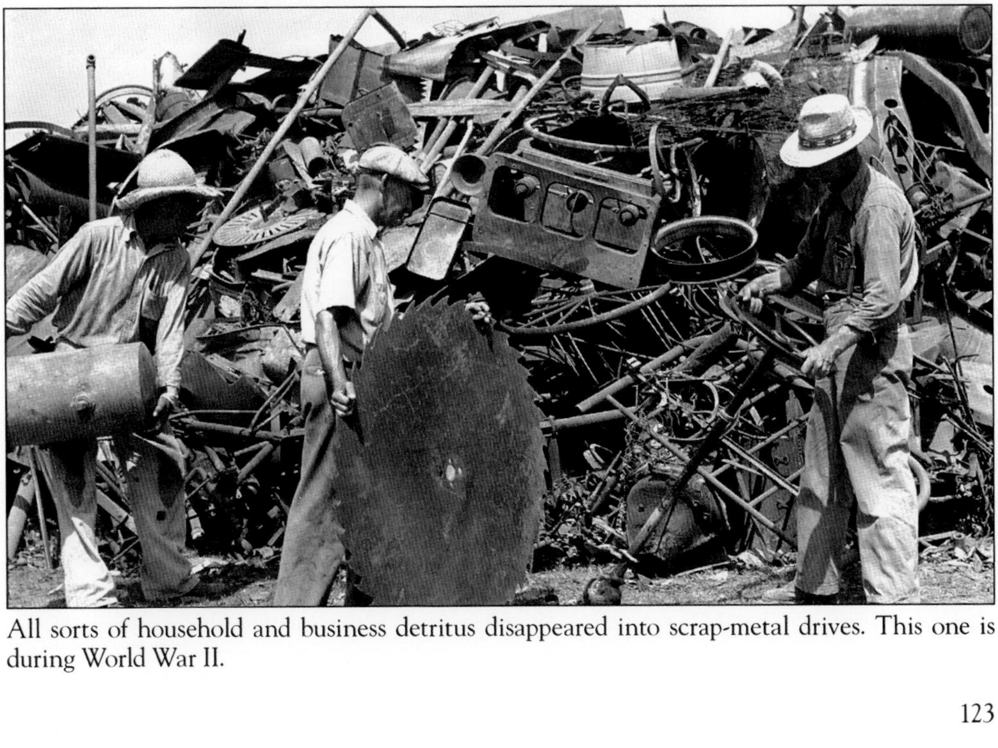

All sorts of household and business detritus disappeared into scrap-metal drives. This one is during World War II.

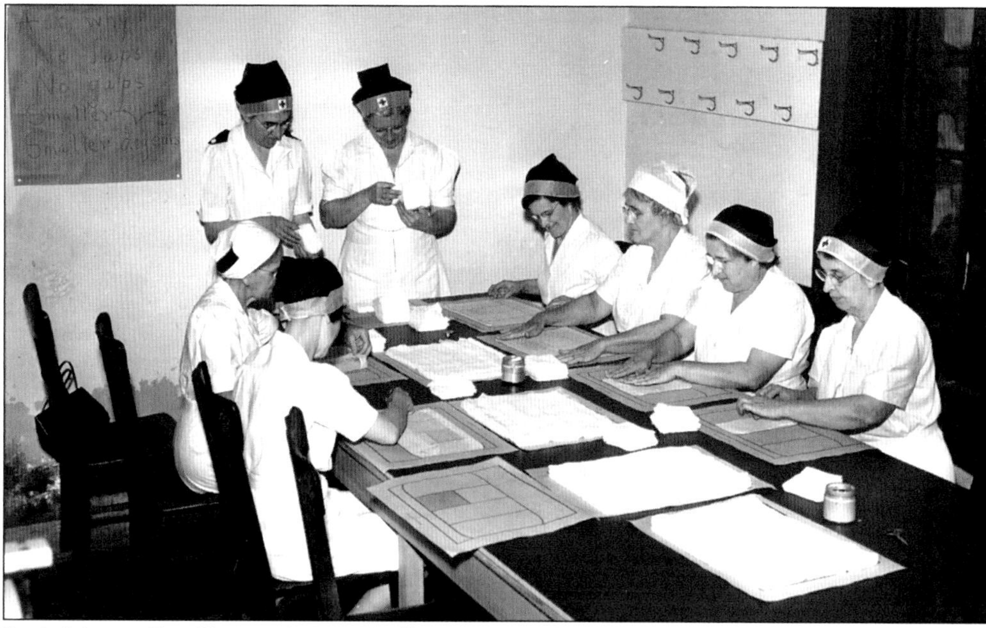

Ruth Morris, Eva Kepner, Lottie Griffin, Mrs. Gordon Walts, Catherine Miller, and Bertha Duley follow Red Cross instructions for folding bandages during World War II.

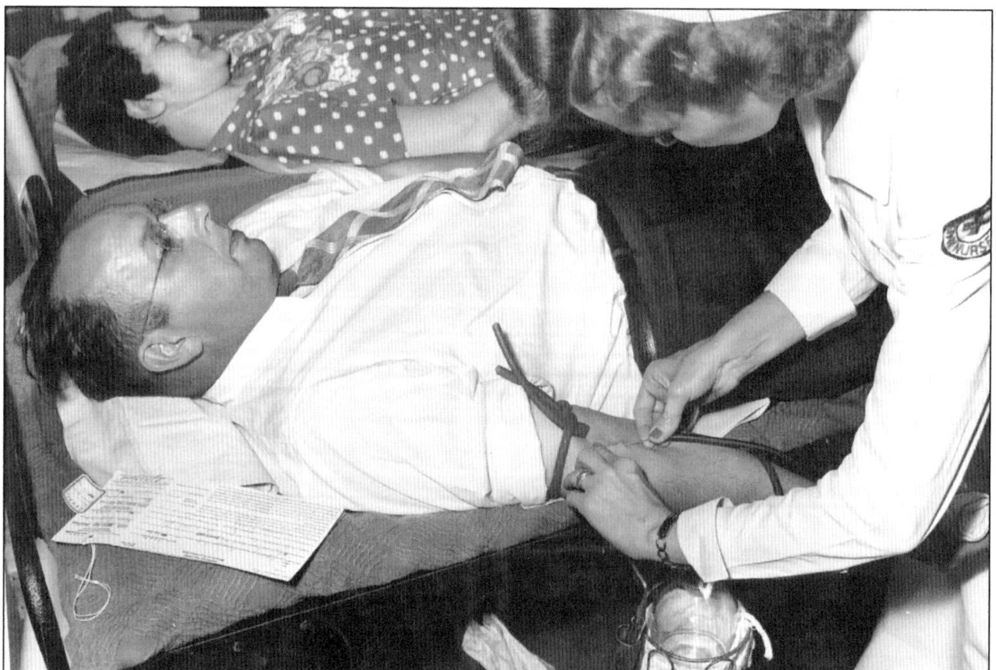

Blood drives were also important national efforts. Blood transfusion had been attempted, sometimes successfully, for several centuries, but it was not until World War II that science and technology combined to identify blood types and store and ship blood, and that fresh blood saved lives on the battlefields. The American Red Cross, then as now, coordinated the efforts, and civilians were eager to help the men at the front. Here Rev. Omar F. J. Rau sets an example by giving blood.

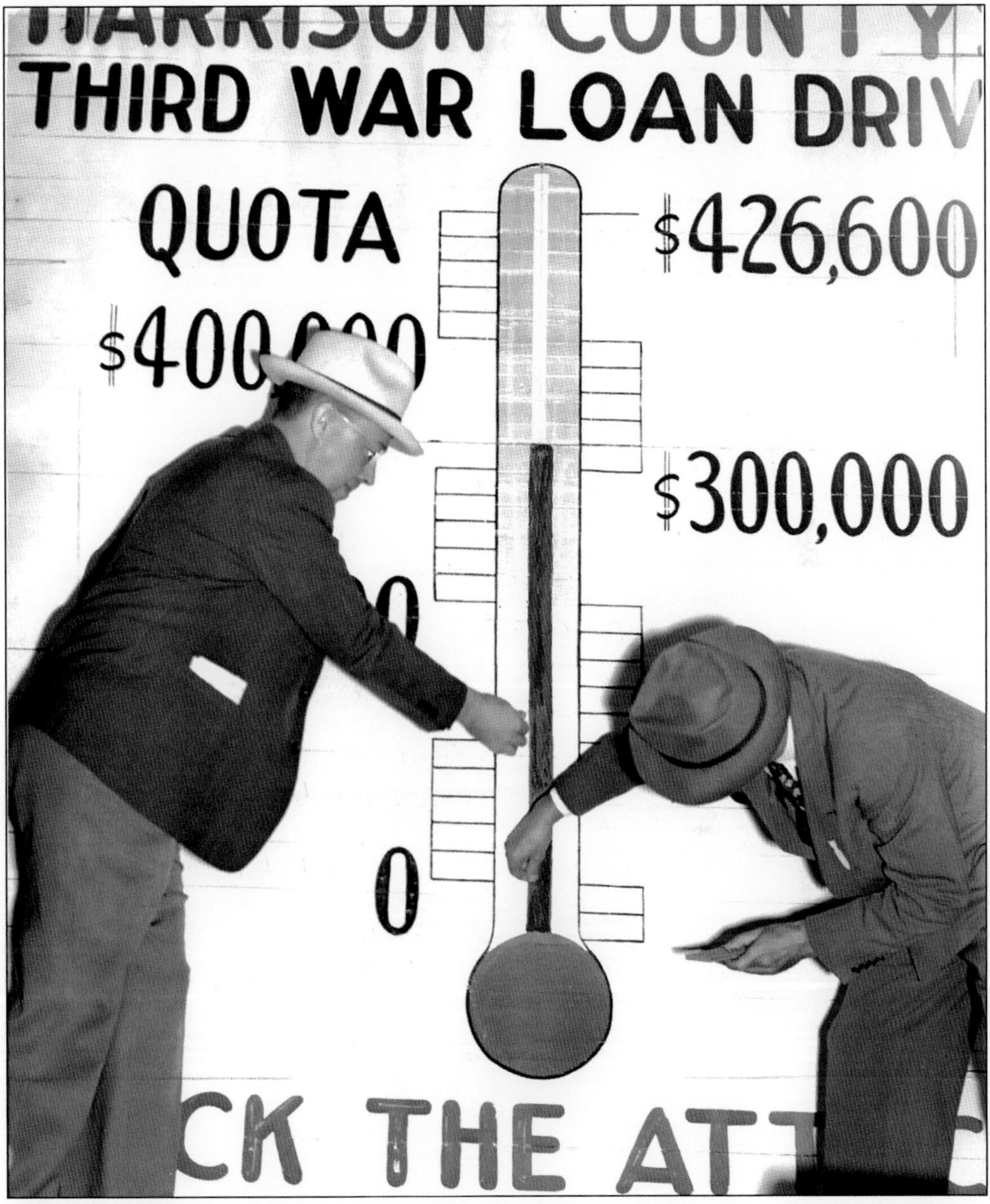

Earl Miller (left) helps chart the success of the Third War Loan Drive. Not only is war expensive in lives, it also costs a lot of money.

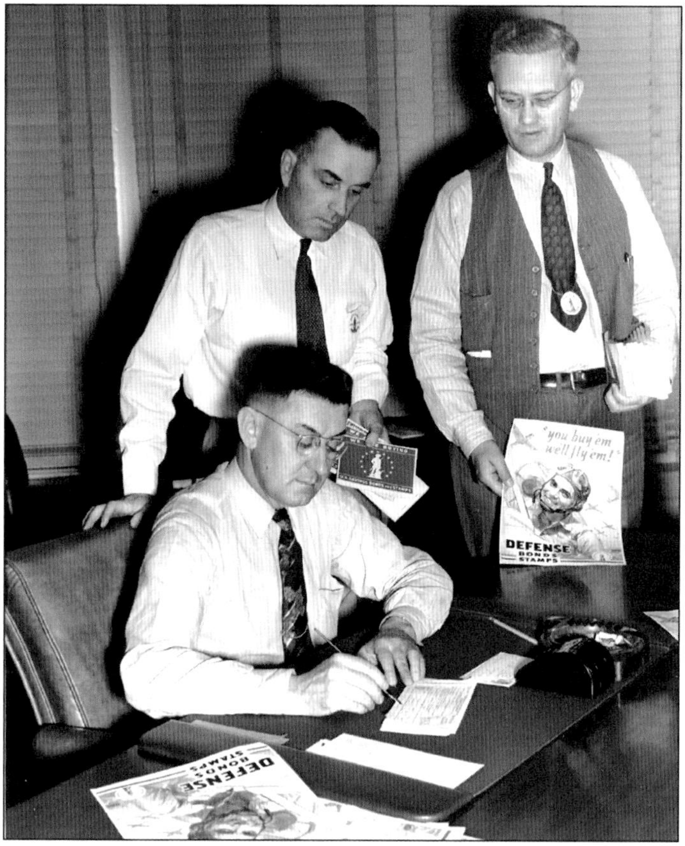

Willis Dome, Jack Miller, and Allen Jordan organize a sale of defense bonds and stamps. World War II was expensive, and to meet the cost, the federal government appealed directly to the American people. War bonds and stamps were sold in organized drives all across the country. Civilians could "do their part" by buying the bonds and stamps. Everyone, including children, housewives, and the elderly, wanted to show their patriotism by paying money for the war, with the promise that the bonds could be redeemed for capital plus interest after the war.

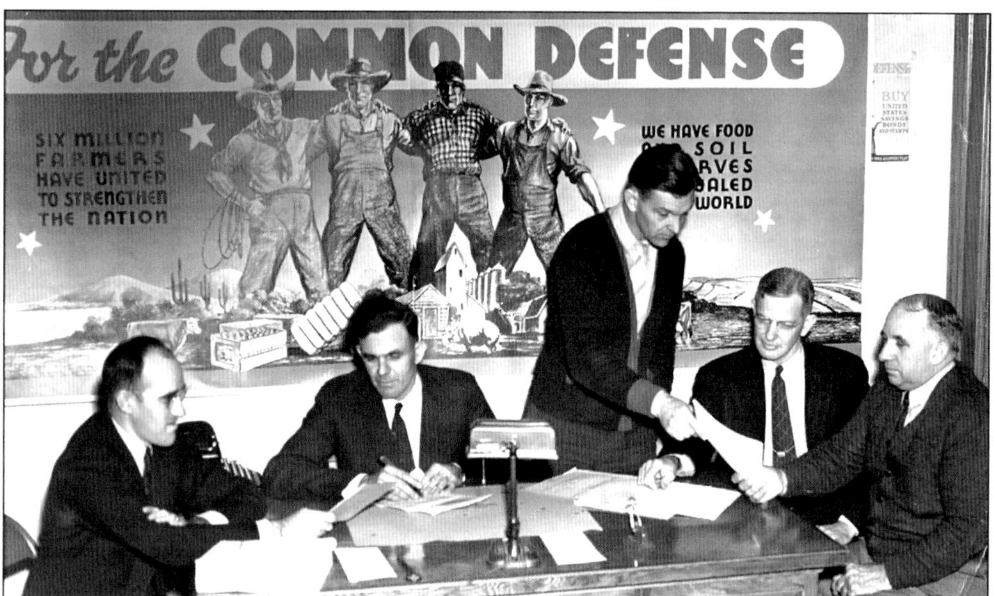

Farming was essential to the war effort and farming communities were proud of their contribution to the national good. Maurice Goode, Frank Hillman, an unidentified man, Arville Miles, and Tom Cooper keep up with the paperwork typical of any government initiative.

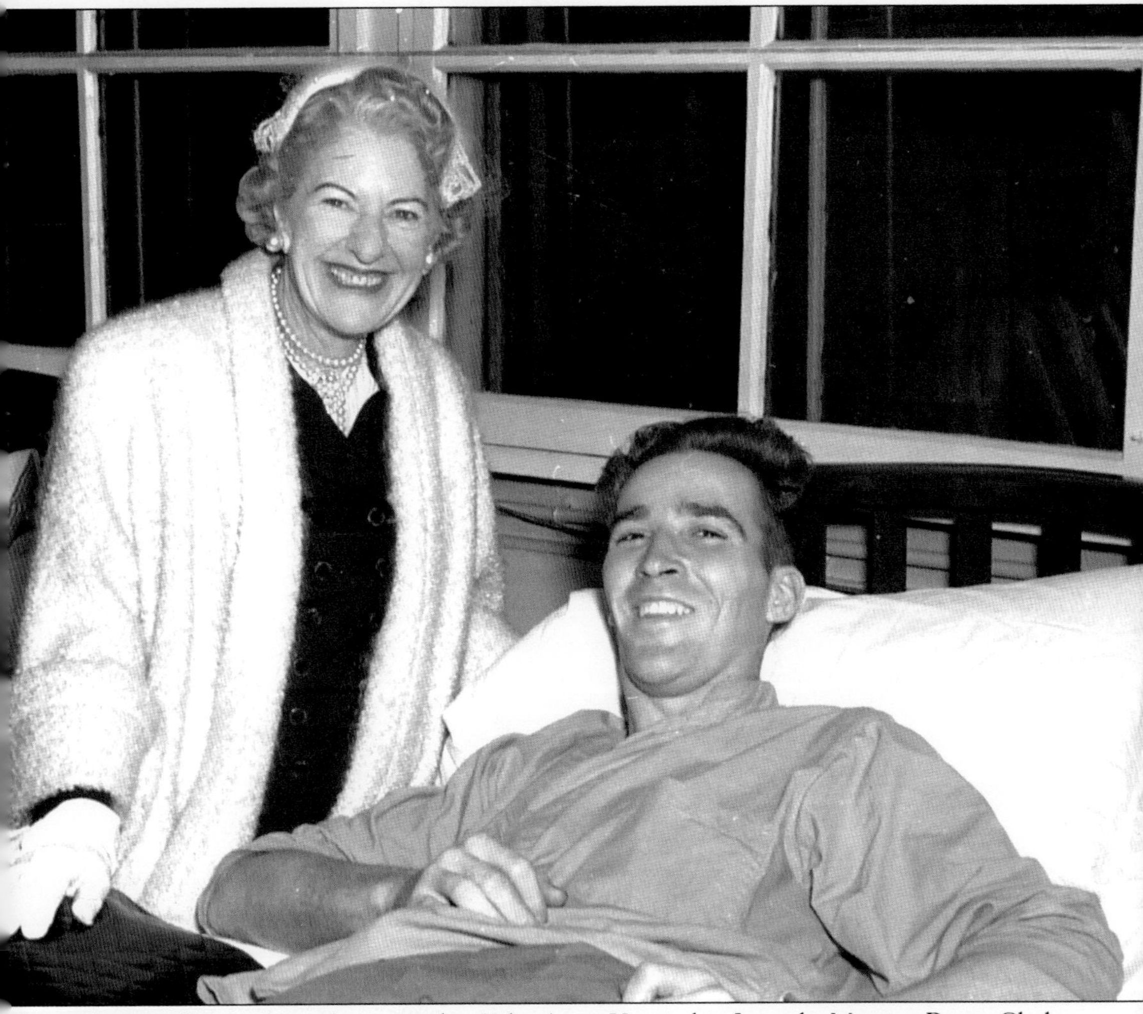

Pfc. Burrell E. McMonigle is visited in Yoko Army Hospital in Japan by Maurine Doran Clark, whose husband, Mark Clark, was commander in chief of the Far East Command during the Korean conflict.